PHILIP K. DICK

PHILIP K. DICK
A COMICS BIOGRAPHY
LAURENT QUEYSSI / MAURO MARCHESI

nbm GRAPHIC NOVELS
Nantier • Beall • Minoustchine
NEW YORK

ISBN 978-1-68112-191-8
Library of Congress Control Number: 2018959630
Initially published in French as *Phil, Une Vie de Philip K. Dick* © Blue Lotus Prod, Paris, 2017 (www.21g.fr)
© 2018 NBM for the English translation
Translation by Edward Gauvin
Lettering by Ortho

Printed in India
1st printing November 2018

This graphic novel is also available as an e-book

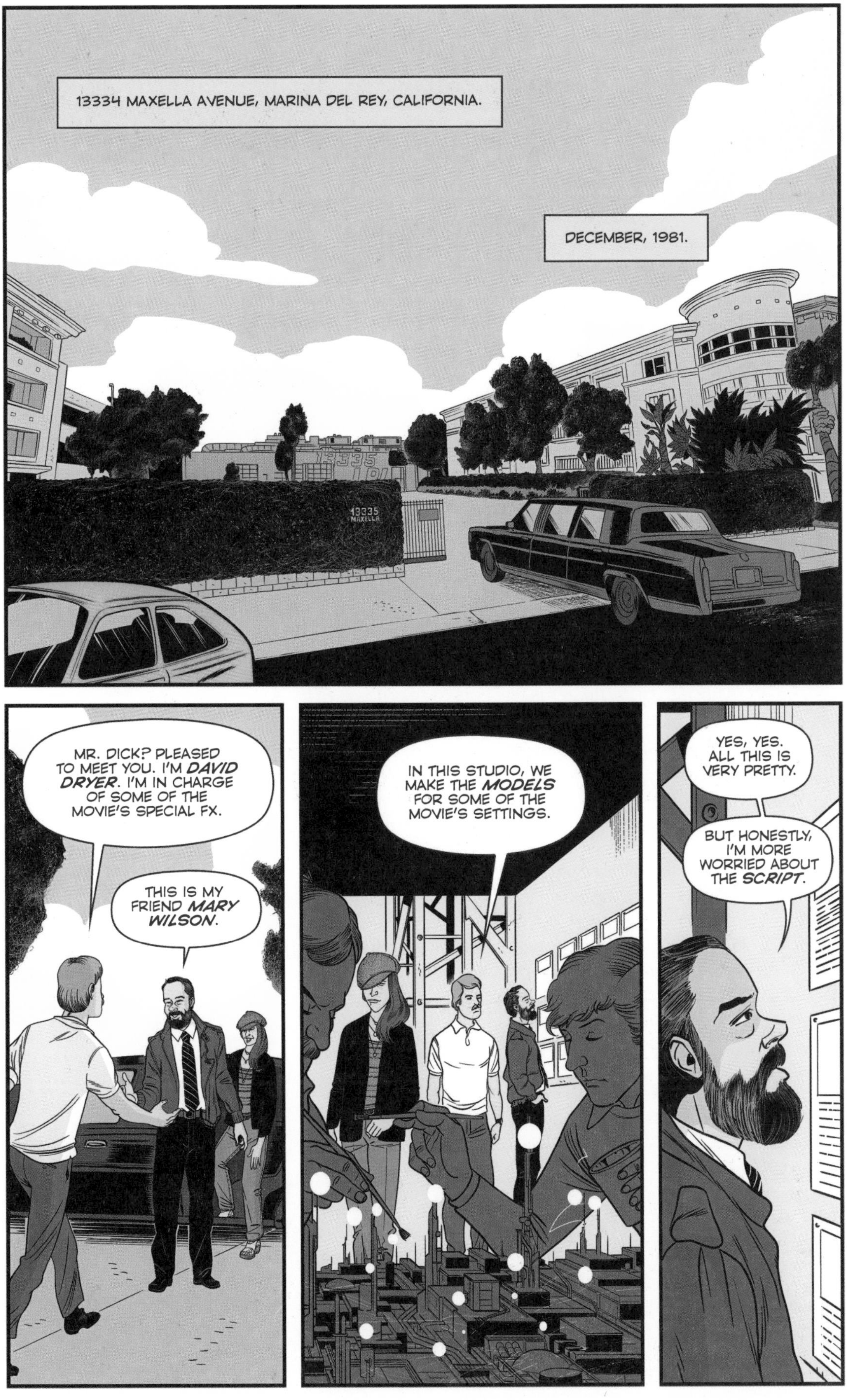
13334 MAXELLA AVENUE, MARINA DEL REY, CALIFORNIA.
DECEMBER, 1981.
13335 MAXELLA
MR. DICK? PLEASED TO MEET YOU. I'M DAVID DRYER. I'M IN CHARGE OF SOME OF THE MOVIE'S SPECIAL FX.
THIS IS MY FRIEND MARY WILSON.
IN THIS STUDIO, WE MAKE THE MODELS FOR SOME OF THE MOVIE'S SETTINGS.
YES, YES. ALL THIS IS VERY PRETTY.
BUT HONESTLY, I'M MORE WORRIED ABOUT THE SCRIPT.

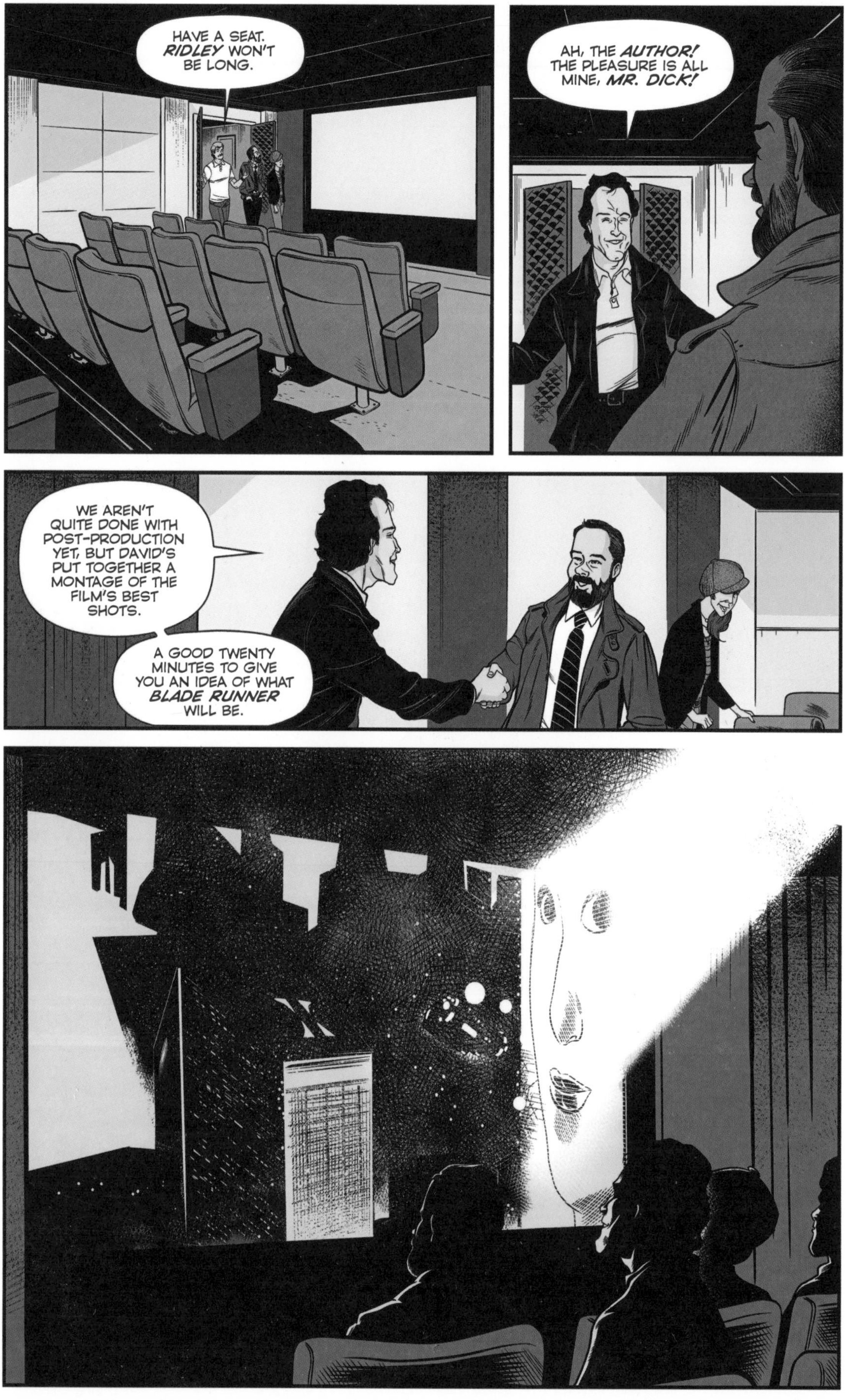
HAVE A SEAT. RIDLEY WON'T BE LONG.
AH, THE AUTHOR! THE PLEASURE IS ALL MINE, MR. DICK!
WE AREN'T QUITE DONE WITH POST-PRODUCTION YET, BUT DAVID'S PUT TOGETHER A MONTAGE OF THE FILM'S BEST SHOTS.
A GOOD TWENTY MINUTES TO GIVE YOU AN IDEA OF WHAT BLADE RUNNER WILL BE.

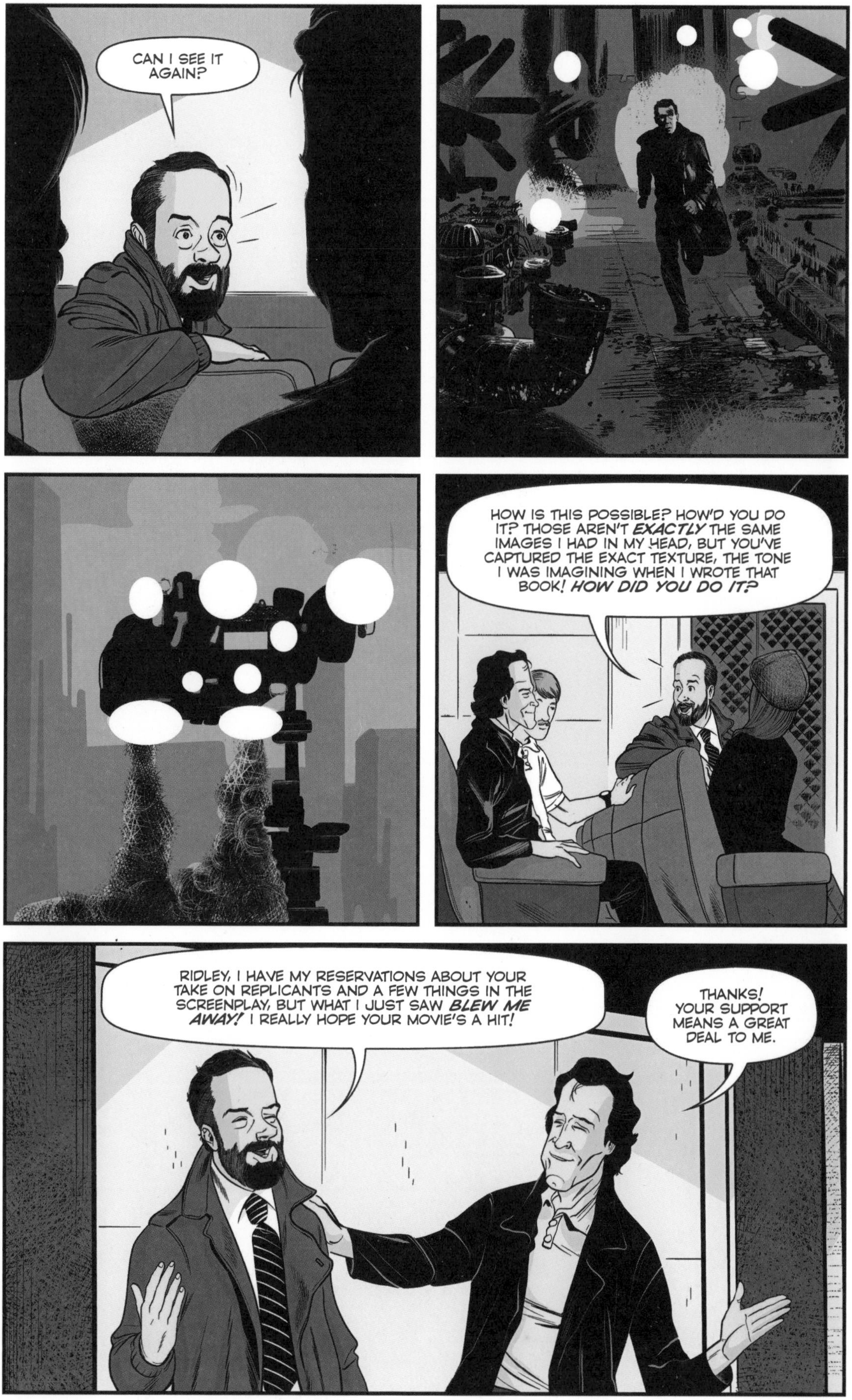
CAN I SEE IT AGAIN?
HOW IS THIS POSSIBLE? HOW'D YOU DO IT? THOSE AREN'T EXACTLY THE SAME IMAGES I HAD IN MY HEAD, BUT YOU'VE CAPTURED THE EXACT TEXTURE, THE TONE I WAS IMAGINING WHEN I WROTE THAT BOOK! HOW DID YOU DO IT?
RIDLEY, I HAVE MY RESERVATIONS ABOUT YOUR TAKE ON REPLICANTS AND A FEW THINGS IN THE SCREENPLAY, BUT WHAT I JUST SAW BLEW ME AWAY! I REALLY HOPE YOUR MOVIE'S A HIT!
THANKS! YOUR SUPPORT MEANS A GREAT DEAL TO ME.

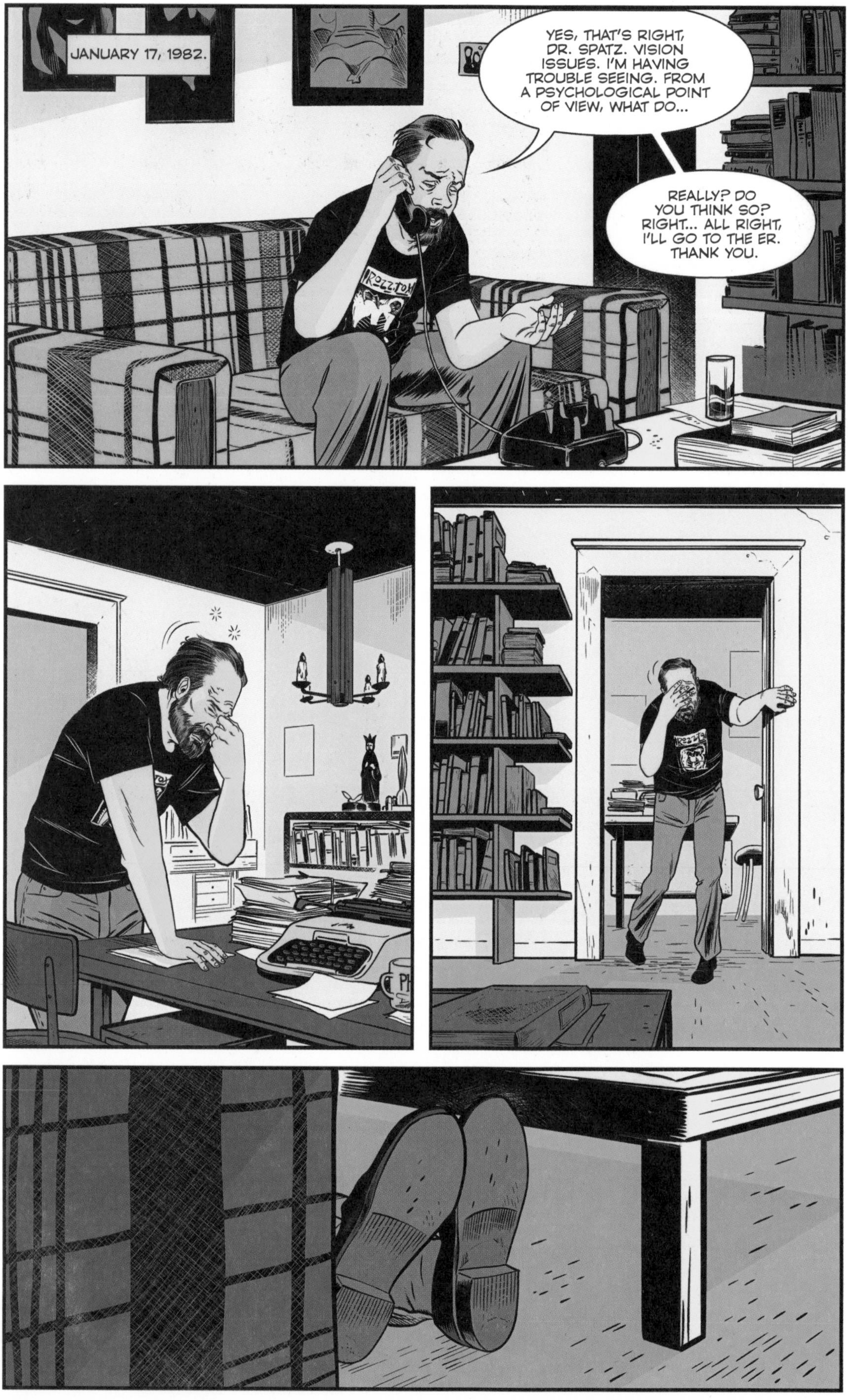
JANUARY 17, 1982.
YES, THAT'S RIGHT, DR. SPATZ. VISION ISSUES. I'M HAVING TROUBLE SEEING. FROM A PSYCHOLOGICAL POINT OF VIEW, WHAT DO...
REALLY? DO YOU THINK SO? RIGHT... ALL RIGHT, I'LL GO TO THE ER. THANK YOU.

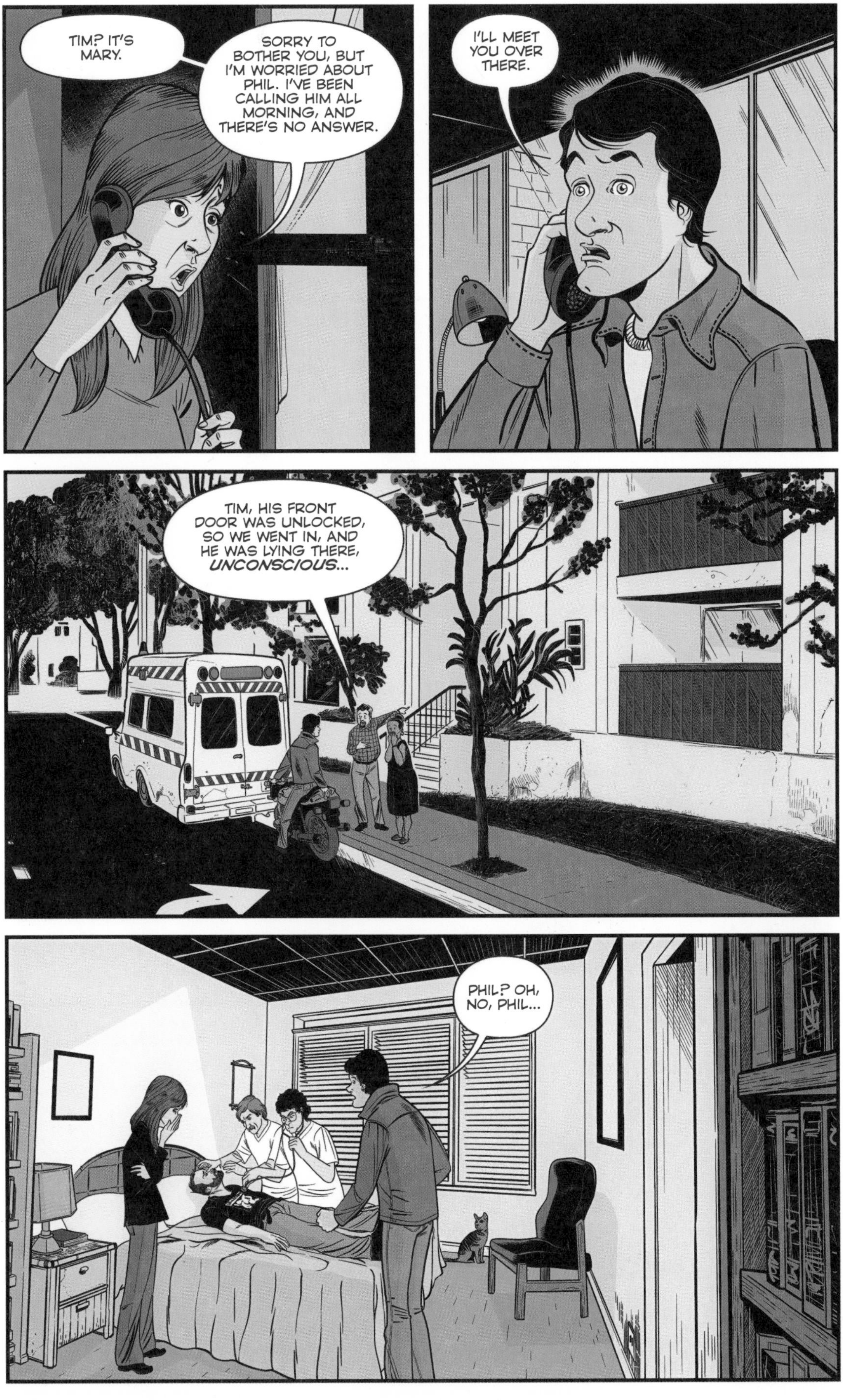
TIM? IT'S MARY.
SORRY TO BOTHER YOU, BUT I'M WORRIED ABOUT PHIL. I'VE BEEN CALLING HIM ALL MORNING, AND THERE'S NO ANSWER.
I'LL MEET YOU OVER THERE.
TIM, HIS FRONT DOOR WAS UNLOCKED, SO WE WENT IN, AND HE WAS LYING THERE, *UNCONSCIOUS*...
PHIL? OH, NO, PHIL...

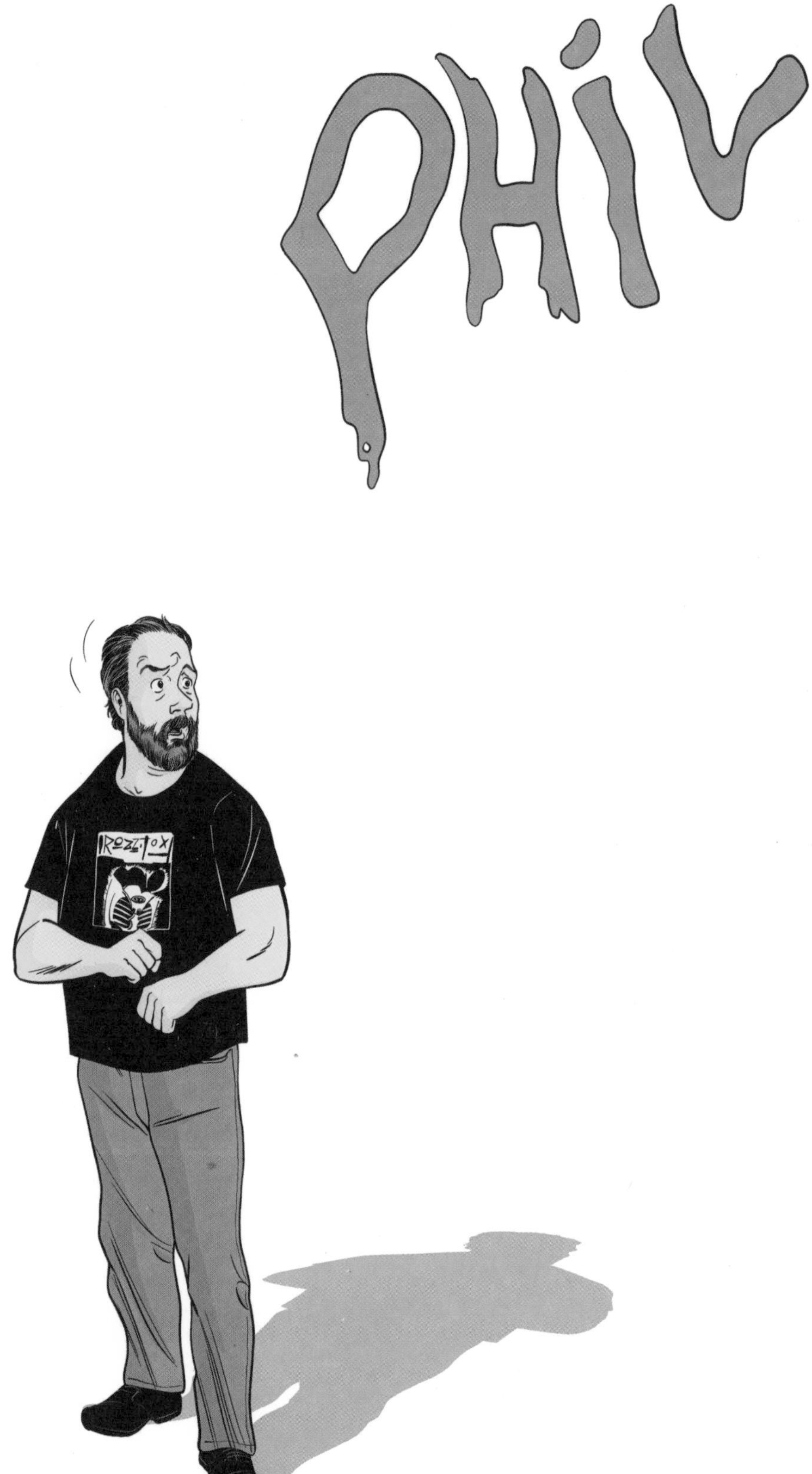
PHIL

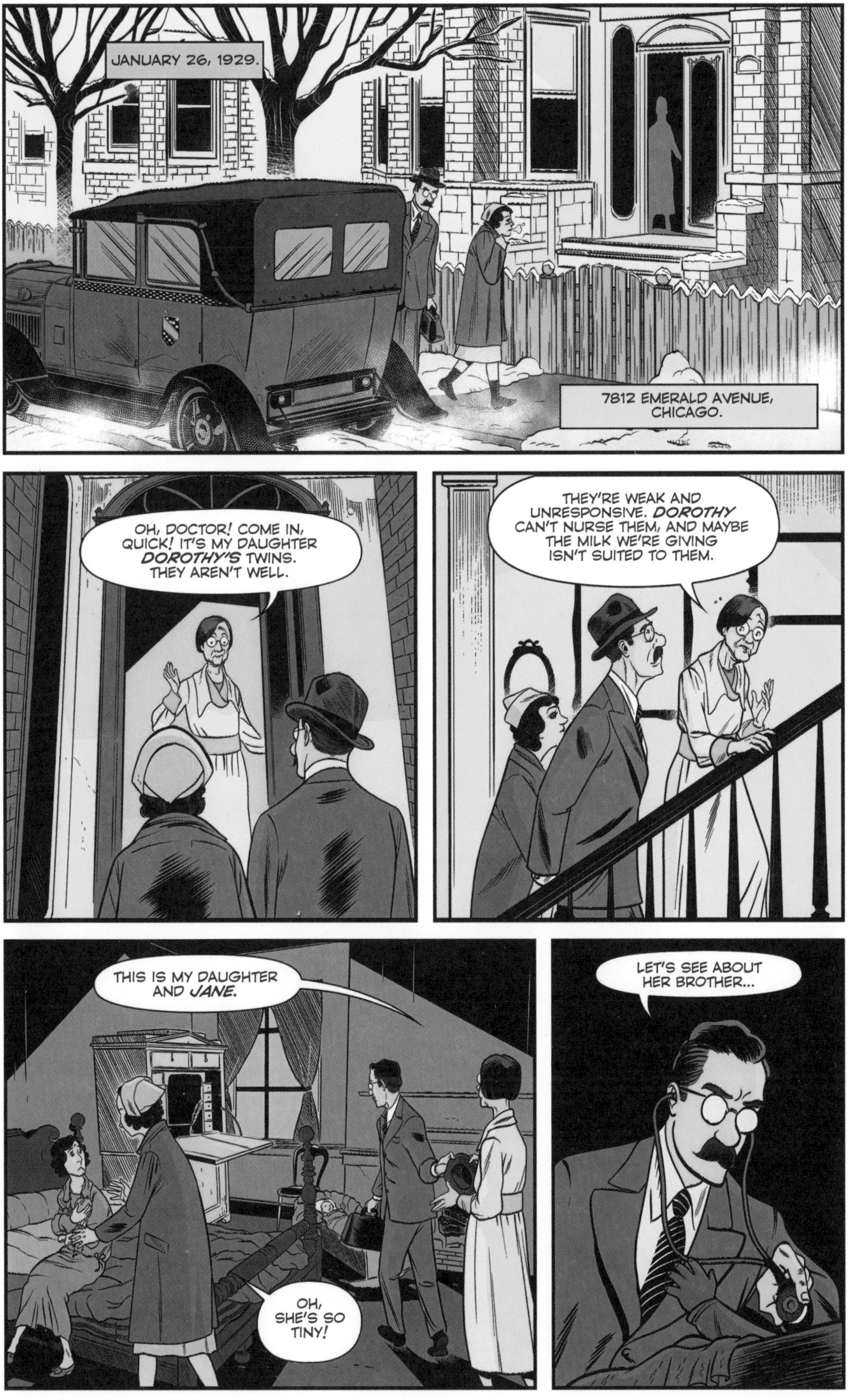
JANUARY 26, 1929.
7812 EMERALD AVENUE, CHICAGO.
OH, DOCTOR! COME IN, QUICK! IT'S MY DAUGHTER *DOROTHY'S* TWINS. THEY AREN'T WELL.
THEY'RE WEAK AND UNRESPONSIVE. *DOROTHY* CAN'T NURSE THEM, AND MAYBE THE MILK WE'RE GIVING ISN'T SUITED TO THEM.
THIS IS MY DAUGHTER AND *JANE*.
OH, SHE'S SO TINY!
LET'S SEE ABOUT HER BROTHER...

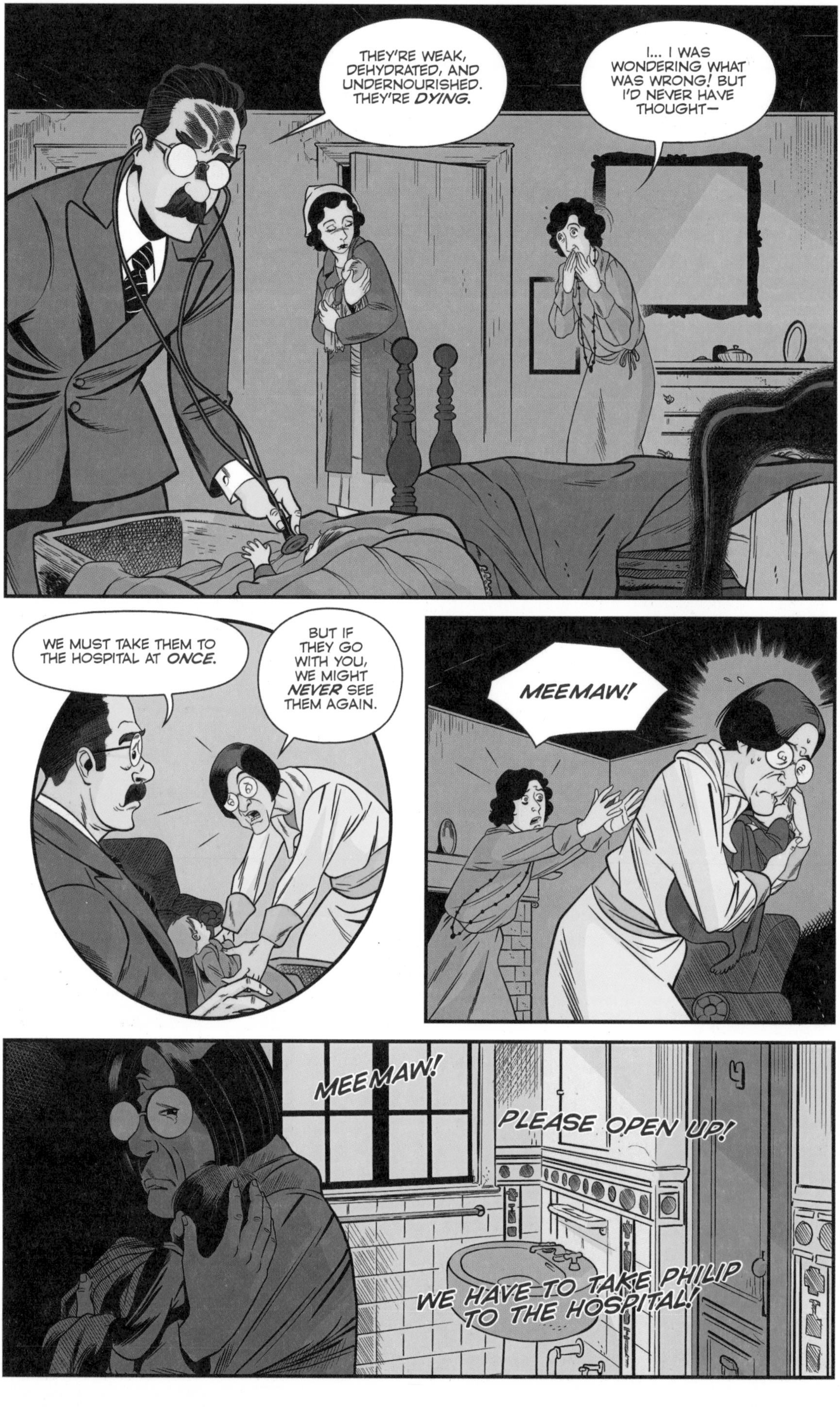
THEY'RE WEAK, DEHYDRATED, AND UNDERNOURISHED. THEY'RE *DYING*.
I... I WAS WONDERING WHAT WAS WRONG! BUT I'D NEVER HAVE THOUGHT—
WE MUST TAKE THEM TO THE HOSPITAL AT *ONCE*.
BUT IF THEY GO WITH YOU, WE MIGHT *NEVER* SEE THEM AGAIN.
MEEMAW!
MEEMAW!
PLEASE OPEN UP!
WE HAVE TO TAKE PHILIP TO THE HOSPITAL!

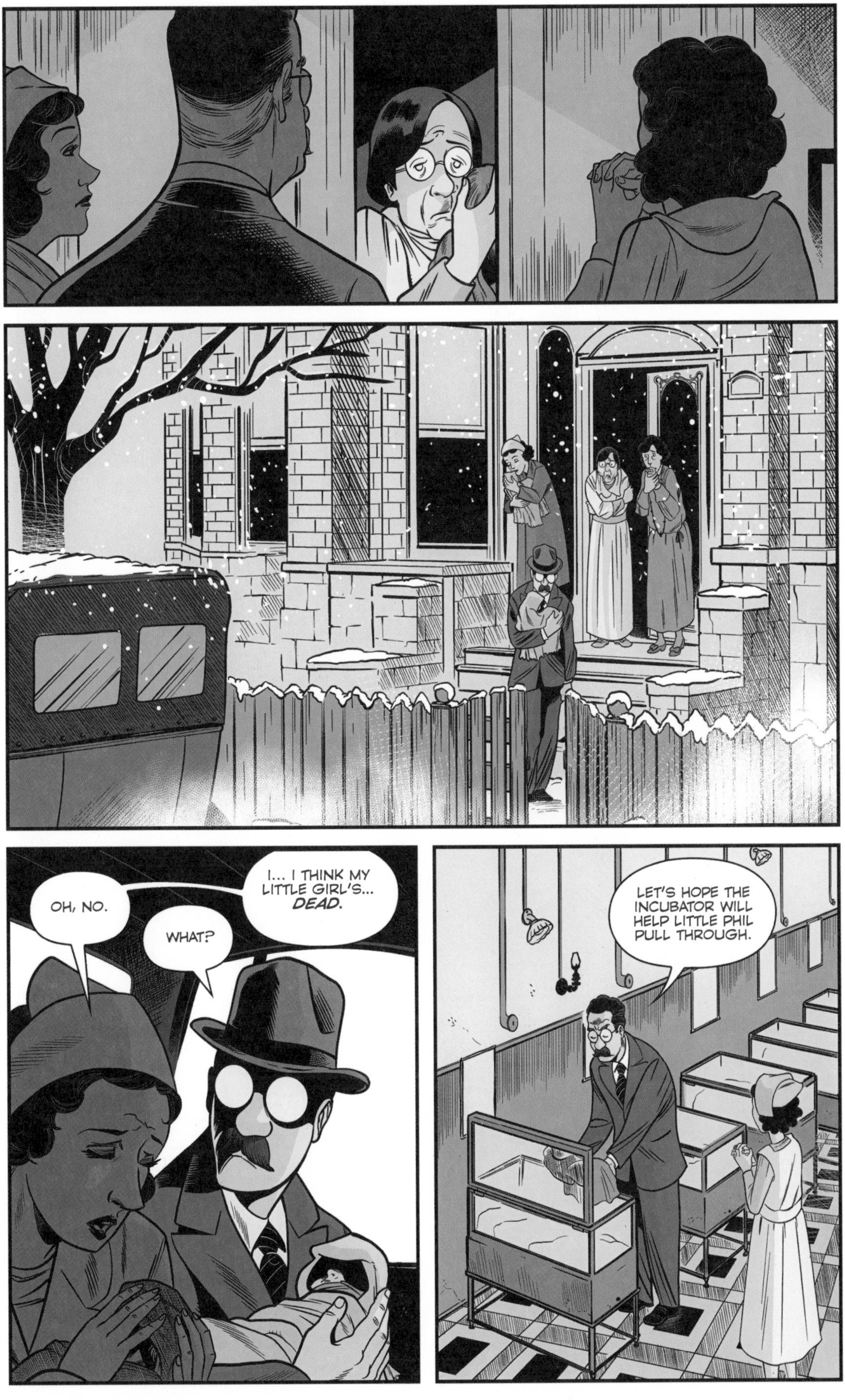
OH, NO.
WHAT?
I... I THINK MY LITTLE GIRL'S... ***DEAD.***
LET'S HOPE THE INCUBATOR WILL HELP LITTLE PHIL PULL THROUGH.

HALF-LIFE

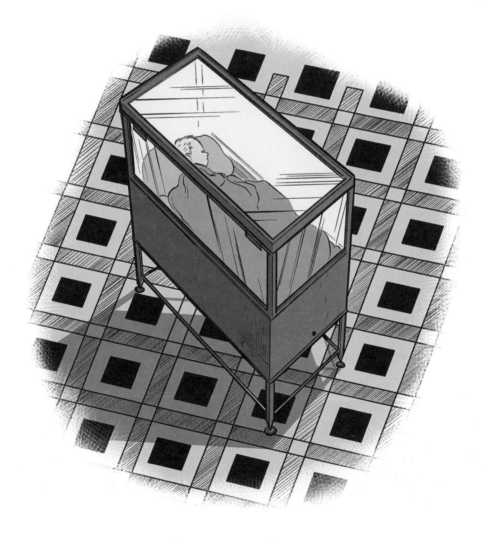

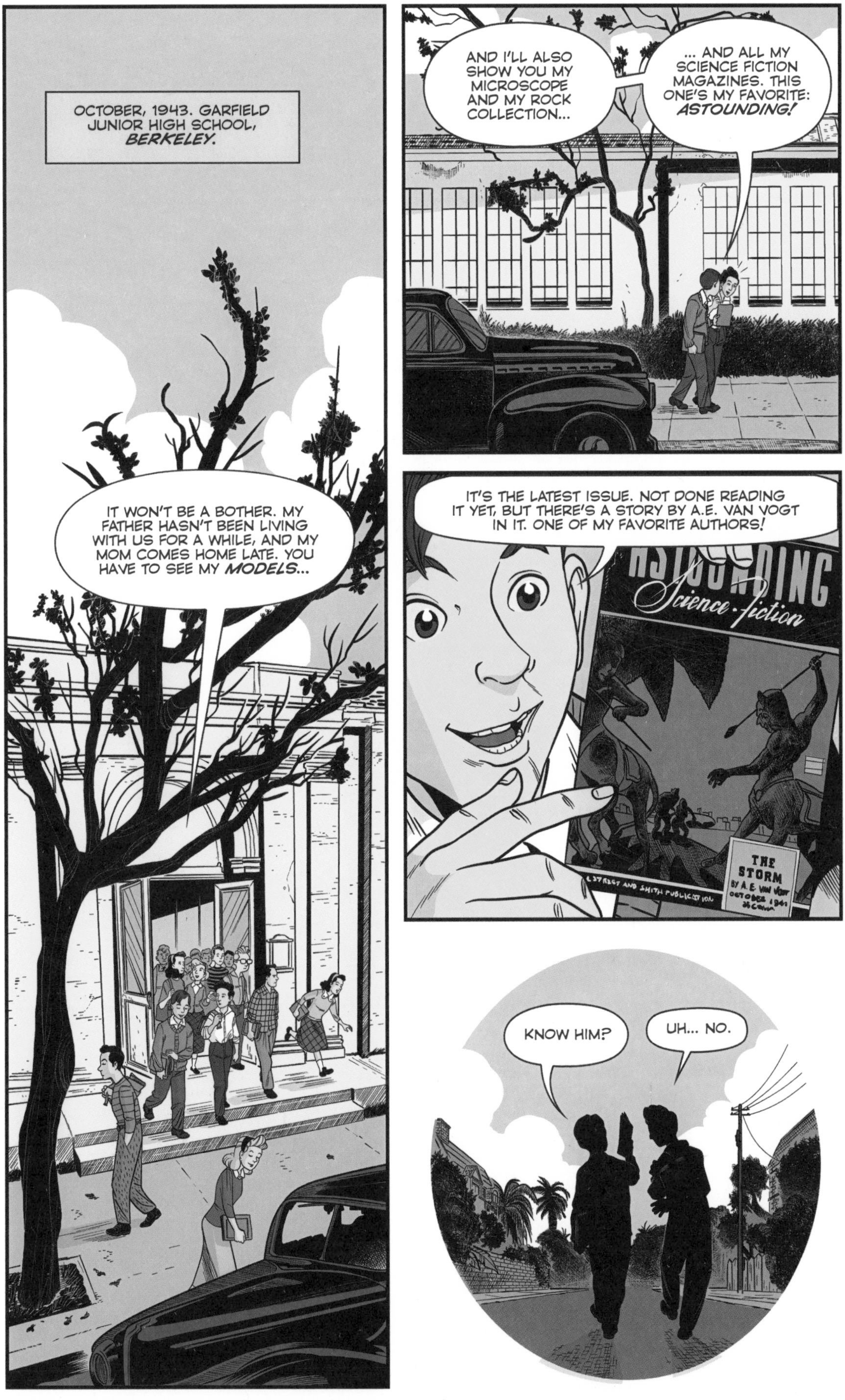
OCTOBER, 1943. GARFIELD JUNIOR HIGH SCHOOL, *BERKELEY.*
IT WON'T BE A BOTHER. MY FATHER HASN'T BEEN LIVING WITH US FOR A WHILE, AND MY MOM COMES HOME LATE. YOU HAVE TO SEE MY *MODELS*...
AND I'LL ALSO SHOW YOU MY MICROSCOPE AND MY ROCK COLLECTION...
... AND ALL MY SCIENCE FICTION MAGAZINES. THIS ONE'S MY FAVORITE: *ASTOUNDING!*
IT'S THE LATEST ISSUE. NOT DONE READING IT YET, BUT THERE'S A STORY BY A.E. VAN VOGT IN IT. ONE OF MY FAVORITE AUTHORS!
Science-Fiction
THE STORM
BY A.E. VAN VOGT
KNOW HIM?
UH... NO.

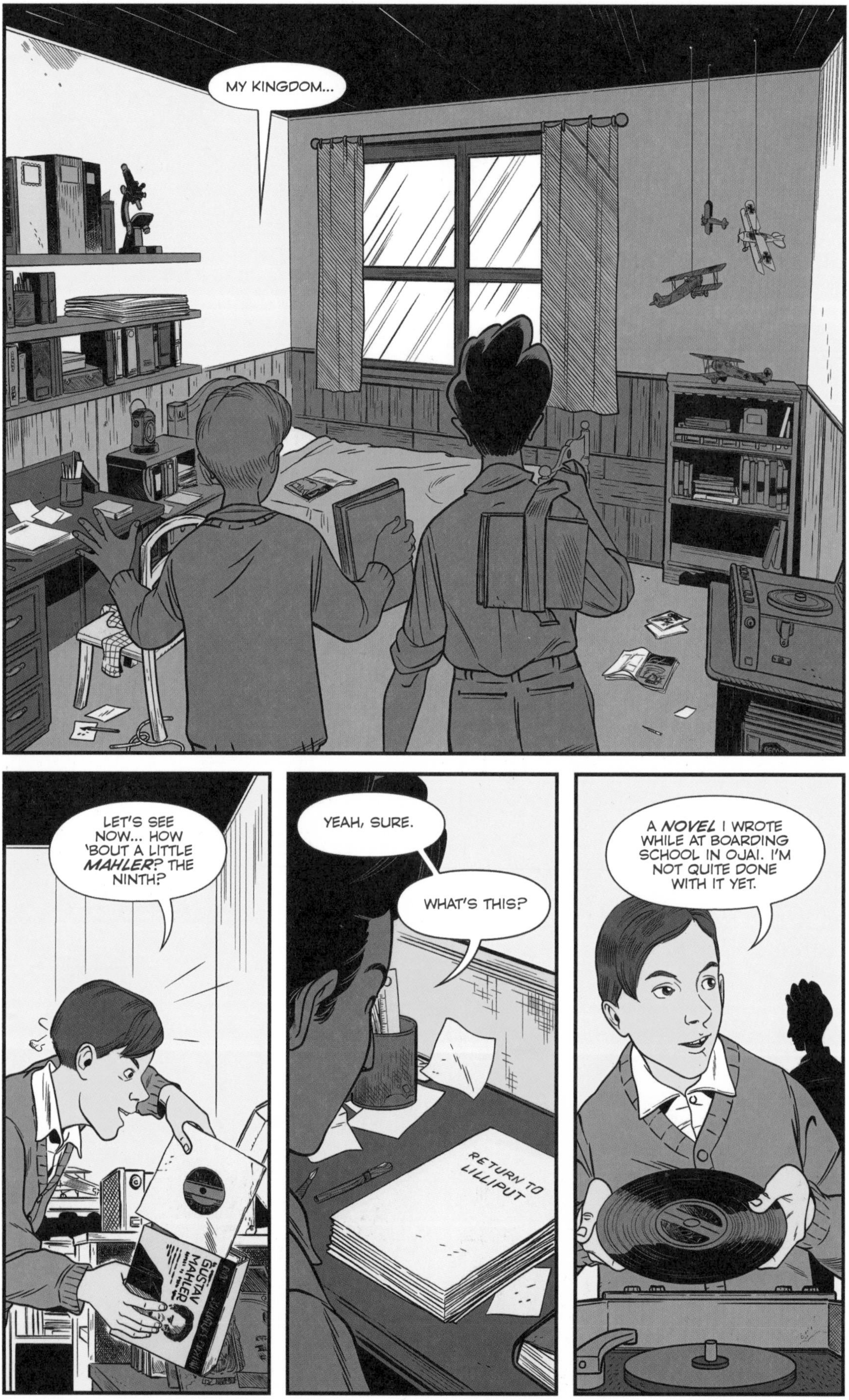
MY KINGDOM...
LET'S SEE NOW... HOW 'BOUT A LITTLE *MAHLER*? THE NINTH?
GUSTAV MAHLER
YEAH, SURE.
WHAT'S THIS?
RETURN TO LILLIPUT
A *NOVEL* I WROTE WHILE AT BOARDING SCHOOL IN OJAI. I'M NOT QUITE DONE WITH IT YET.

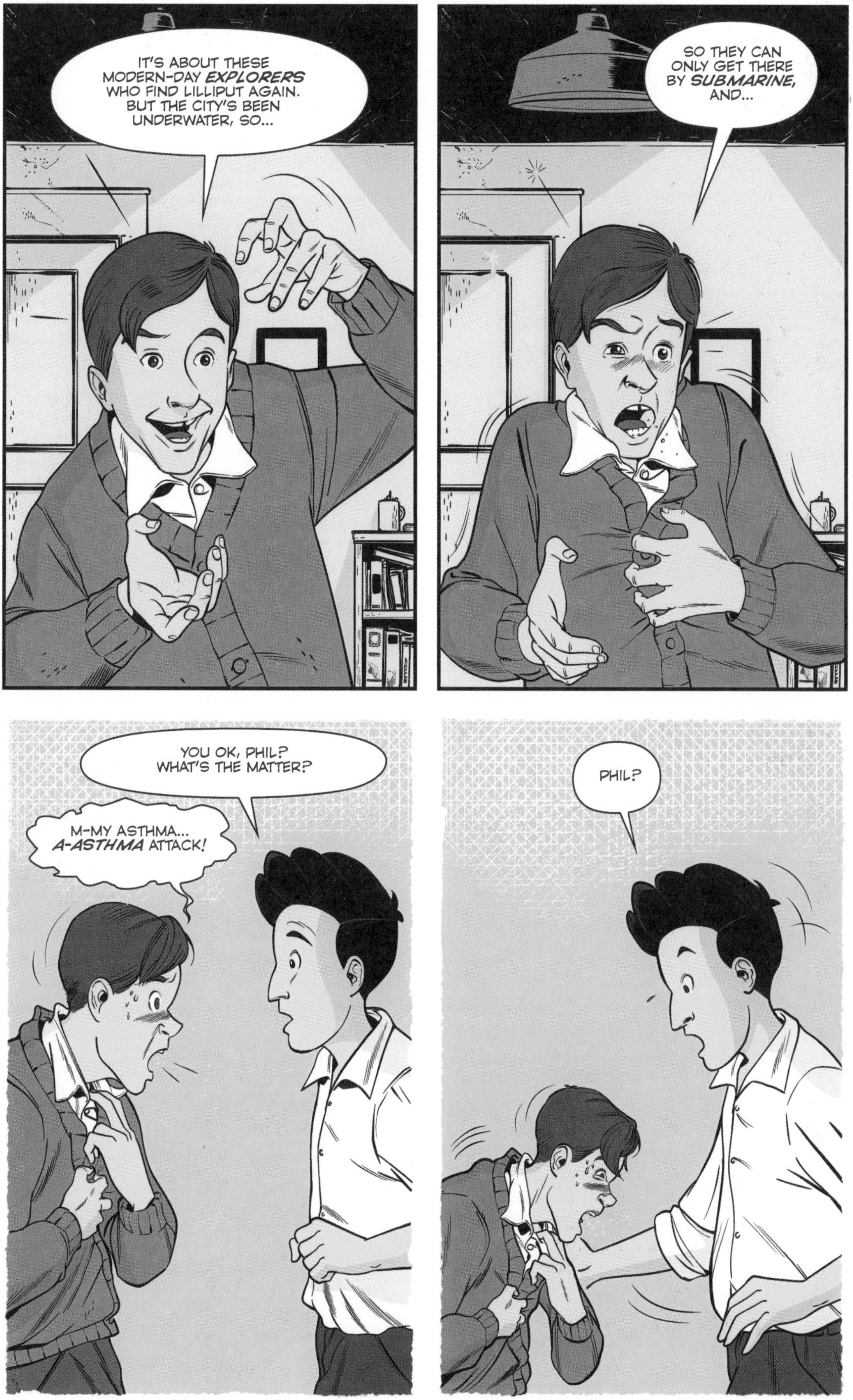
IT'S ABOUT THESE MODERN-DAY EXPLORERS WHO FIND LILLIPUT AGAIN. BUT THE CITY'S BEEN UNDERWATER, SO...
SO THEY CAN ONLY GET THERE BY SUBMARINE, AND...
YOU OK, PHIL? WHAT'S THE MATTER?
M-MY ASTHMA... A-ASTHMA ATTACK!
PHIL?

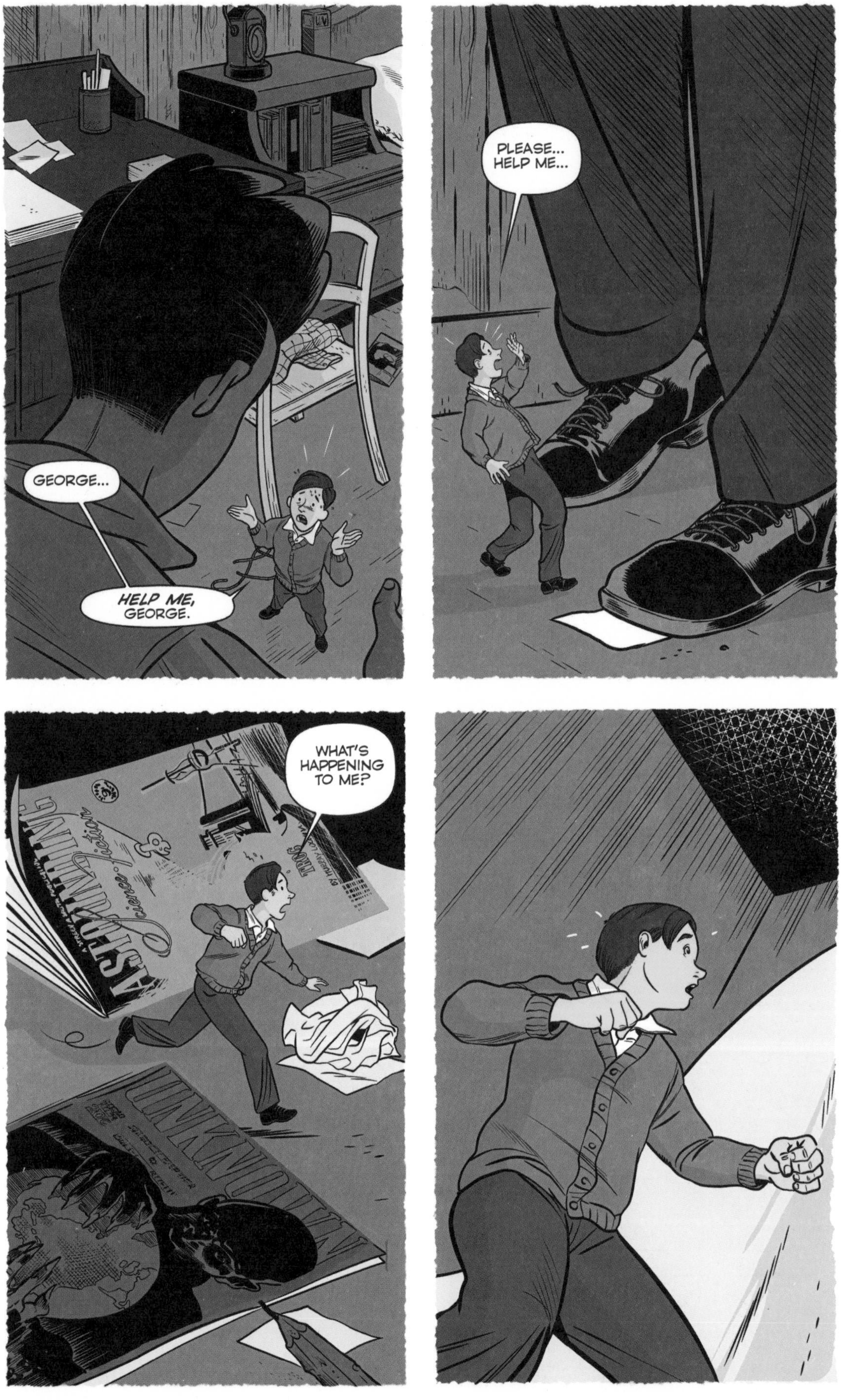
GEORGE...
HELP ME, GEORGE.
PLEASE... HELP ME...
WHAT'S HAPPENING TO ME?

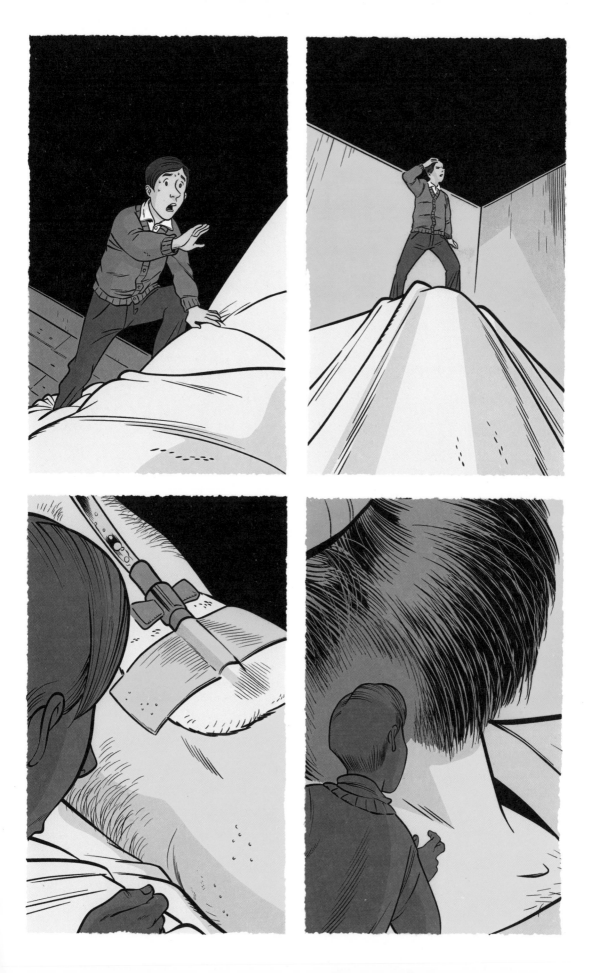

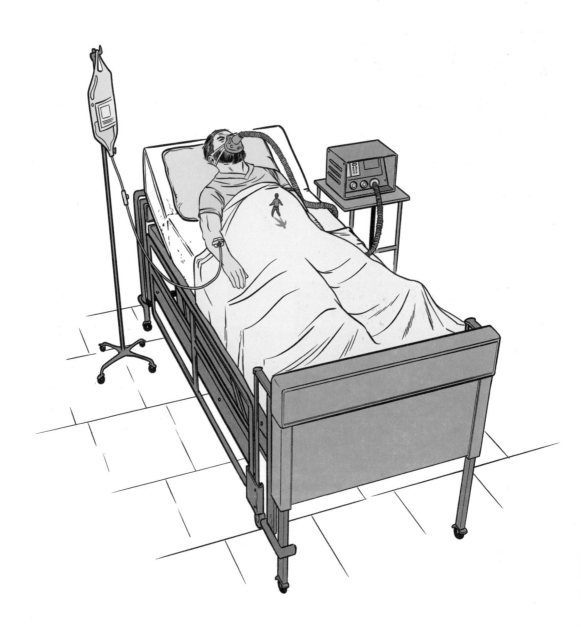

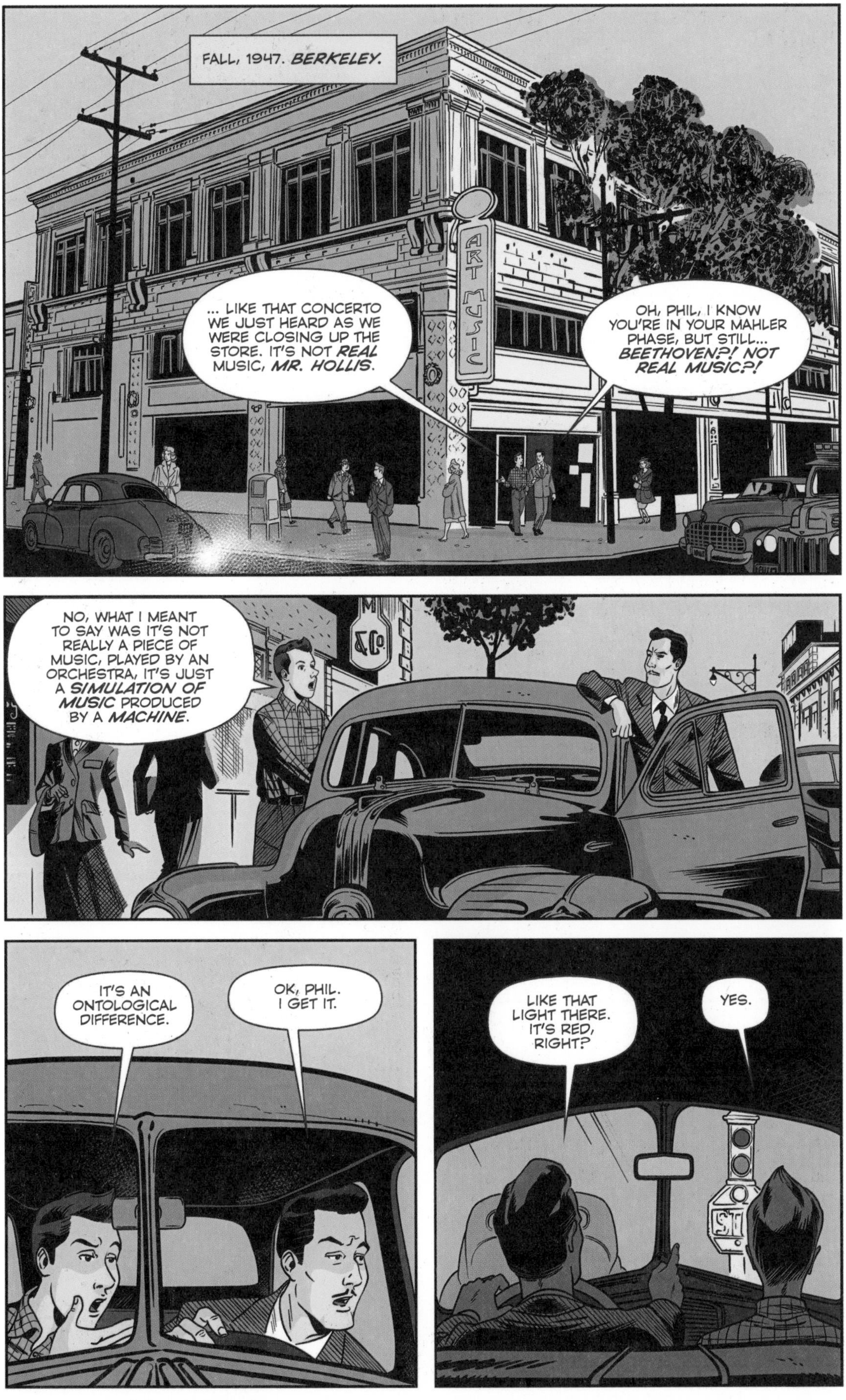
FALL, 1947. BERKELEY.
ART MUSIC
... LIKE THAT CONCERTO WE JUST HEARD AS WE WERE CLOSING UP THE STORE. IT'S NOT REAL MUSIC, MR. HOLLIS.
OH, PHIL, I KNOW YOU'RE IN YOUR MAHLER PHASE, BUT STILL... BEETHOVEN?! NOT REAL MUSIC?!
NO, WHAT I MEANT TO SAY WAS IT'S NOT REALLY A PIECE OF MUSIC, PLAYED BY AN ORCHESTRA, IT'S JUST A SIMULATION OF MUSIC PRODUCED BY A MACHINE.
IT'S AN ONTOLOGICAL DIFFERENCE.
OK, PHIL. I GET IT.
LIKE THAT LIGHT THERE. IT'S RED, RIGHT?
YES.

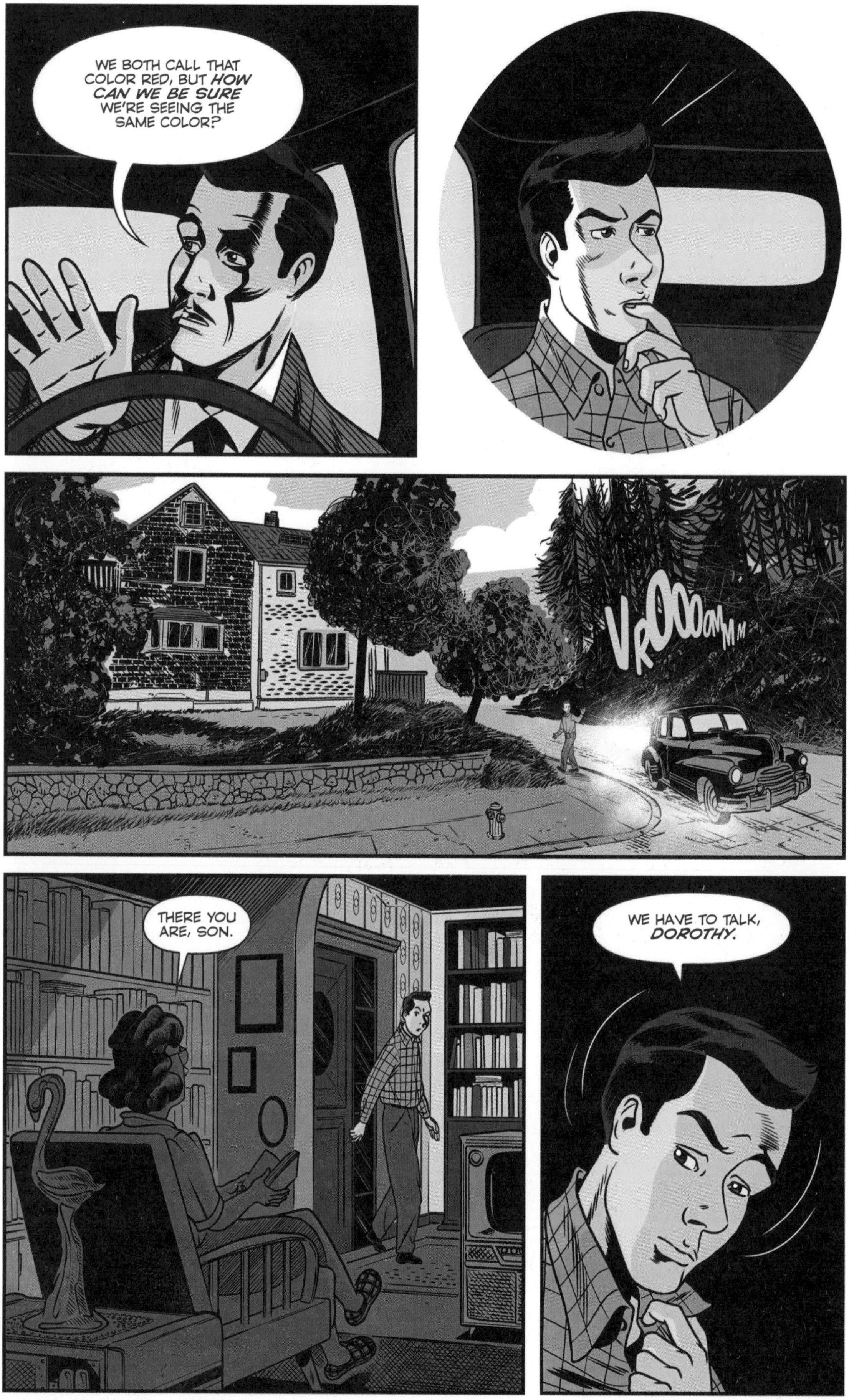
WE BOTH CALL THAT COLOR RED, BUT HOW CAN WE BE SURE WE'RE SEEING THE SAME COLOR?
VROOOOMMM
THERE YOU ARE, SON.
WE HAVE TO TALK, DOROTHY.

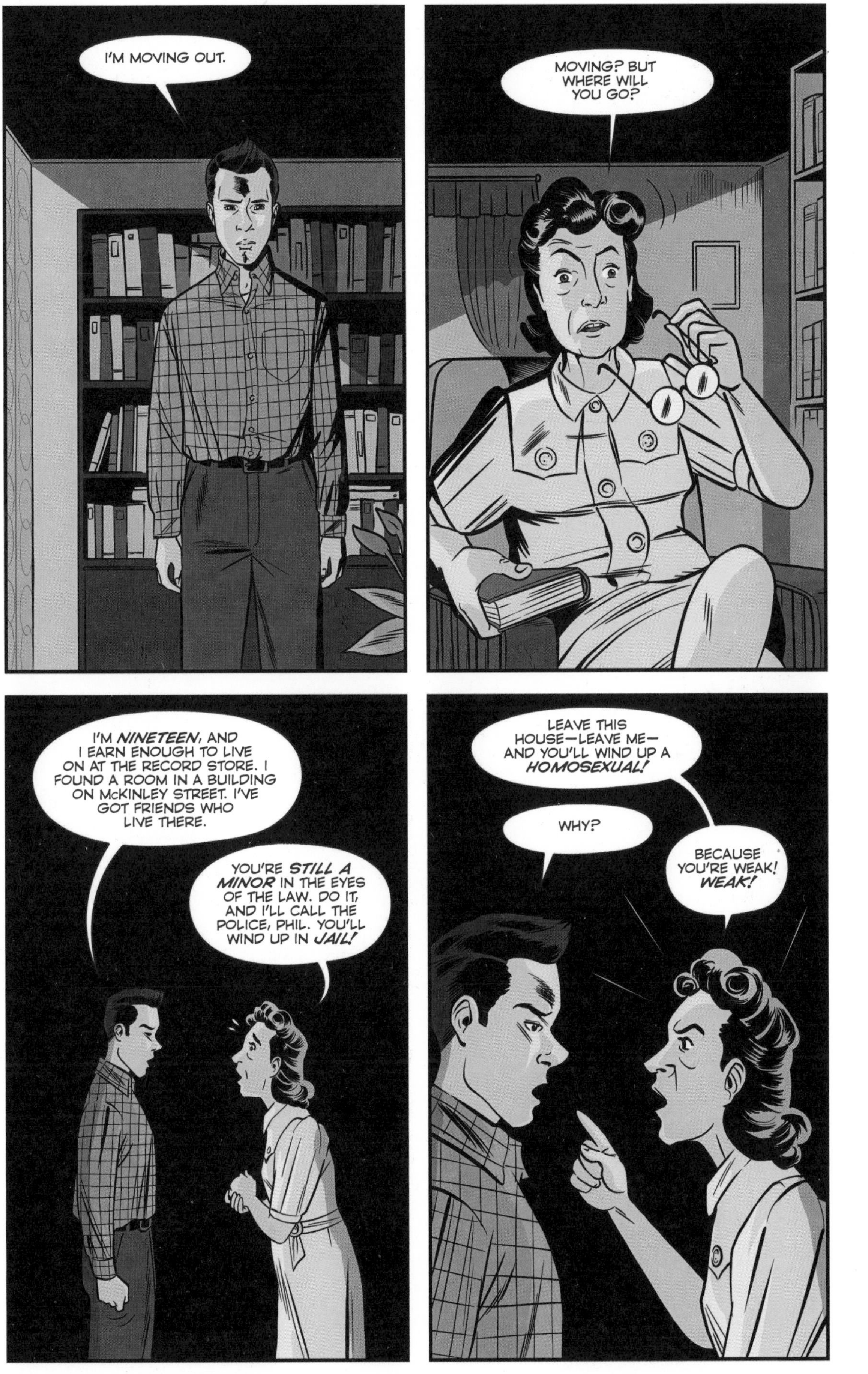
I'M MOVING OUT.
MOVING? BUT WHERE WILL YOU GO?
I'M NINETEEN, AND I EARN ENOUGH TO LIVE ON AT THE RECORD STORE. I FOUND A ROOM IN A BUILDING ON McKINLEY STREET. I'VE GOT FRIENDS WHO LIVE THERE.
YOU'RE STILL A MINOR IN THE EYES OF THE LAW. DO IT, AND I'LL CALL THE POLICE, PHIL. YOU'LL WIND UP IN JAIL!
LEAVE THIS HOUSE—LEAVE ME—AND YOU'LL WIND UP A HOMOSEXUAL!
WHY?
BECAUSE YOU'RE WEAK! WEAK!

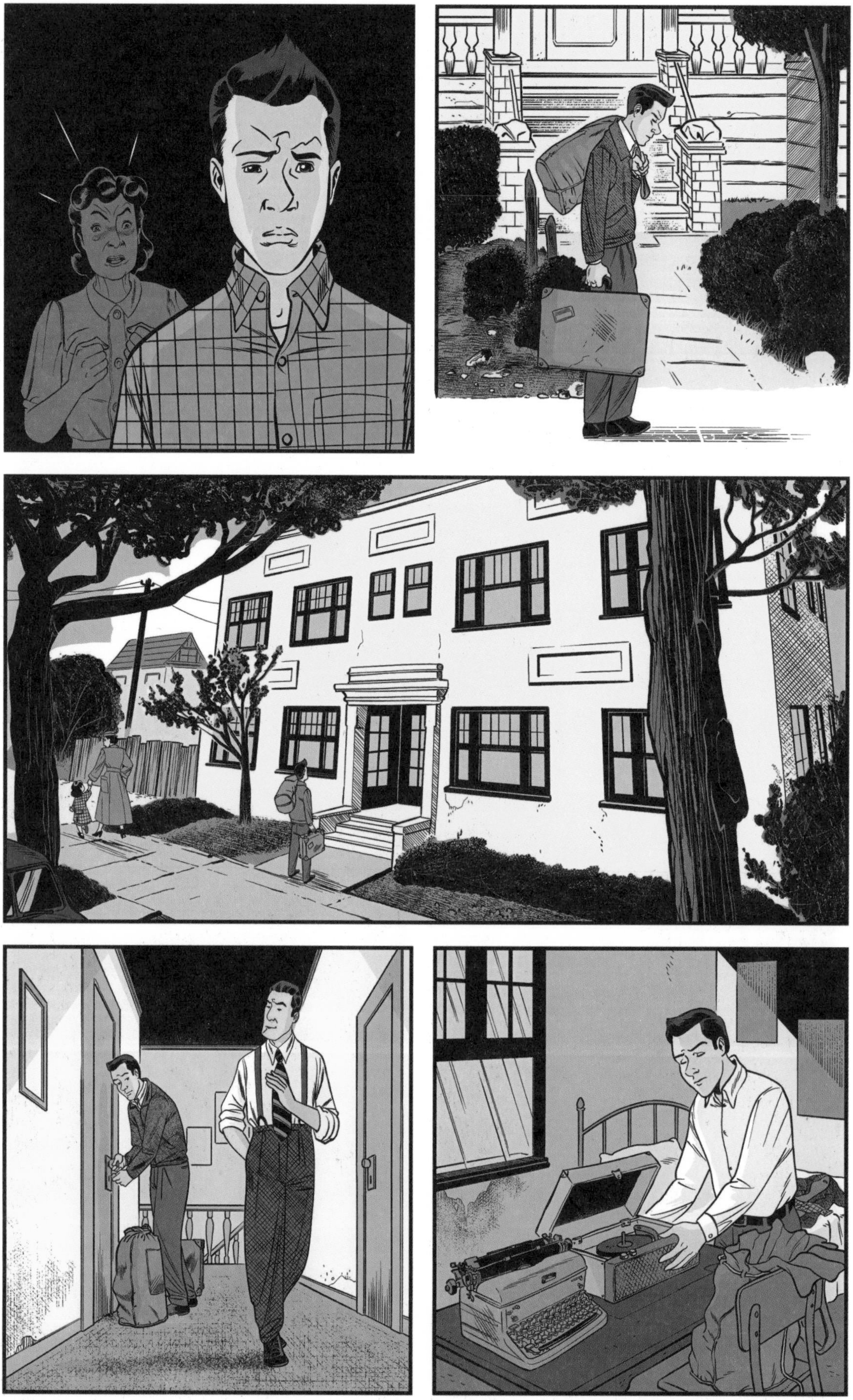

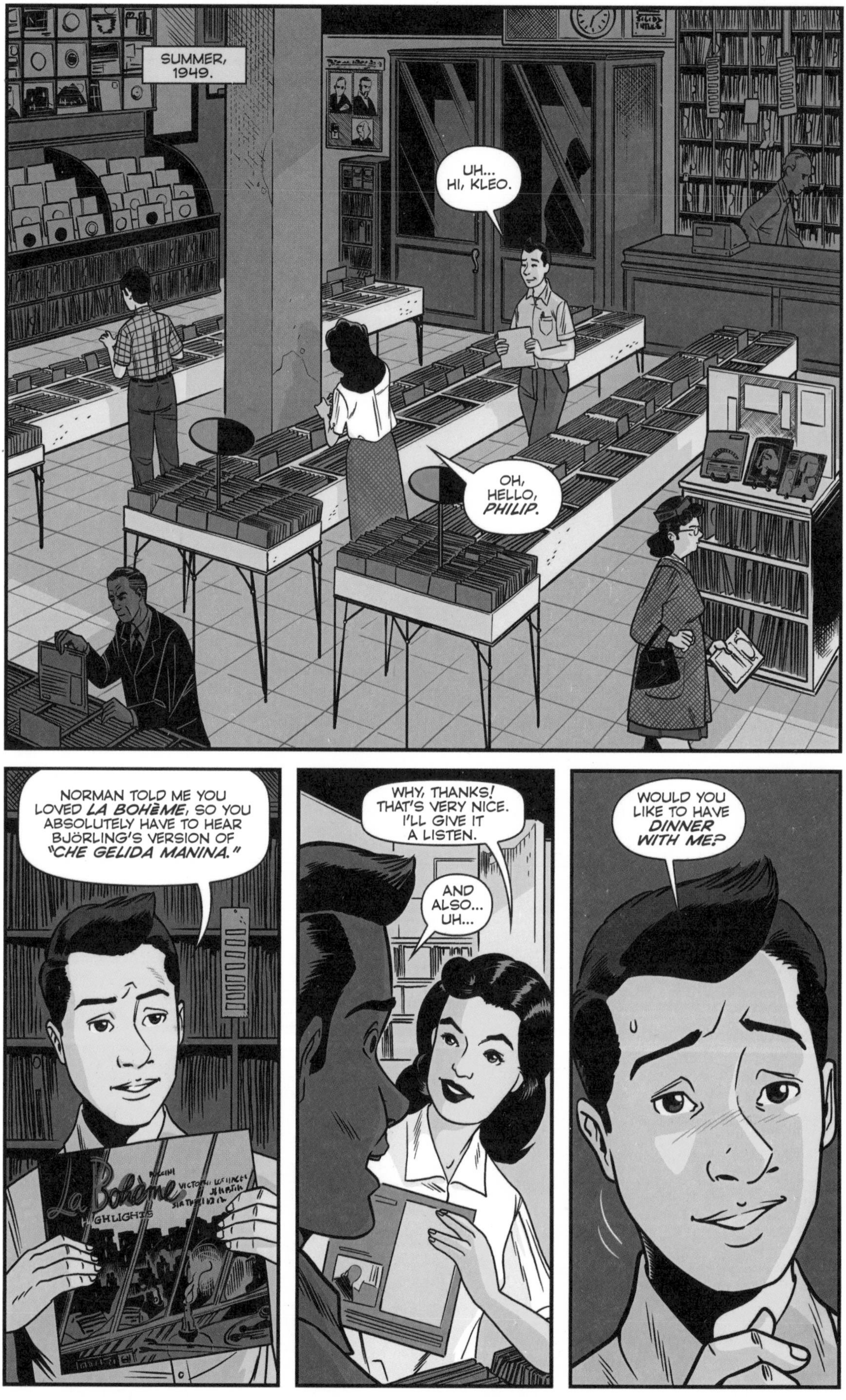
SUMMER, 1949.
UH... HI, KLEO.
OH, HELLO, PHILIP.
NORMAN TOLD ME YOU LOVED LA BOHÈME, SO YOU ABSOLUTELY HAVE TO HEAR BJÖRLING'S VERSION OF "CHE GELIDA MANINA."
La Bohème
HIGHLIGHTS
WHY, THANKS! THAT'S VERY NICE. I'LL GIVE IT A LISTEN.
AND ALSO... UH...
WOULD YOU LIKE TO HAVE DINNER WITH ME?

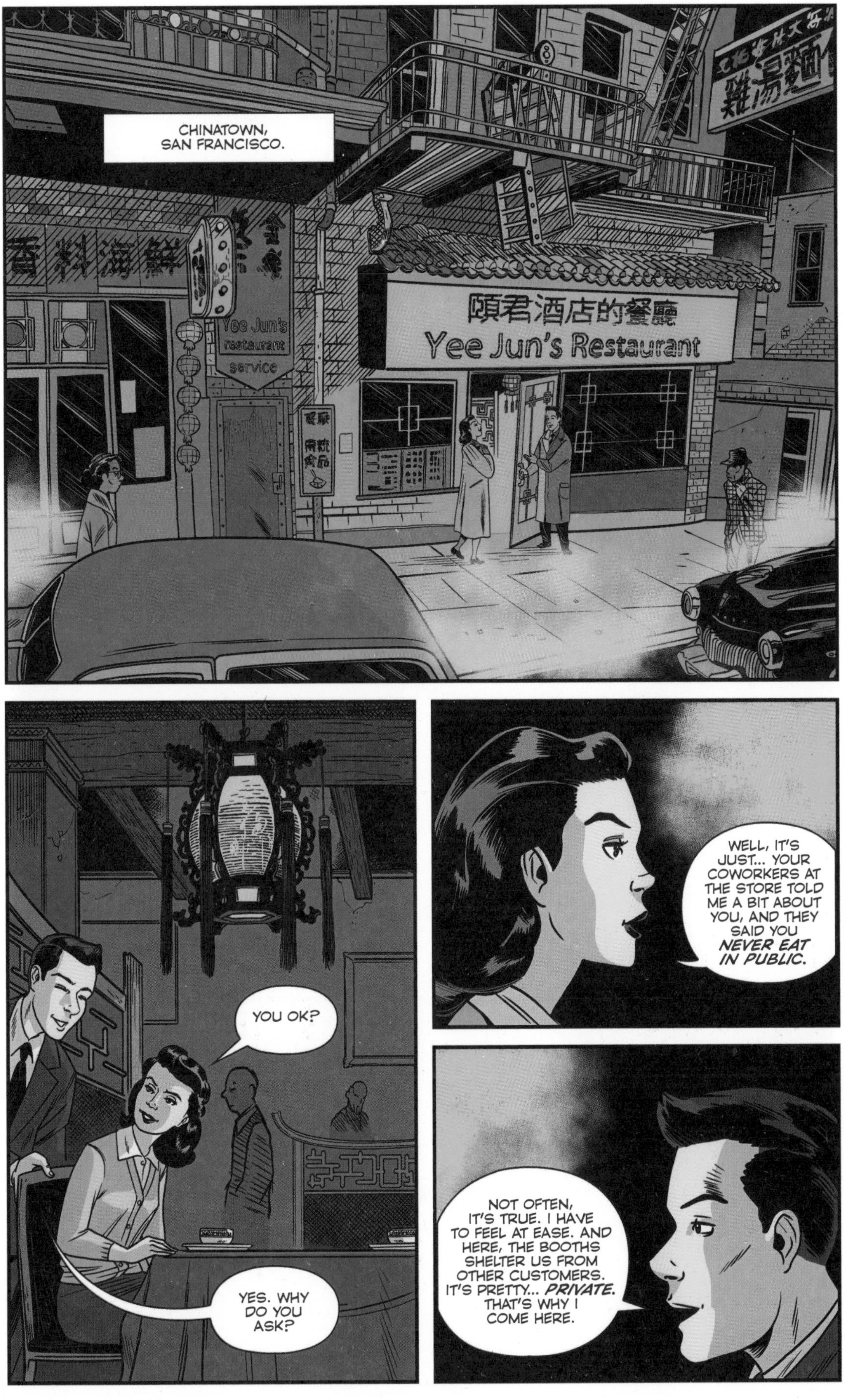

CHINATOWN, SAN FRANCISCO.
頤君酒店的餐廳
Yee Jun's Restaurant
Yee Jun's restaurant service
YOU OK?
YES. WHY DO YOU ASK?
WELL, IT'S JUST... YOUR COWORKERS AT THE STORE TOLD ME A BIT ABOUT YOU, AND THEY SAID YOU ***NEVER EAT IN PUBLIC***.
NOT OFTEN, IT'S TRUE. I HAVE TO FEEL AT EASE. AND HERE, THE BOOTHS SHELTER US FROM OTHER CUSTOMERS. IT'S PRETTY... ***PRIVATE***. THAT'S WHY I COME HERE.

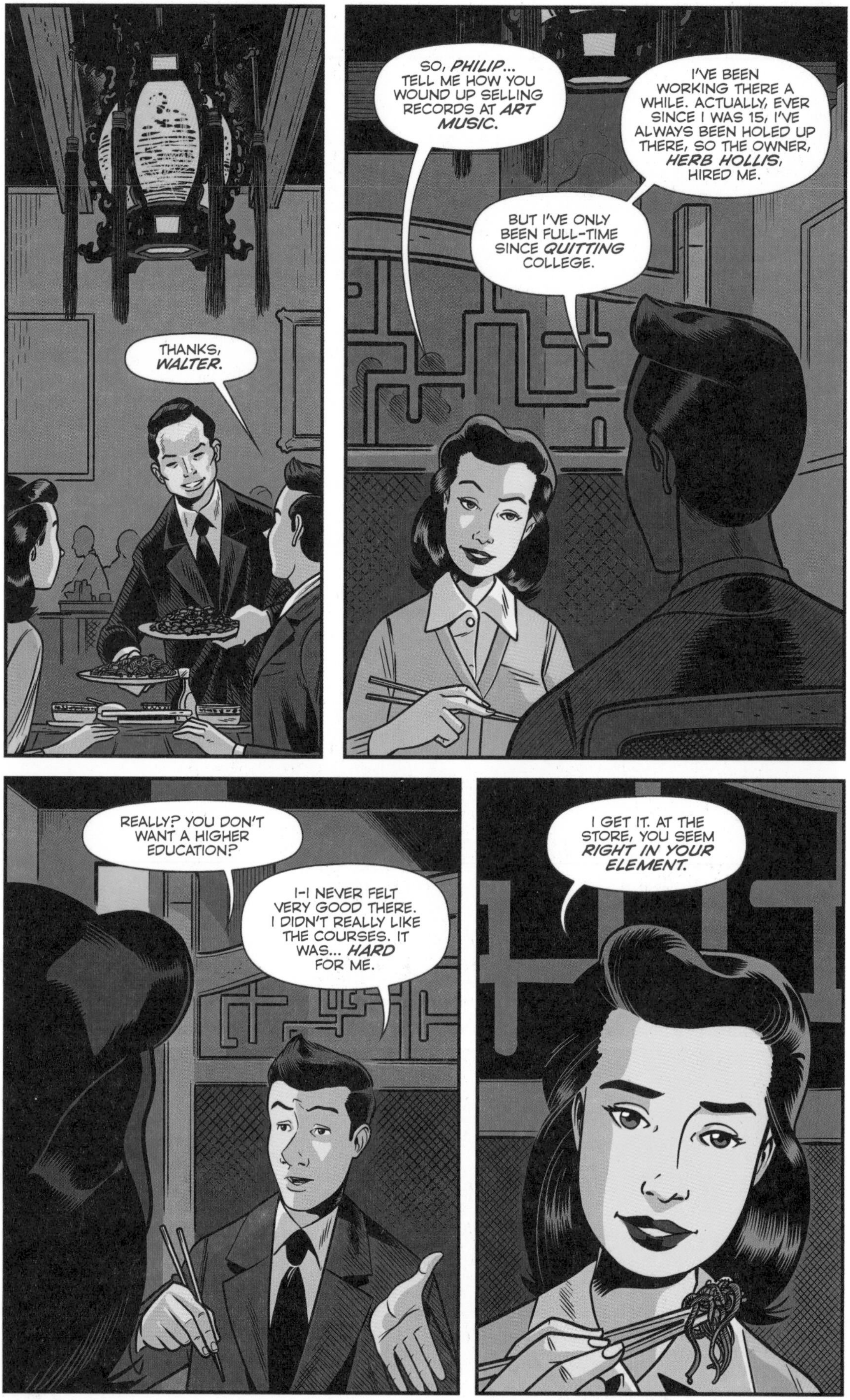
THANKS, WALTER.
SO, PHILIP... TELL ME HOW YOU WOUND UP SELLING RECORDS AT ART MUSIC.
I'VE BEEN WORKING THERE A WHILE. ACTUALLY, EVER SINCE I WAS 15, I'VE ALWAYS BEEN HOLED UP THERE, SO THE OWNER, HERB HOLLIS, HIRED ME.
BUT I'VE ONLY BEEN FULL-TIME SINCE QUITTING COLLEGE.
REALLY? YOU DON'T WANT A HIGHER EDUCATION?
I-I NEVER FELT VERY GOOD THERE. I DIDN'T REALLY LIKE THE COURSES. IT WAS... HARD FOR ME.
I GET IT. AT THE STORE, YOU SEEM RIGHT IN YOUR ELEMENT.

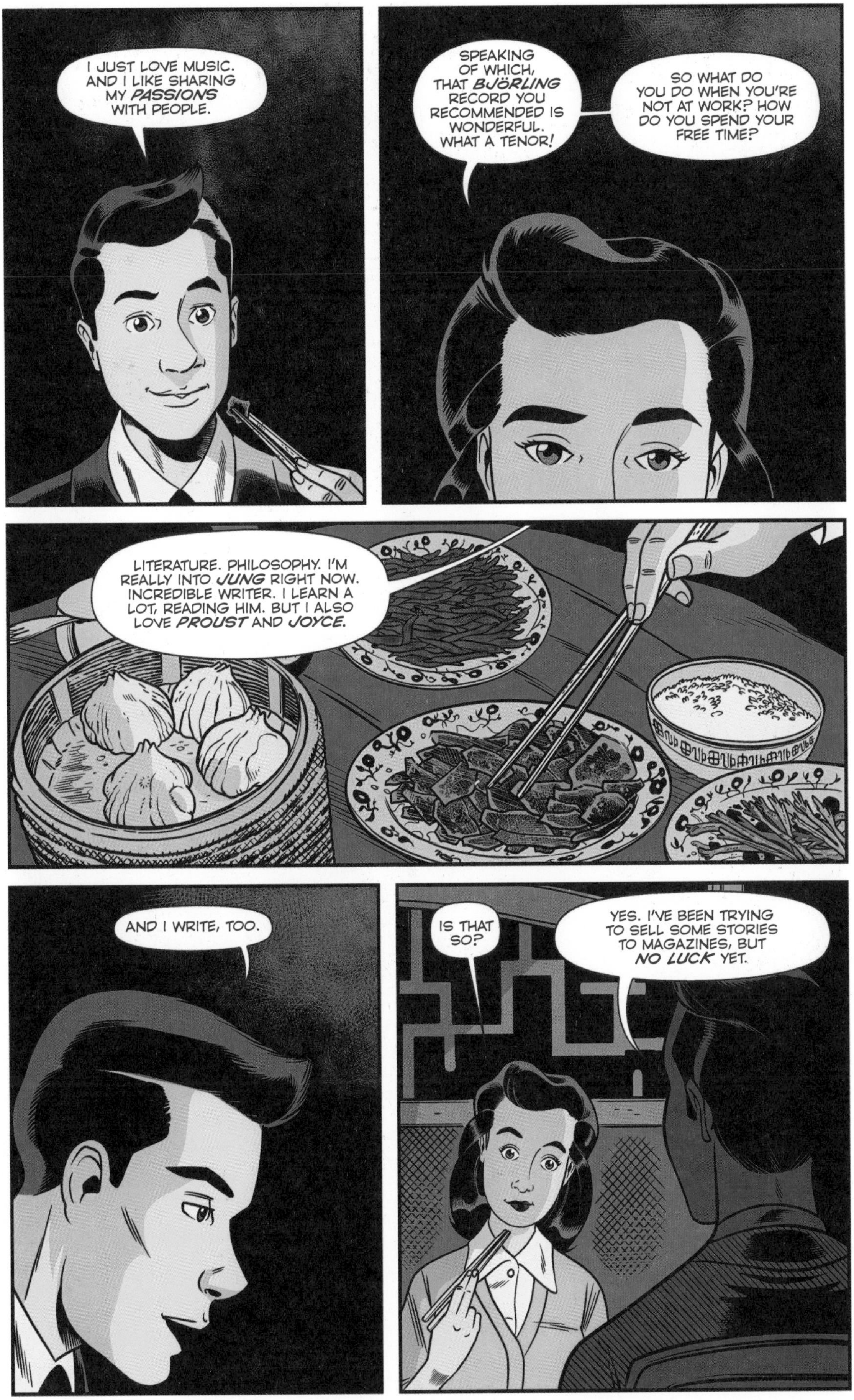
I JUST LOVE MUSIC. AND I LIKE SHARING MY PASSIONS WITH PEOPLE.
SPEAKING OF WHICH, THAT BJÖRLING RECORD YOU RECOMMENDED IS WONDERFUL. WHAT A TENOR!
SO WHAT DO YOU DO WHEN YOU'RE NOT AT WORK? HOW DO YOU SPEND YOUR FREE TIME?
LITERATURE. PHILOSOPHY. I'M REALLY INTO JUNG RIGHT NOW. INCREDIBLE WRITER. I LEARN A LOT, READING HIM. BUT I ALSO LOVE PROUST AND JOYCE.
AND I WRITE, TOO.
IS THAT SO?
YES. I'VE BEEN TRYING TO SELL SOME STORIES TO MAGAZINES, BUT NO LUCK YET.

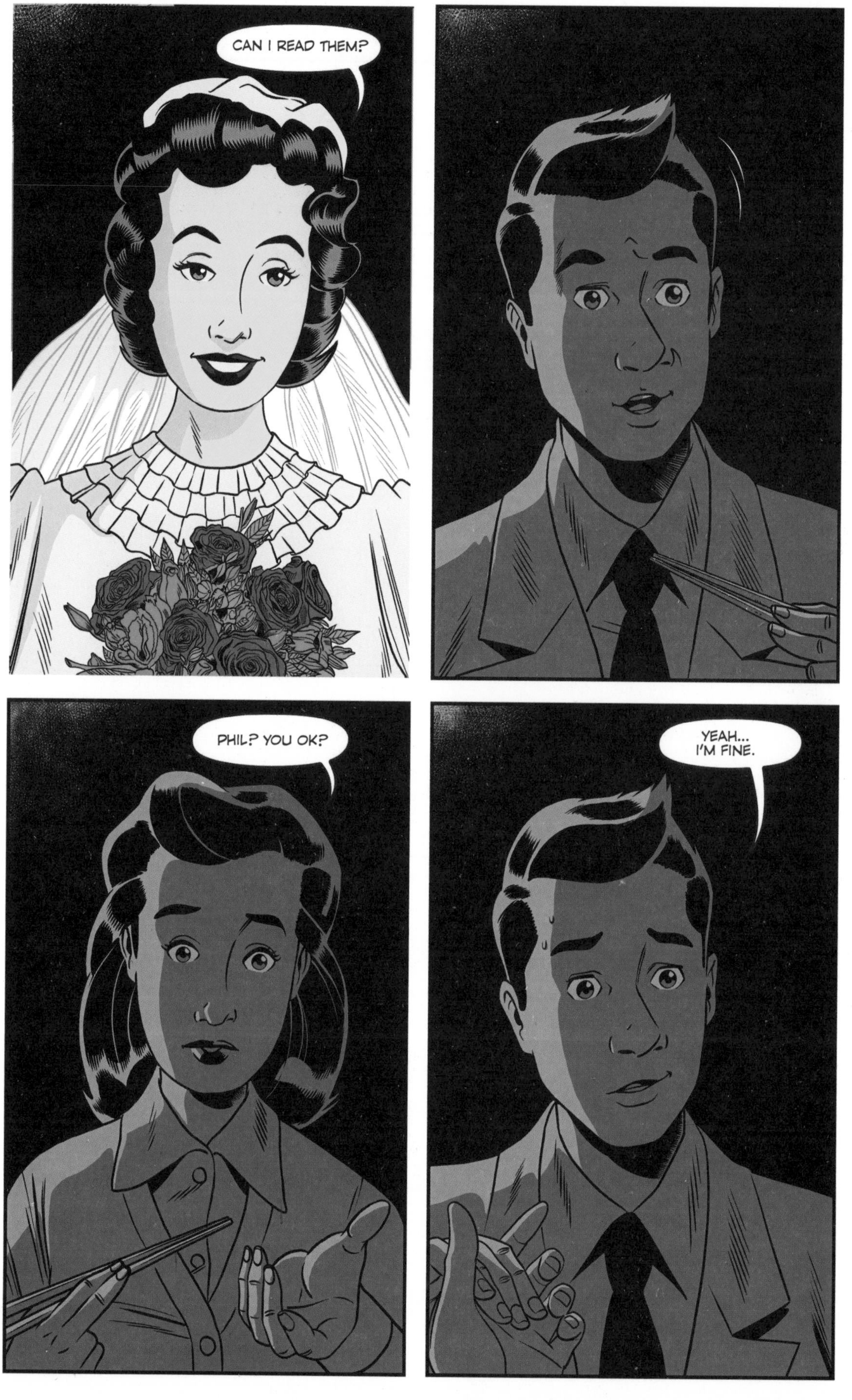
CAN I READ THEM?
PHIL? YOU OK?
YEAH...
I'M FINE.

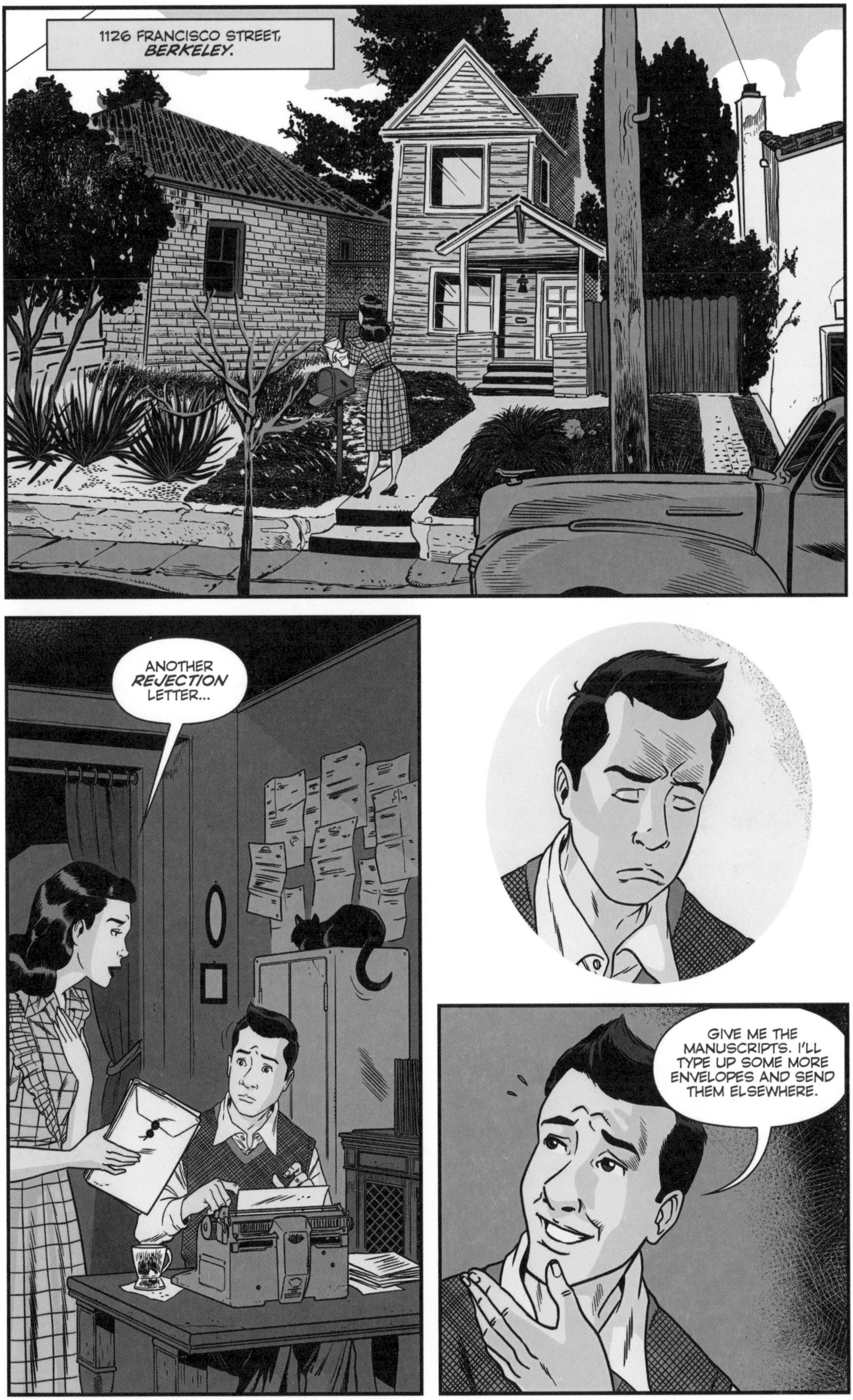
1126 FRANCISCO STREET, *BERKELEY.*
ANOTHER *REJECTION* LETTER...
GIVE ME THE MANUSCRIPTS. I'LL TYPE UP SOME MORE ENVELOPES AND SEND THEM ELSEWHERE.

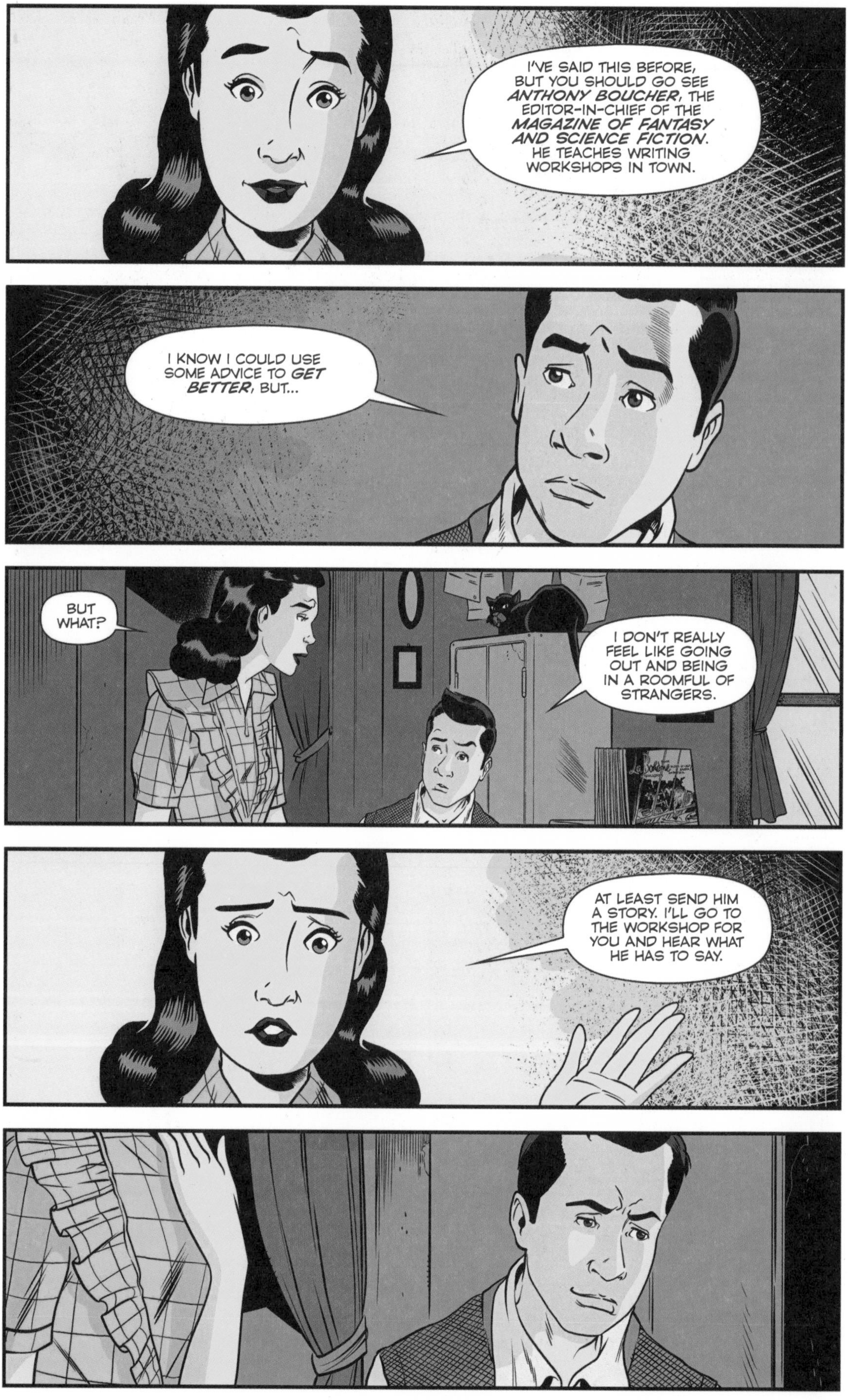
I'VE SAID THIS BEFORE, BUT YOU SHOULD GO SEE ANTHONY BOUCHER, THE EDITOR-IN-CHIEF OF THE MAGAZINE OF FANTASY AND SCIENCE FICTION. HE TEACHES WRITING WORKSHOPS IN TOWN.
I KNOW I COULD USE SOME ADVICE TO GET BETTER, BUT...
BUT WHAT?
I DON'T REALLY FEEL LIKE GOING OUT AND BEING IN A ROOMFUL OF STRANGERS.
AT LEAST SEND HIM A STORY. I'LL GO TO THE WORKSHOP FOR YOU AND HEAR WHAT HE HAS TO SAY.

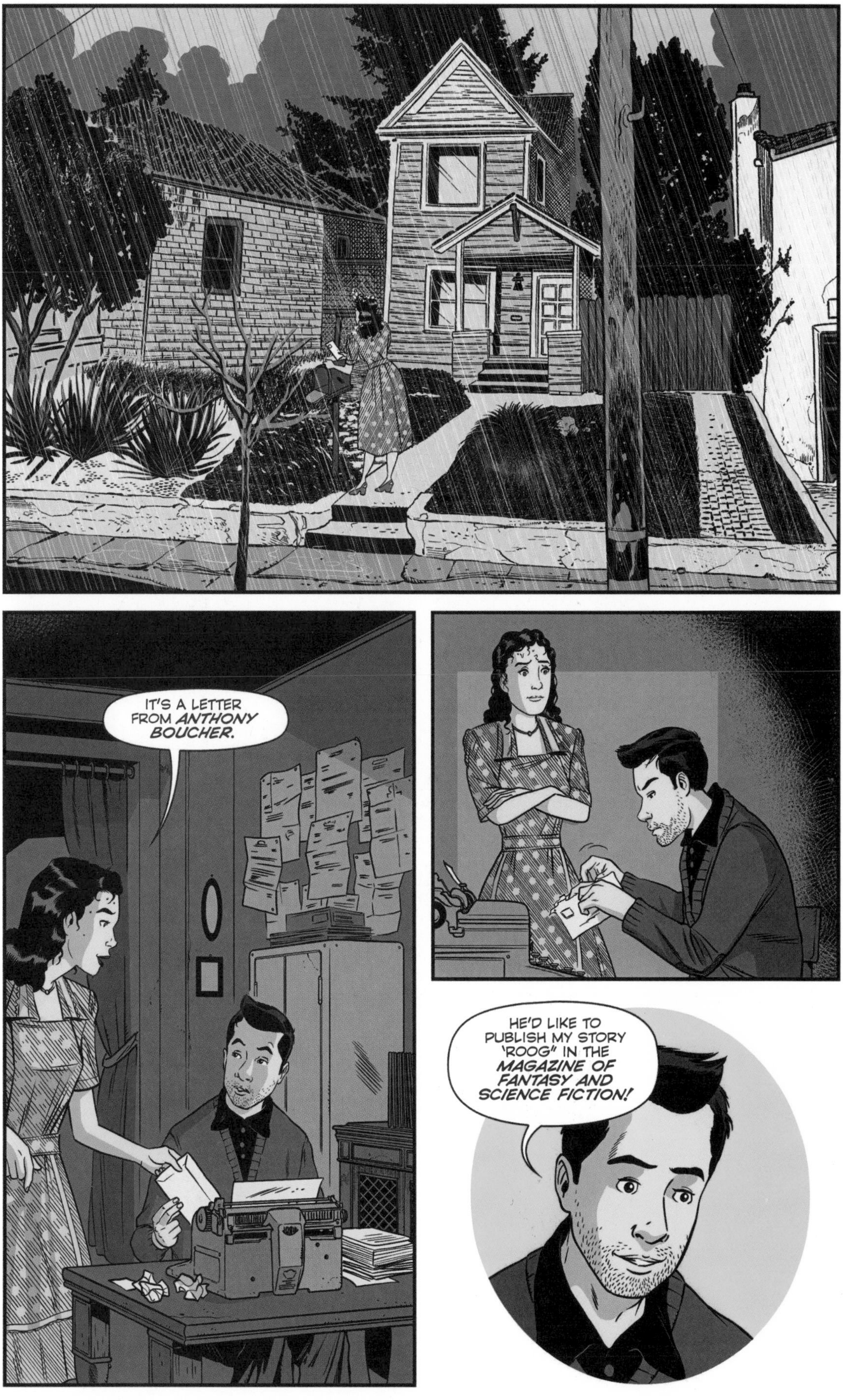
IT'S A LETTER FROM ANTHONY BOUCHER.
HE'D LIKE TO PUBLISH MY STORY 'ROOG" IN THE MAGAZINE OF FANTASY AND SCIENCE FICTION!

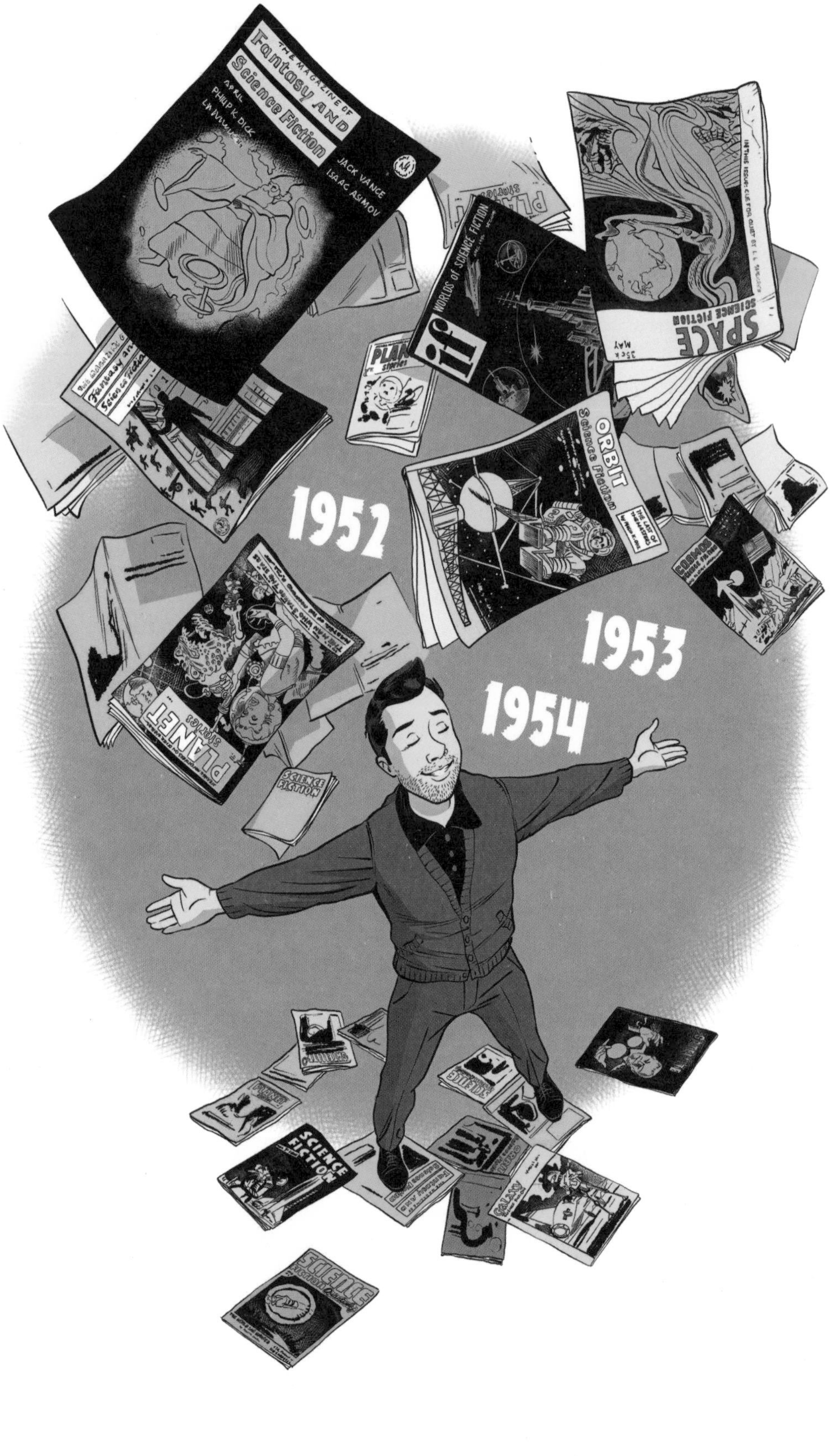

THE MAGAZINE OF
Fantasy AND
Science Fiction
APRIL
PHILIP K. DICK
JACK VANCE
ISAAC ASIMOV
WORLDS of SCIENCE FICTION
if
SPACE
SCIENCE FICTION
MAY
35¢
ORBIT
Science Fiction
PLANET
stories
SCIENCE
FICTION
1952
1953
1954

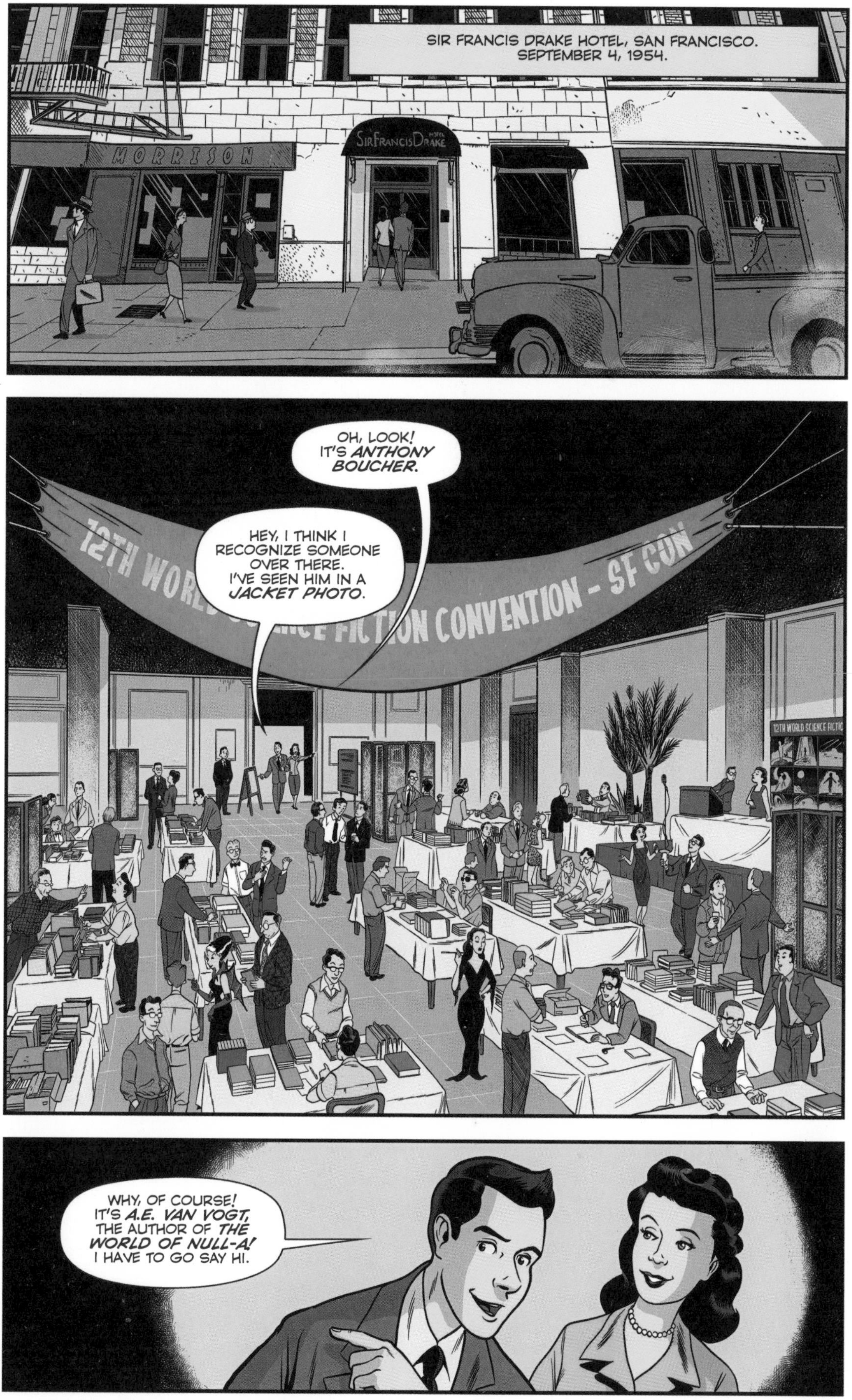
SIR FRANCIS DRAKE HOTEL, SAN FRANCISCO.
SEPTEMBER 4, 1954.
SIR FRANCIS DRAKE HOTEL
MORRISON
OH, LOOK! IT'S *ANTHONY BOUCHER.*
HEY, I THINK I RECOGNIZE SOMEONE OVER THERE. I'VE SEEN HIM IN A *JACKET PHOTO*.
12TH WORLD
FICTION CONVENTION - SF CON
12TH WORLD SCIENCE FICTION
WHY, OF COURSE! IT'S *A.E. VAN VOGT,* THE AUTHOR OF *THE WORLD OF NULL-A!* I HAVE TO GO SAY HI.

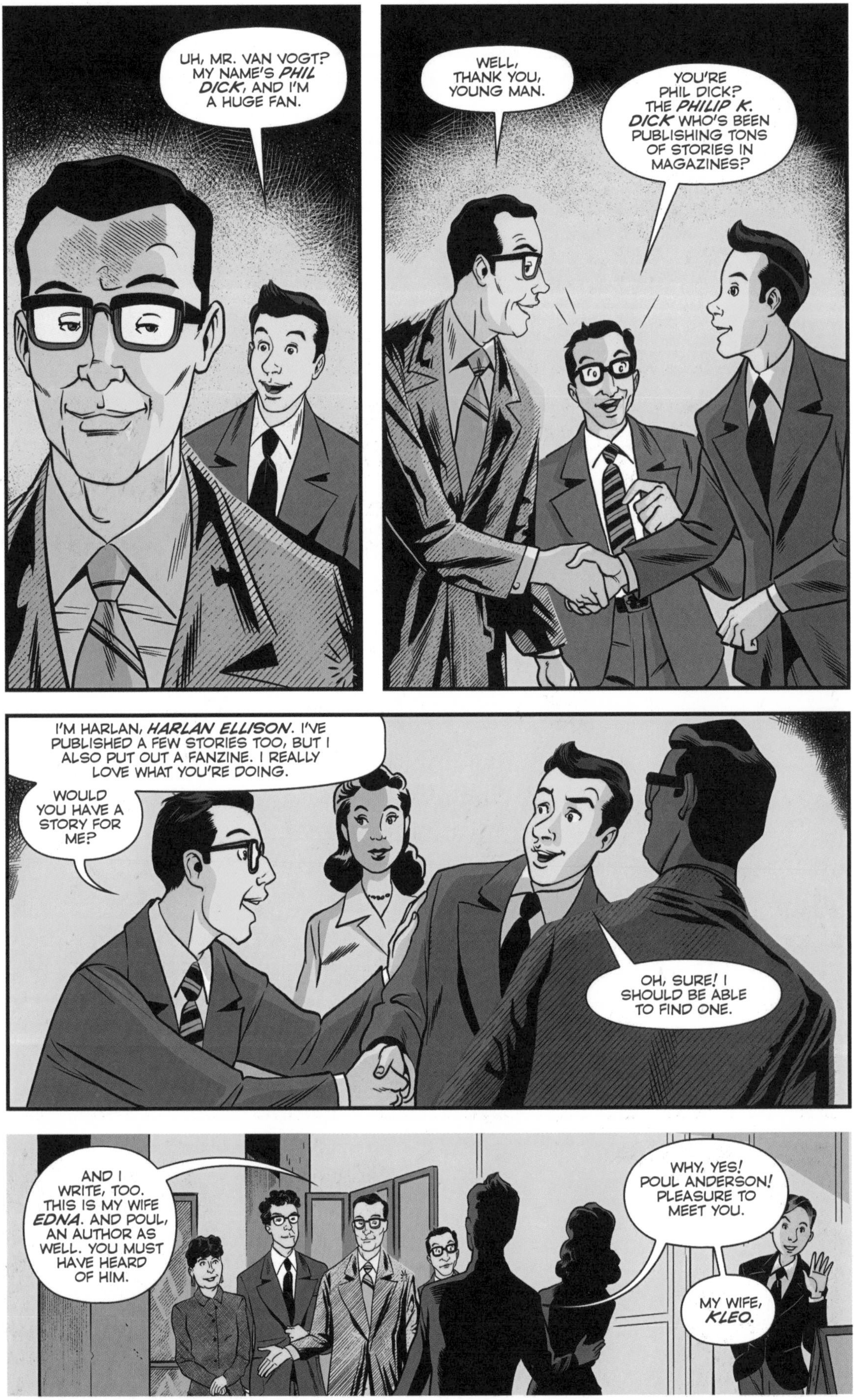
UH, MR. VAN VOGT? MY NAME'S PHIL DICK, AND I'M A HUGE FAN.
WELL, THANK YOU, YOUNG MAN.
YOU'RE PHIL DICK? THE PHILIP K. DICK WHO'S BEEN PUBLISHING TONS OF STORIES IN MAGAZINES?
I'M HARLAN, HARLAN ELLISON. I'VE PUBLISHED A FEW STORIES TOO, BUT I ALSO PUT OUT A FANZINE. I REALLY LOVE WHAT YOU'RE DOING.
WOULD YOU HAVE A STORY FOR ME?
OH, SURE! I SHOULD BE ABLE TO FIND ONE.
AND I WRITE, TOO. THIS IS MY WIFE EDNA. AND POUL, AN AUTHOR AS WELL. YOU MUST HAVE HEARD OF HIM.
WHY, YES! POUL ANDERSON! PLEASURE TO MEET YOU.
MY WIFE, KLEO.

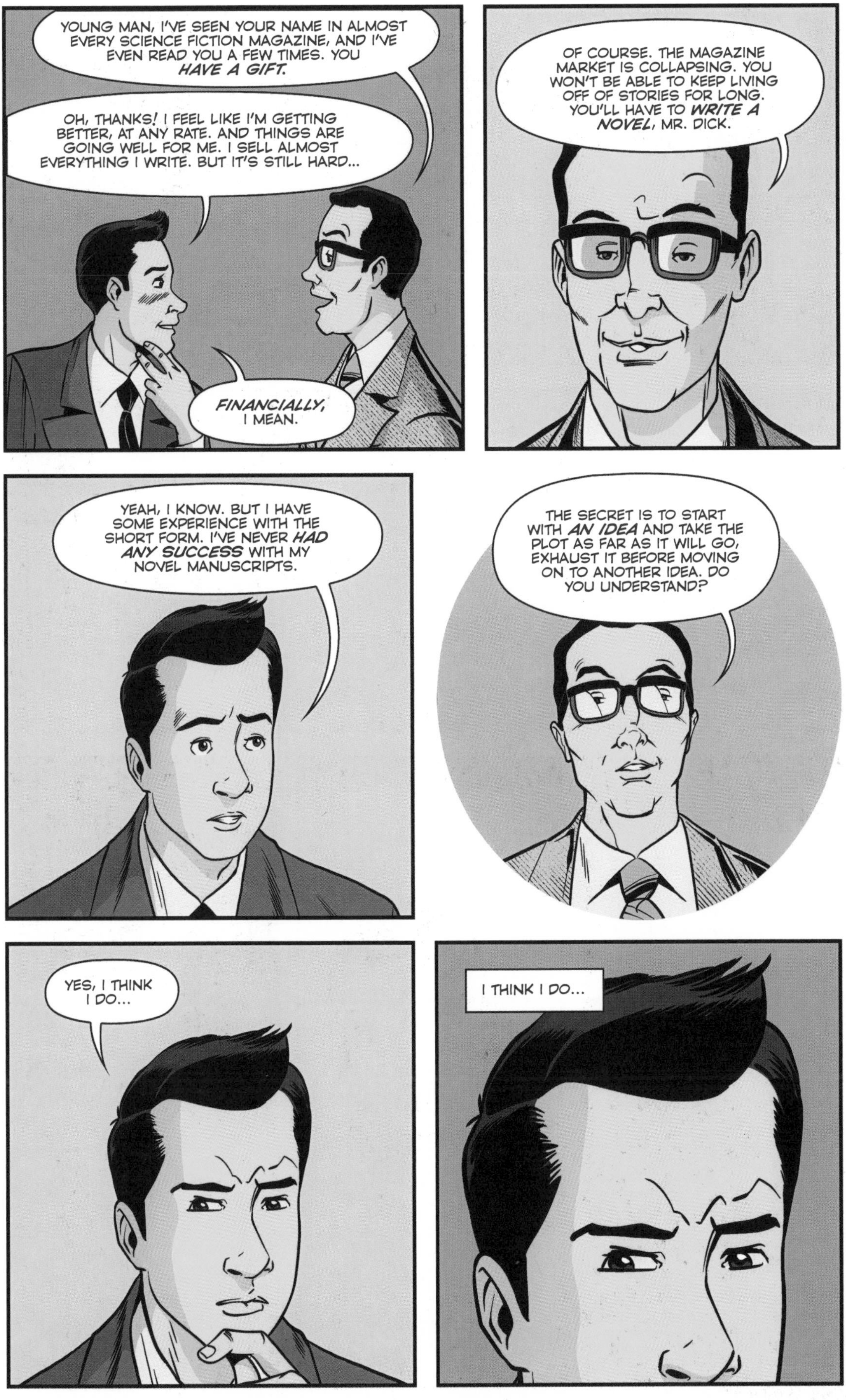
YOUNG MAN, I'VE SEEN YOUR NAME IN ALMOST EVERY SCIENCE FICTION MAGAZINE, AND I'VE EVEN READ YOU A FEW TIMES. YOU *HAVE A GIFT.*
OH, THANKS! I FEEL LIKE I'M GETTING BETTER, AT ANY RATE. AND THINGS ARE GOING WELL FOR ME. I SELL ALMOST EVERYTHING I WRITE. BUT IT'S STILL HARD...
FINANCIALLY, I MEAN.
OF COURSE. THE MAGAZINE MARKET IS COLLAPSING. YOU WON'T BE ABLE TO KEEP LIVING OFF OF STORIES FOR LONG. YOU'LL HAVE TO *WRITE A NOVEL,* MR. DICK.
YEAH, I KNOW. BUT I HAVE SOME EXPERIENCE WITH THE SHORT FORM. I'VE NEVER *HAD ANY SUCCESS* WITH MY NOVEL MANUSCRIPTS.
THE SECRET IS TO START WITH *AN IDEA* AND TAKE THE PLOT AS FAR AS IT WILL GO, EXHAUST IT BEFORE MOVING ON TO ANOTHER IDEA. DO YOU UNDERSTAND?
YES, I THINK I DO...
I THINK I DO...

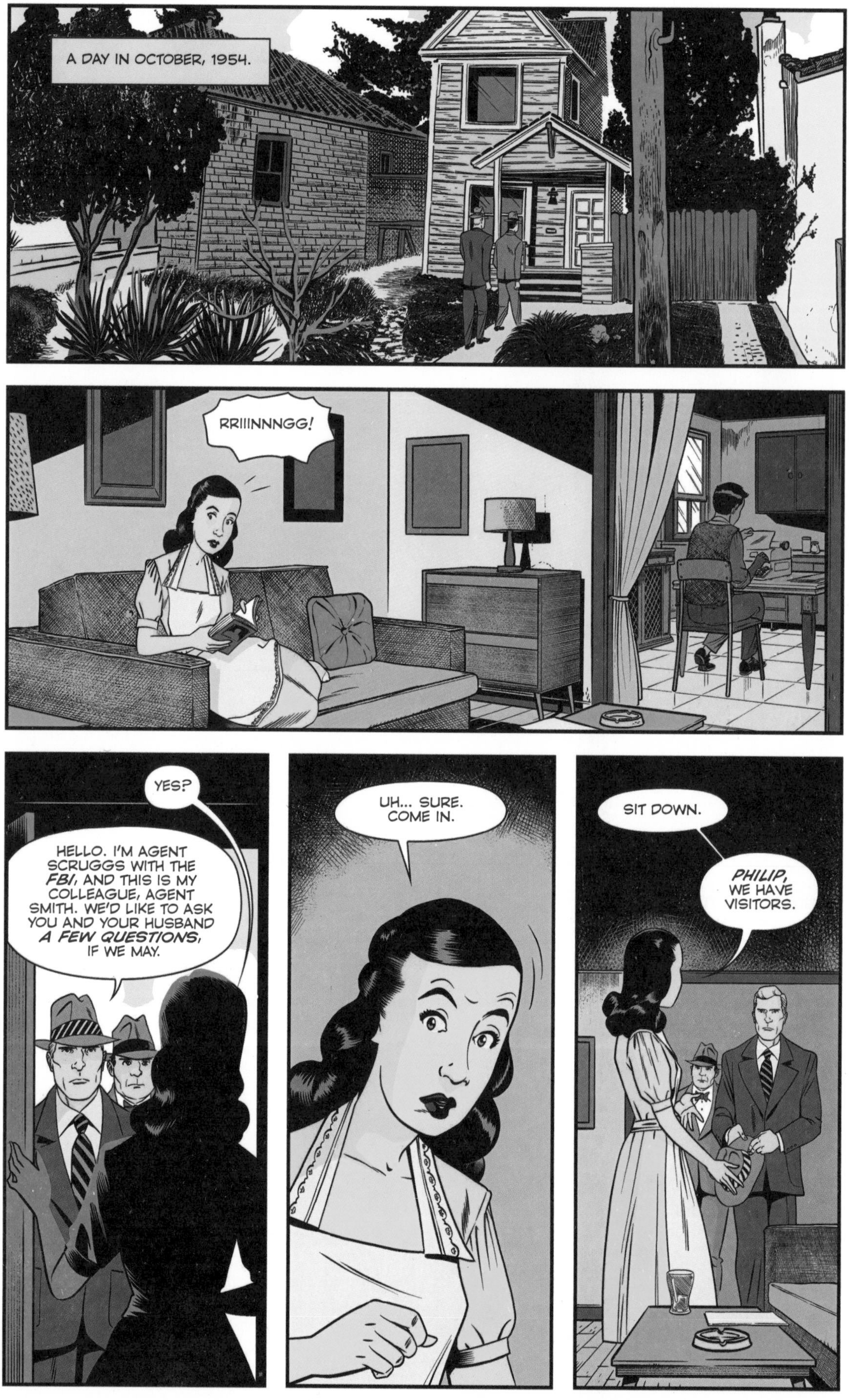
A DAY IN OCTOBER, 1954.
RRIIINNNGG!
YES?
HELLO. I'M AGENT SCRUGGS WITH THE *FBI*, AND THIS IS MY COLLEAGUE, AGENT SMITH. WE'D LIKE TO ASK YOU AND YOUR HUSBAND *A FEW QUESTIONS*, IF WE MAY.
UH... SURE. COME IN.
SIT DOWN.
PHILIP, WE HAVE VISITORS.

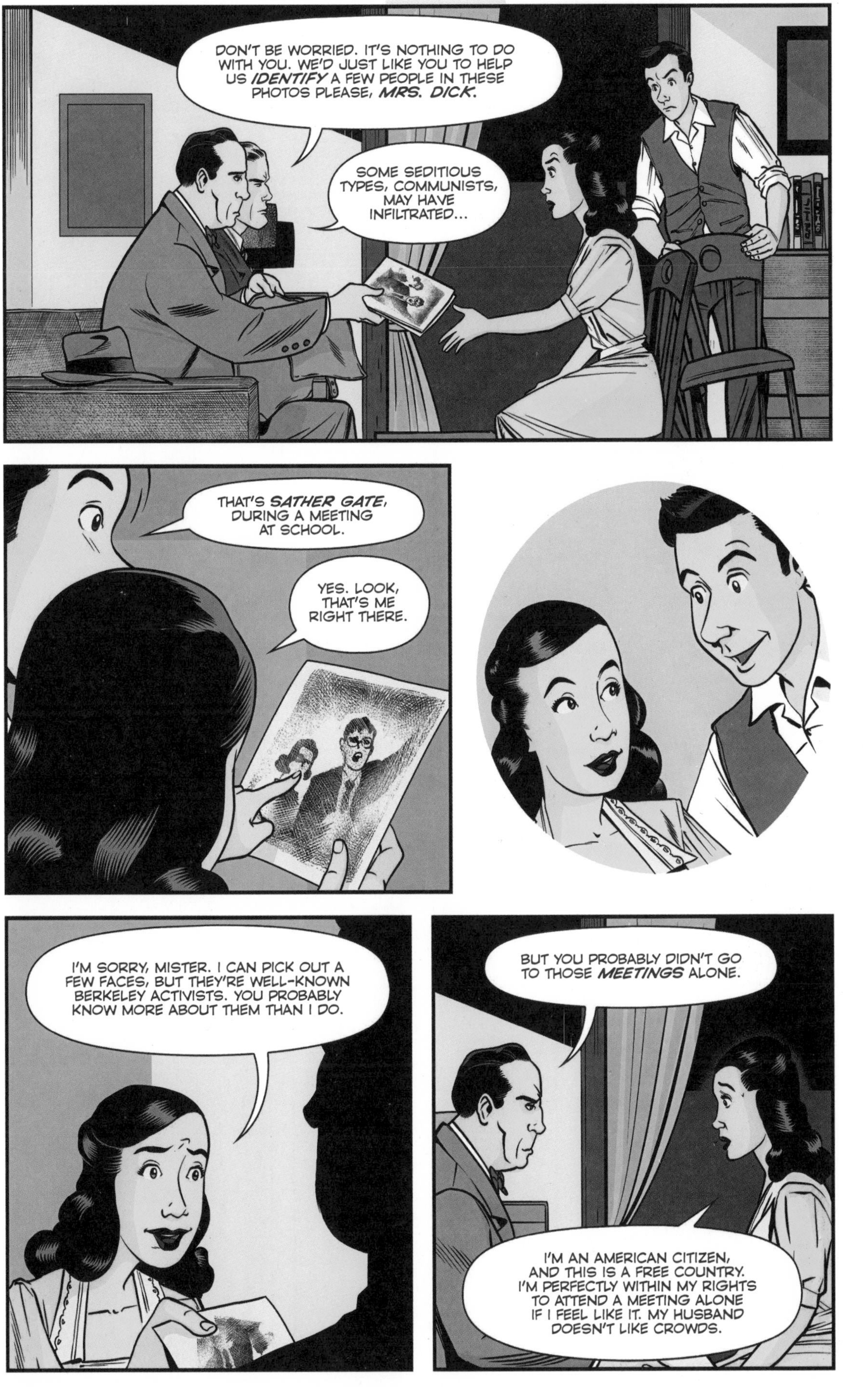
DON'T BE WORRIED. IT'S NOTHING TO DO WITH YOU. WE'D JUST LIKE YOU TO HELP US *IDENTIFY* A FEW PEOPLE IN THESE PHOTOS PLEASE, *MRS. DICK.*
SOME SEDITIOUS TYPES, COMMUNISTS, MAY HAVE INFILTRATED...
THAT'S *SATHER GATE*, DURING A MEETING AT SCHOOL.
YES. LOOK, THAT'S ME RIGHT THERE.
I'M SORRY, MISTER. I CAN PICK OUT A FEW FACES, BUT THEY'RE WELL-KNOWN BERKELEY ACTIVISTS. YOU PROBABLY KNOW MORE ABOUT THEM THAN I DO.
BUT YOU PROBABLY DIDN'T GO TO THOSE *MEETINGS* ALONE.
I'M AN AMERICAN CITIZEN, AND THIS IS A FREE COUNTRY. I'M PERFECTLY WITHIN MY RIGHTS TO ATTEND A MEETING ALONE IF I FEEL LIKE IT. MY HUSBAND DOESN'T LIKE CROWDS.

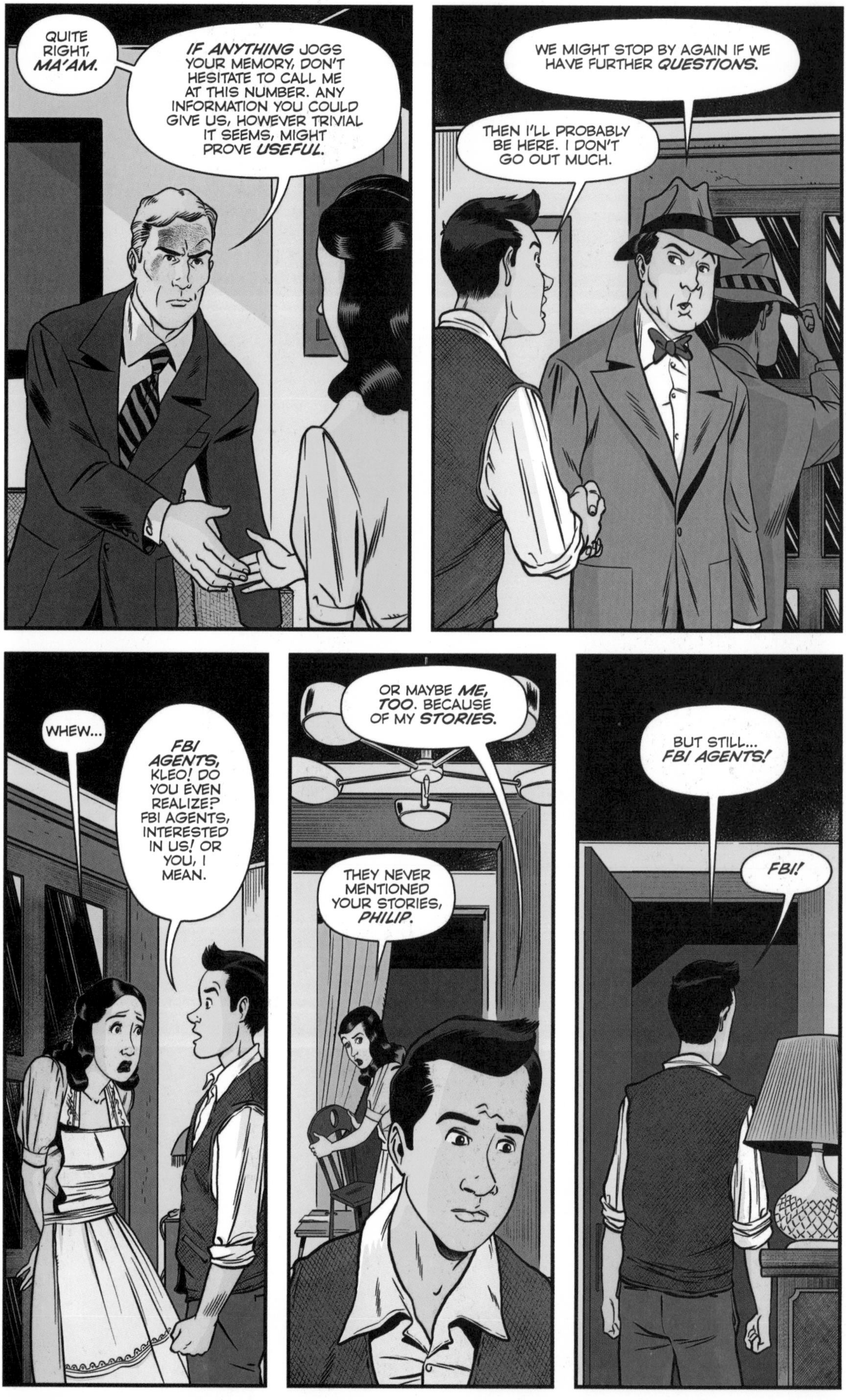
QUITE RIGHT, MA'AM.
IF ANYTHING JOGS YOUR MEMORY, DON'T HESITATE TO CALL ME AT THIS NUMBER. ANY INFORMATION YOU COULD GIVE US, HOWEVER TRIVIAL IT SEEMS, MIGHT PROVE USEFUL.
WE MIGHT STOP BY AGAIN IF WE HAVE FURTHER QUESTIONS.
THEN I'LL PROBABLY BE HERE. I DON'T GO OUT MUCH.
WHEW...
FBI AGENTS, KLEO! DO YOU EVEN REALIZE? FBI AGENTS, INTERESTED IN US! OR YOU, I MEAN.
OR MAYBE ME, TOO. BECAUSE OF MY STORIES.
THEY NEVER MENTIONED YOUR STORIES, PHILIP.
BUT STILL... FBI AGENTS!
FBI!

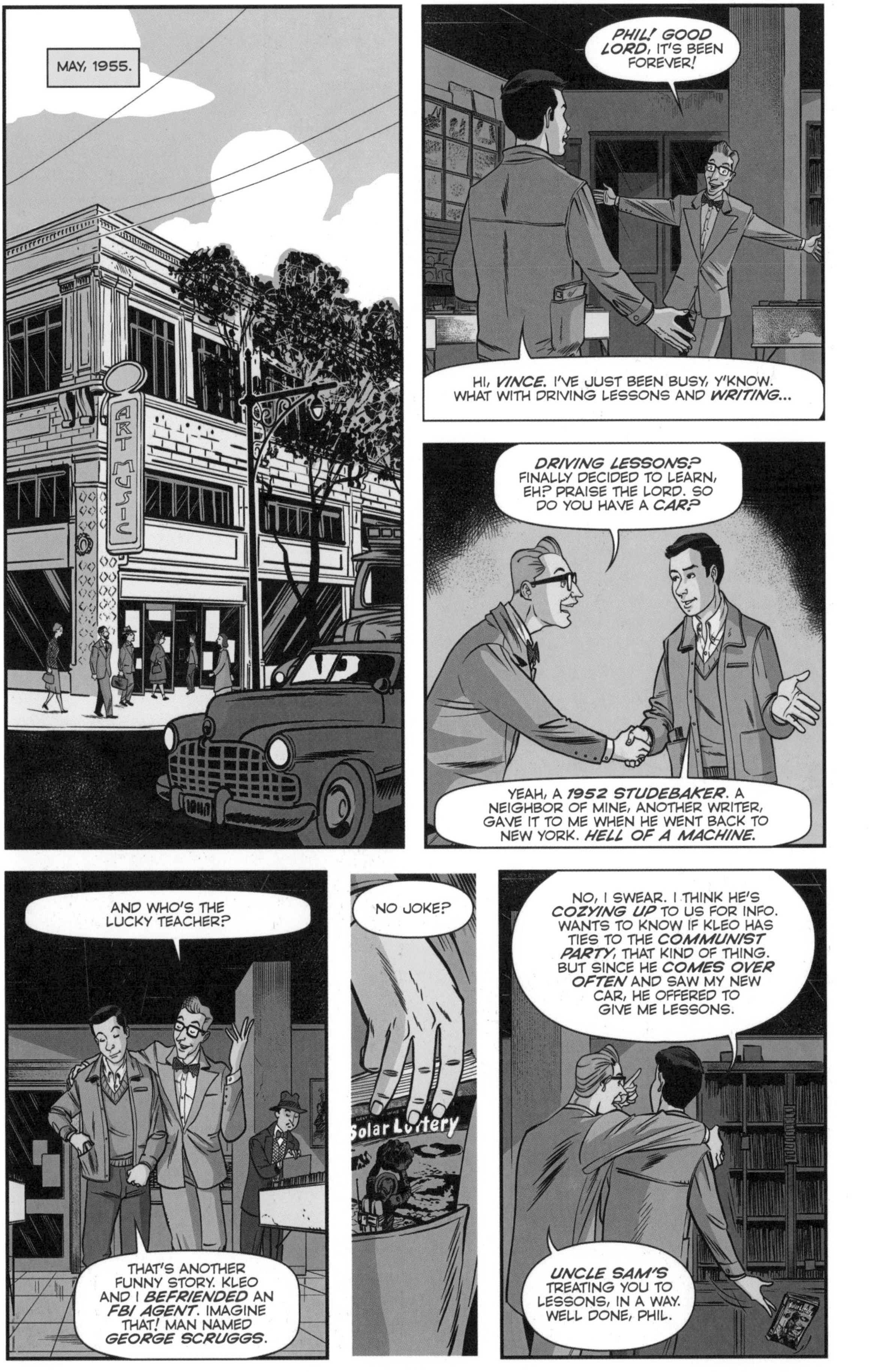
MAY, 1955.
ART MUSIC
PHIL! GOOD LORD, IT'S BEEN FOREVER!
HI, VINCE. I'VE JUST BEEN BUSY, Y'KNOW. WHAT WITH DRIVING LESSONS AND WRITING...
DRIVING LESSONS? FINALLY DECIDED TO LEARN, EH? PRAISE THE LORD. SO DO YOU HAVE A CAR?
YEAH, A 1952 STUDEBAKER. A NEIGHBOR OF MINE, ANOTHER WRITER, GAVE IT TO ME WHEN HE WENT BACK TO NEW YORK. HELL OF A MACHINE.
AND WHO'S THE LUCKY TEACHER?
THAT'S ANOTHER FUNNY STORY. KLEO AND I BEFRIENDED AN FBI AGENT. IMAGINE THAT! MAN NAMED GEORGE SCRUGGS.
NO JOKE?
Solar Lottery
NO, I SWEAR. I THINK HE'S COZYING UP TO US FOR INFO. WANTS TO KNOW IF KLEO HAS TIES TO THE COMMUNIST PARTY, THAT KIND OF THING. BUT SINCE HE COMES OVER OFTEN AND SAW MY NEW CAR, HE OFFERED TO GIVE ME LESSONS.
UNCLE SAM'S TREATING YOU TO LESSONS, IN A WAY. WELL DONE, PHIL.

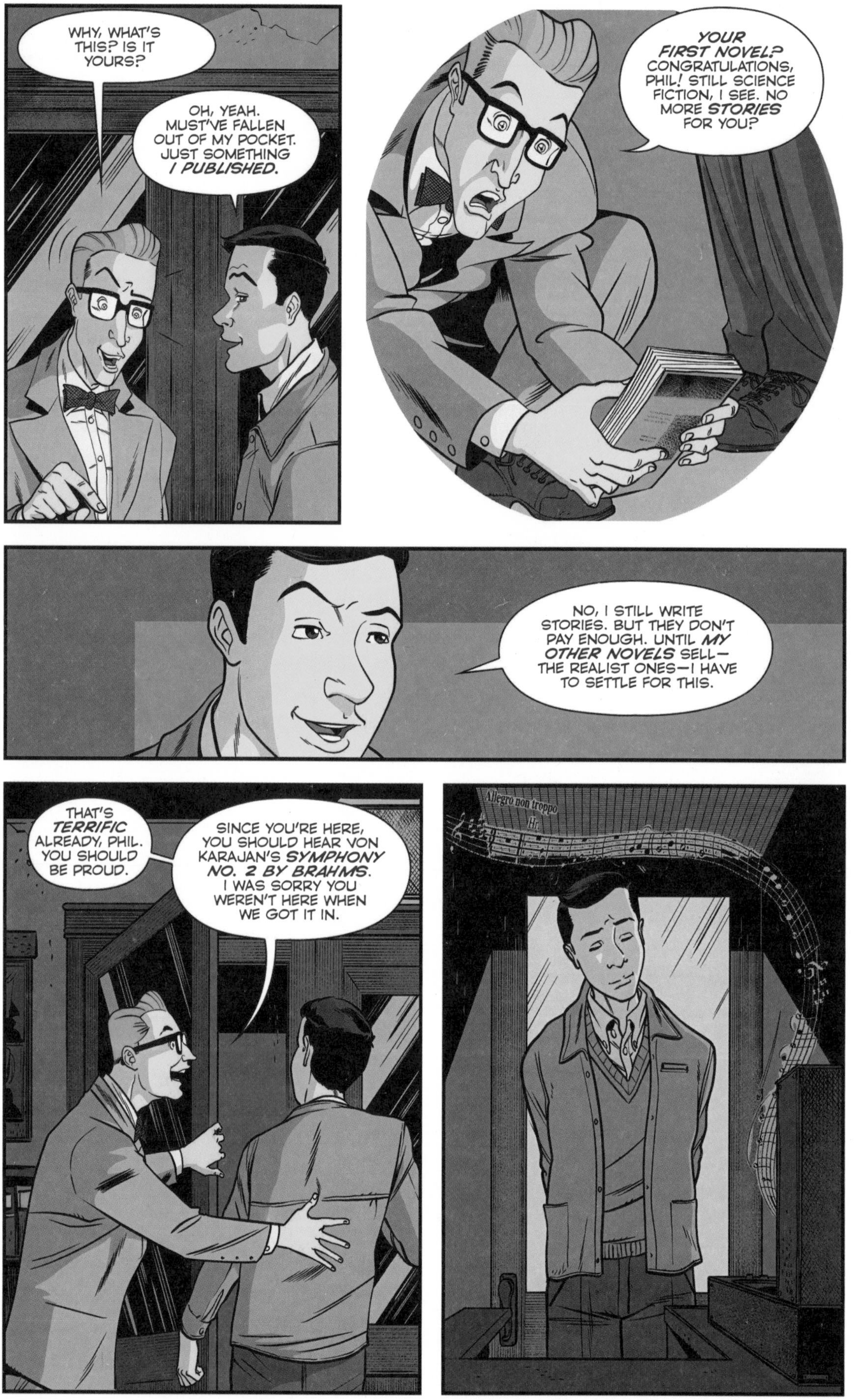
WHY, WHAT'S THIS? IS IT YOURS?
OH, YEAH. MUST'VE FALLEN OUT OF MY POCKET. JUST SOMETHING *I PUBLISHED.*
YOUR FIRST NOVEL? CONGRATULATIONS, PHIL! STILL SCIENCE FICTION, I SEE. NO MORE *STORIES* FOR YOU?
NO, I STILL WRITE STORIES. BUT THEY DON'T PAY ENOUGH. UNTIL *MY OTHER NOVELS* SELL—THE REALIST ONES—I HAVE TO SETTLE FOR THIS.
THAT'S *TERRIFIC* ALREADY, PHIL. YOU SHOULD BE PROUD.
SINCE YOU'RE HERE, YOU SHOULD HEAR VON KARAJAN'S *SYMPHONY NO. 2 BY BRAHMS*. I WAS SORRY YOU WEREN'T HERE WHEN WE GOT IT IN.
Allegro non troppo

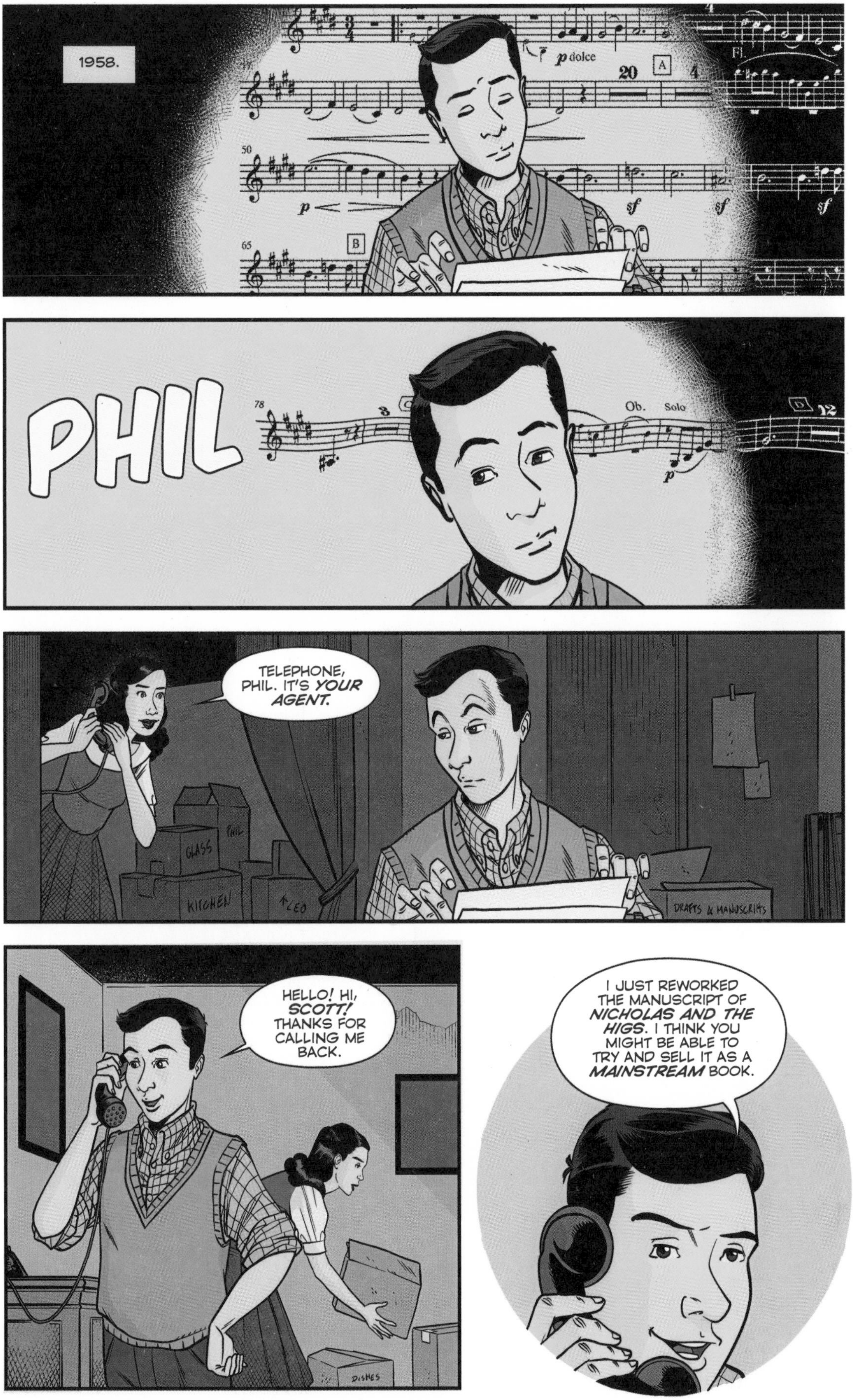

1958.
PHIL
TELEPHONE, PHIL. IT'S YOUR AGENT.
GLASS
PHIL
KITCHEN
LEO
DRAFTS & MANUSCRIPTS
HELLO! HI, SCOTT! THANKS FOR CALLING ME BACK.
DISHES
I JUST REWORKED THE MANUSCRIPT OF NICHOLAS AND THE HIGS. I THINK YOU MIGHT BE ABLE TO TRY AND SELL IT AS A MAINSTREAM BOOK.

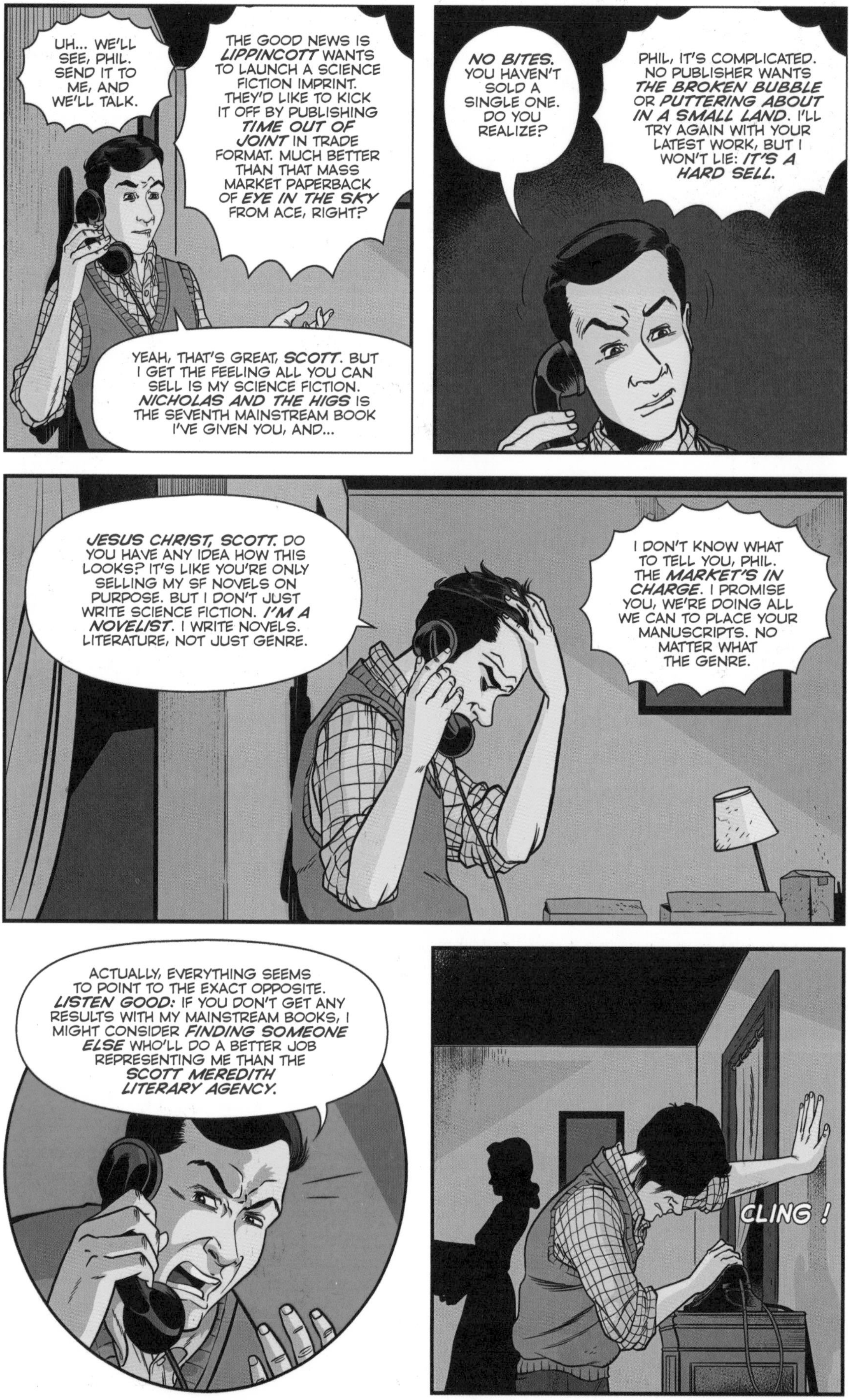

UH... WE'LL SEE, PHIL. SEND IT TO ME, AND WE'LL TALK.
THE GOOD NEWS IS LIPPINCOTT WANTS TO LAUNCH A SCIENCE FICTION IMPRINT. THEY'D LIKE TO KICK IT OFF BY PUBLISHING TIME OUT OF JOINT IN TRADE FORMAT. MUCH BETTER THAN THAT MASS MARKET PAPERBACK OF EYE IN THE SKY FROM ACE, RIGHT?
YEAH, THAT'S GREAT, SCOTT. BUT I GET THE FEELING ALL YOU CAN SELL IS MY SCIENCE FICTION. NICHOLAS AND THE HIGS IS THE SEVENTH MAINSTREAM BOOK I'VE GIVEN YOU, AND...
NO BITES. YOU HAVEN'T SOLD A SINGLE ONE. DO YOU REALIZE?
PHIL, IT'S COMPLICATED. NO PUBLISHER WANTS THE BROKEN BUBBLE OR PUTTERING ABOUT IN A SMALL LAND. I'LL TRY AGAIN WITH YOUR LATEST WORK, BUT I WON'T LIE: IT'S A HARD SELL.
JESUS CHRIST, SCOTT. DO YOU HAVE ANY IDEA HOW THIS LOOKS? IT'S LIKE YOU'RE ONLY SELLING MY SF NOVELS ON PURPOSE. BUT I DON'T JUST WRITE SCIENCE FICTION. I'M A NOVELIST. I WRITE NOVELS. LITERATURE, NOT JUST GENRE.
I DON'T KNOW WHAT TO TELL YOU, PHIL. THE MARKET'S IN CHARGE. I PROMISE YOU, WE'RE DOING ALL WE CAN TO PLACE YOUR MANUSCRIPTS. NO MATTER WHAT THE GENRE.
ACTUALLY, EVERYTHING SEEMS TO POINT TO THE EXACT OPPOSITE. LISTEN GOOD: IF YOU DON'T GET ANY RESULTS WITH MY MAINSTREAM BOOKS, I MIGHT CONSIDER FINDING SOMEONE ELSE WHO'LL DO A BETTER JOB REPRESENTING ME THAN THE SCOTT MEREDITH LITERARY AGENCY.
CLING !

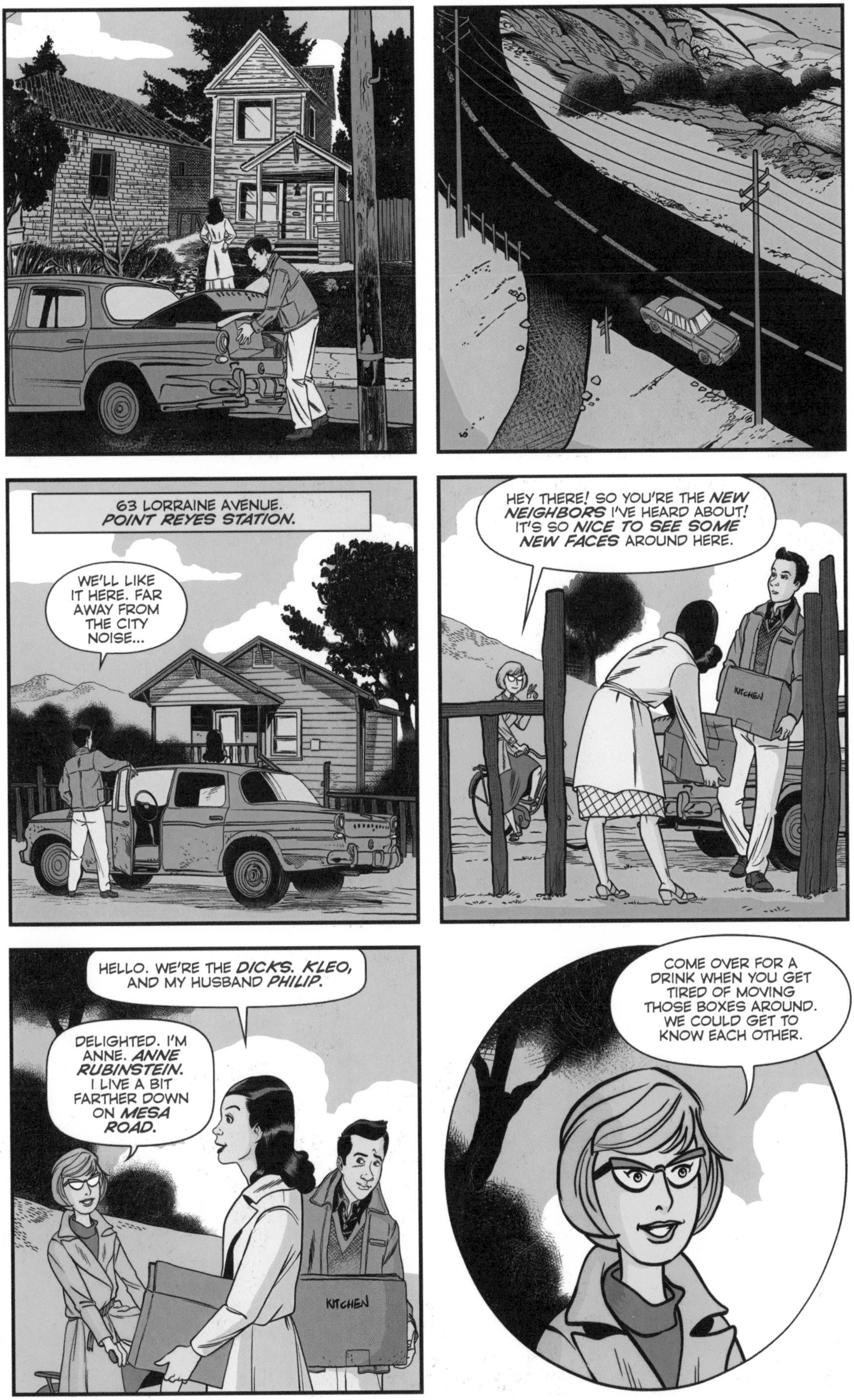
63 LORRAINE AVENUE.
POINT REYES STATION.
WE'LL LIKE IT HERE. FAR AWAY FROM THE CITY NOISE...
HEY THERE! SO YOU'RE THE *NEW NEIGHBORS* I'VE HEARD ABOUT! IT'S SO *NICE TO SEE SOME NEW FACES* AROUND HERE.
KITCHEN
HELLO. WE'RE THE *DICKS. KLEO,* AND MY HUSBAND *PHILIP.*
DELIGHTED. I'M ANNE. *ANNE RUBINSTEIN.* I LIVE A BIT FARTHER DOWN ON *MESA ROAD.*
KITCHEN
COME OVER FOR A DRINK WHEN YOU GET TIRED OF MOVING THOSE BOXES AROUND. WE COULD GET TO KNOW EACH OTHER.

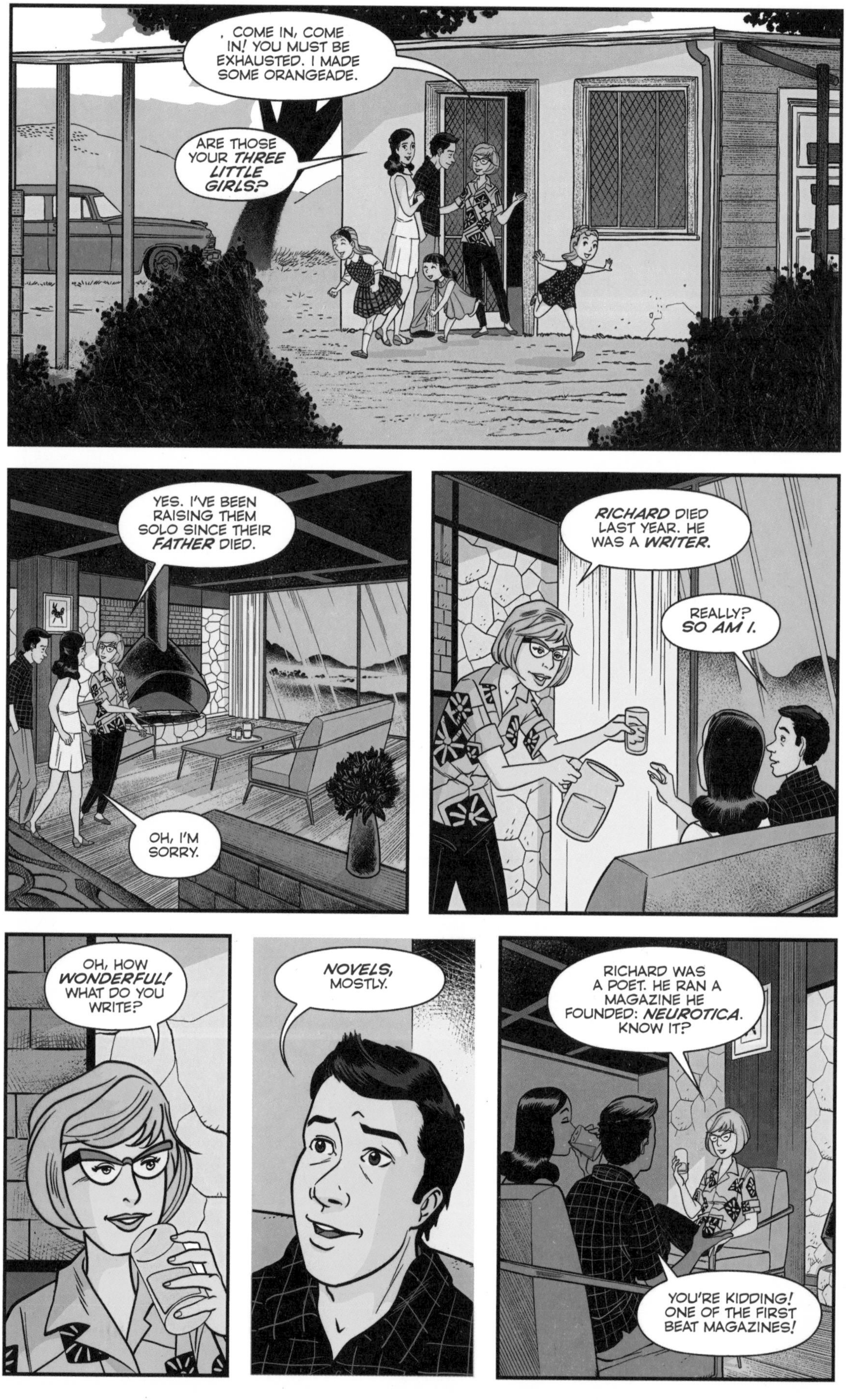
COME IN, COME IN! YOU MUST BE EXHAUSTED. I MADE SOME ORANGEADE.
ARE THOSE YOUR *THREE LITTLE GIRLS?*
YES. I'VE BEEN RAISING THEM SOLO SINCE THEIR *FATHER* DIED.
OH, I'M SORRY.
RICHARD DIED LAST YEAR. HE WAS A *WRITER.*
REALLY? *SO AM I.*
OH, HOW *WONDERFUL!* WHAT DO YOU WRITE?
NOVELS, MOSTLY.
RICHARD WAS A POET. HE RAN A MAGAZINE HE FOUNDED: *NEUROTICA*. KNOW IT?
YOU'RE KIDDING! ONE OF THE FIRST BEAT MAGAZINES!

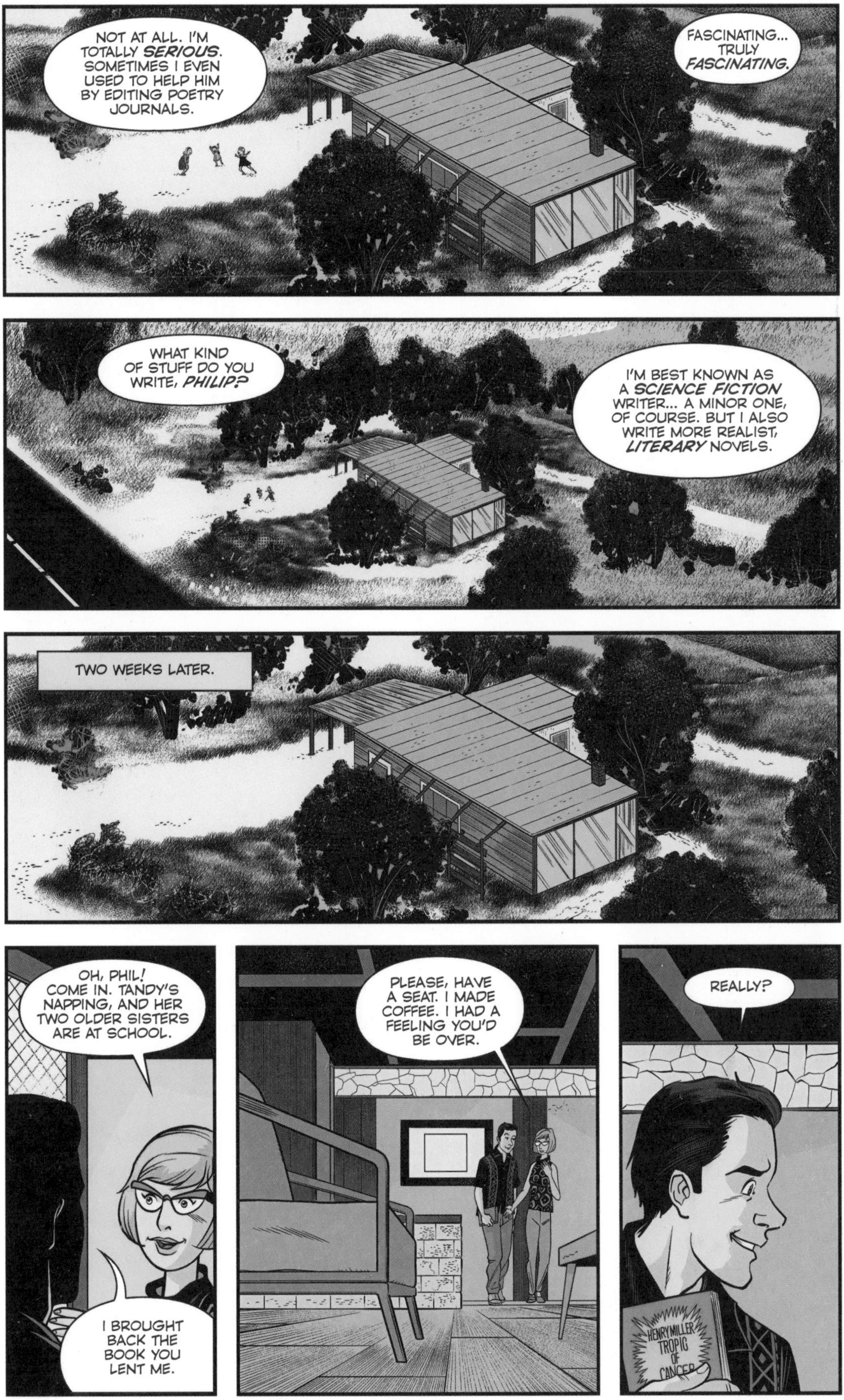
NOT AT ALL. I'M TOTALLY *SERIOUS*. SOMETIMES I EVEN USED TO HELP HIM BY EDITING POETRY JOURNALS.
FASCINATING... TRULY *FASCINATING*.
WHAT KIND OF STUFF DO YOU WRITE, *PHILIP?*
I'M BEST KNOWN AS A *SCIENCE FICTION* WRITER... A MINOR ONE, OF COURSE. BUT I ALSO WRITE MORE REALIST, *LITERARY* NOVELS.
TWO WEEKS LATER.
OH, PHIL! COME IN. TANDY'S NAPPING, AND HER TWO OLDER SISTERS ARE AT SCHOOL.
I BROUGHT BACK THE BOOK YOU LENT ME.
PLEASE, HAVE A SEAT. I MADE COFFEE. I HAD A FEELING YOU'D BE OVER.
REALLY?
HENRY MILLER TROPIC OF CANCER

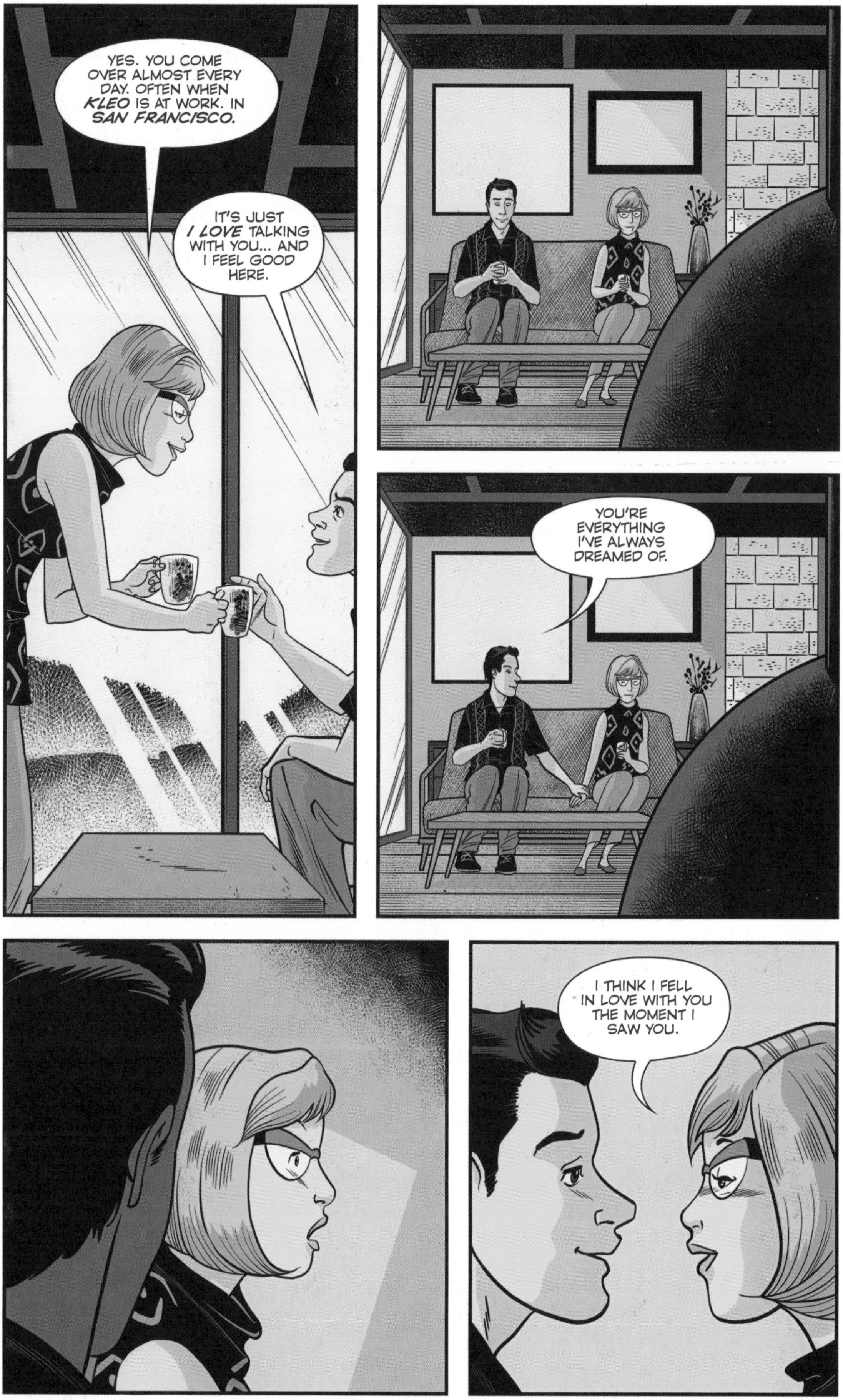
YES. YOU COME OVER ALMOST EVERY DAY. OFTEN WHEN *KLEO* IS AT WORK. IN *SAN FRANCISCO.*
IT'S JUST *I LOVE* TALKING WITH YOU... AND I FEEL GOOD HERE.
YOU'RE EVERYTHING I'VE ALWAYS DREAMED OF.
I THINK I FELL IN LOVE WITH YOU THE MOMENT I SAW YOU.

A FEW MONTHS LATER...

PHILIP!

WHERE ARE YOU, *PHILIP?!*

KLEO... WHAT ARE YOU DOING HERE?

CHRIST, PHILIP, DON'T I COUNT FOR ANYTHING?

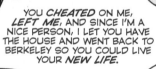

YOU *CHEATED* ON ME, *LEFT ME*, AND SINCE I'M A NICE PERSON, I LET YOU HAVE THE HOUSE AND WENT BACK TO BERKELEY SO YOU COULD LIVE YOUR *NEW LIFE.*

PLEASE, KLEO, CALM DOWN...

I LEFT YOU EVERYTHING, *PHILIP!* EVERYTHING! EVEN THE HOUSE! ALL I TOOK WAS *THE CAR.* AND YOU—

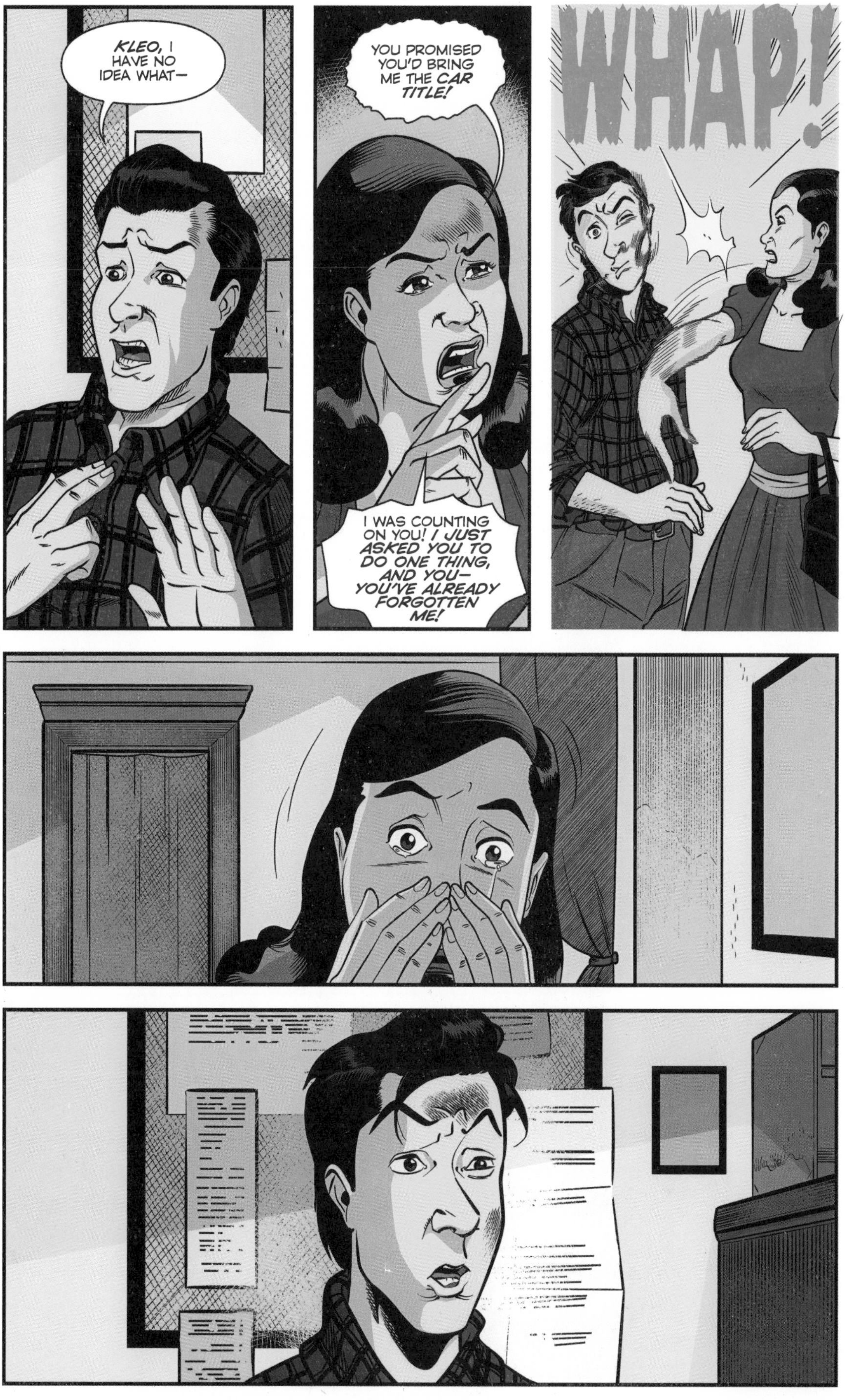
KLEO, I HAVE NO IDEA WHAT—
YOU PROMISED YOU'D BRING ME THE CAR TITLE!
I WAS COUNTING ON YOU! I JUST ASKED YOU TO DO ONE THING, AND YOU— YOU'VE ALREADY FORGOTTEN ME!
WHAP!

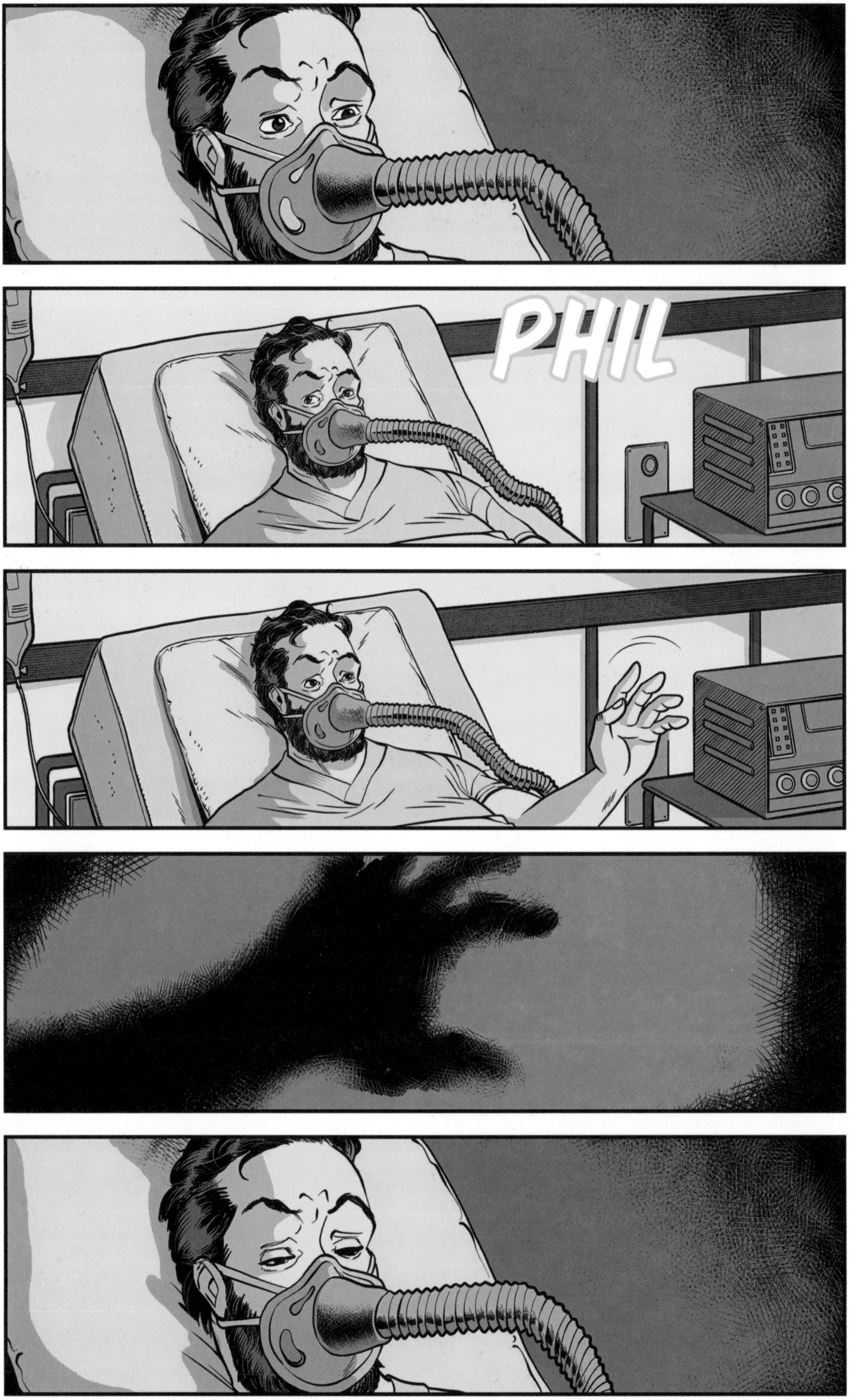
PHIL

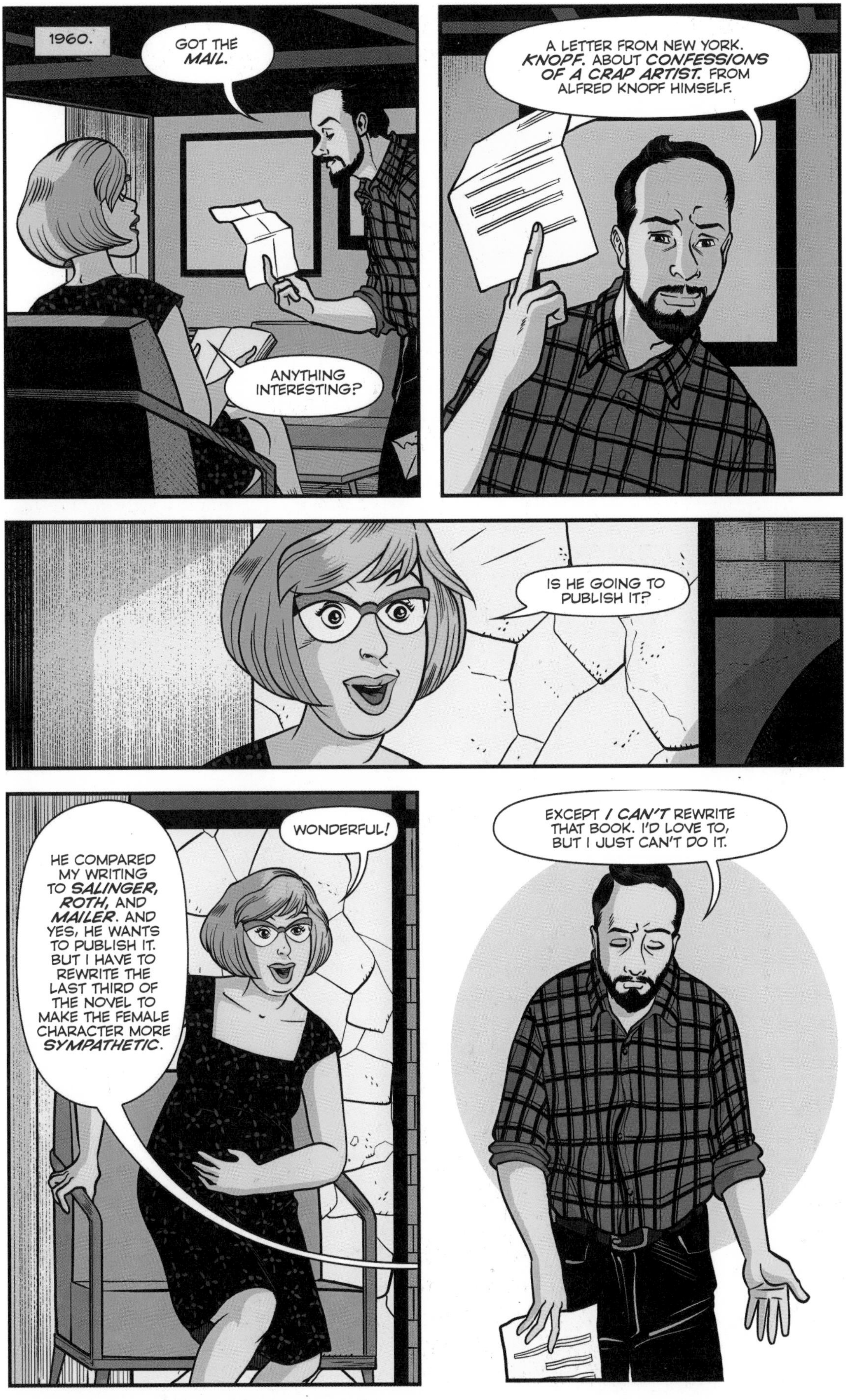
1960.
GOT THE MAIL.
ANYTHING INTERESTING?
A LETTER FROM NEW YORK. KNOPF. ABOUT CONFESSIONS OF A CRAP ARTIST. FROM ALFRED KNOPF HIMSELF.
IS HE GOING TO PUBLISH IT?
HE COMPARED MY WRITING TO SALINGER, ROTH, AND MAILER. AND YES, HE WANTS TO PUBLISH IT. BUT I HAVE TO REWRITE THE LAST THIRD OF THE NOVEL TO MAKE THE FEMALE CHARACTER MORE SYMPATHETIC.
WONDERFUL!
EXCEPT I CAN'T REWRITE THAT BOOK. I'D LOVE TO, BUT I JUST CAN'T DO IT.

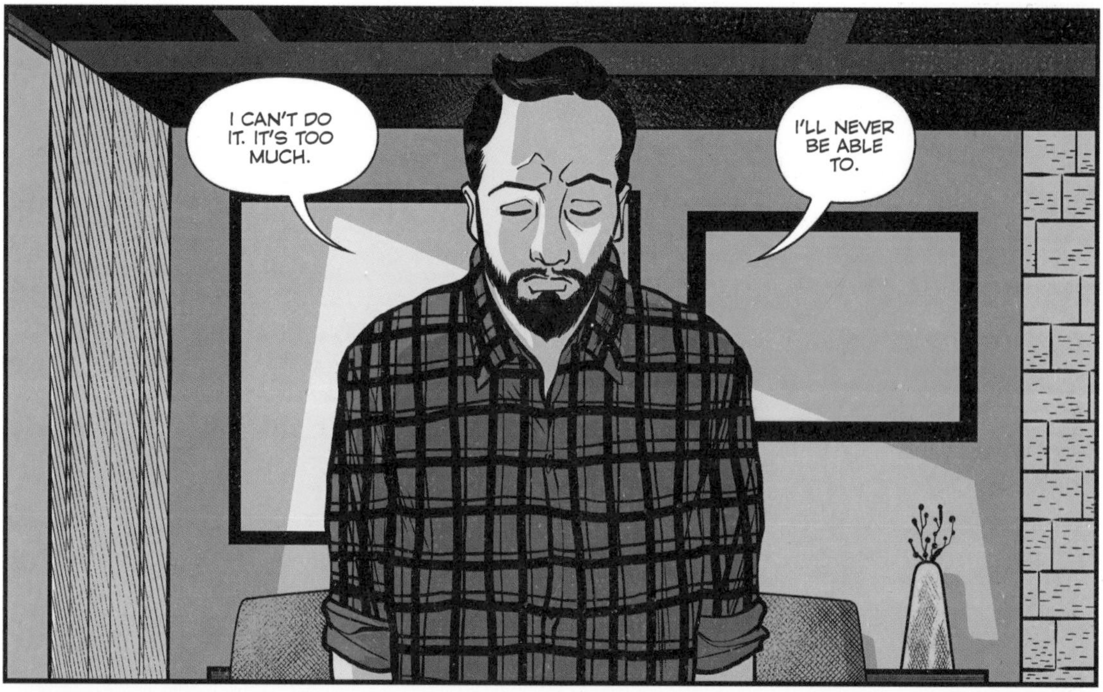
I CAN'T DO IT. IT'S TOO MUCH.
I'LL NEVER BE ABLE TO.

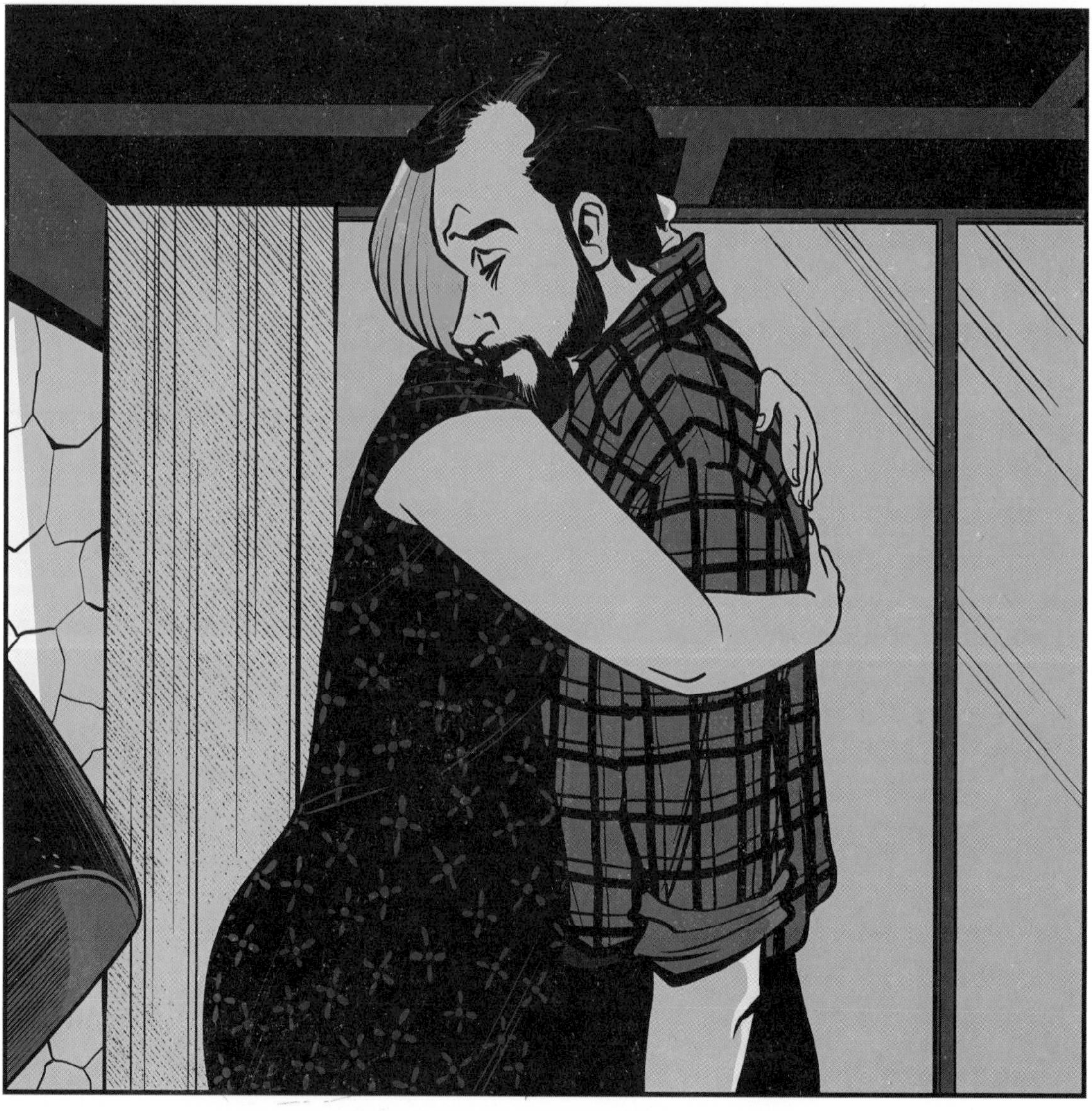

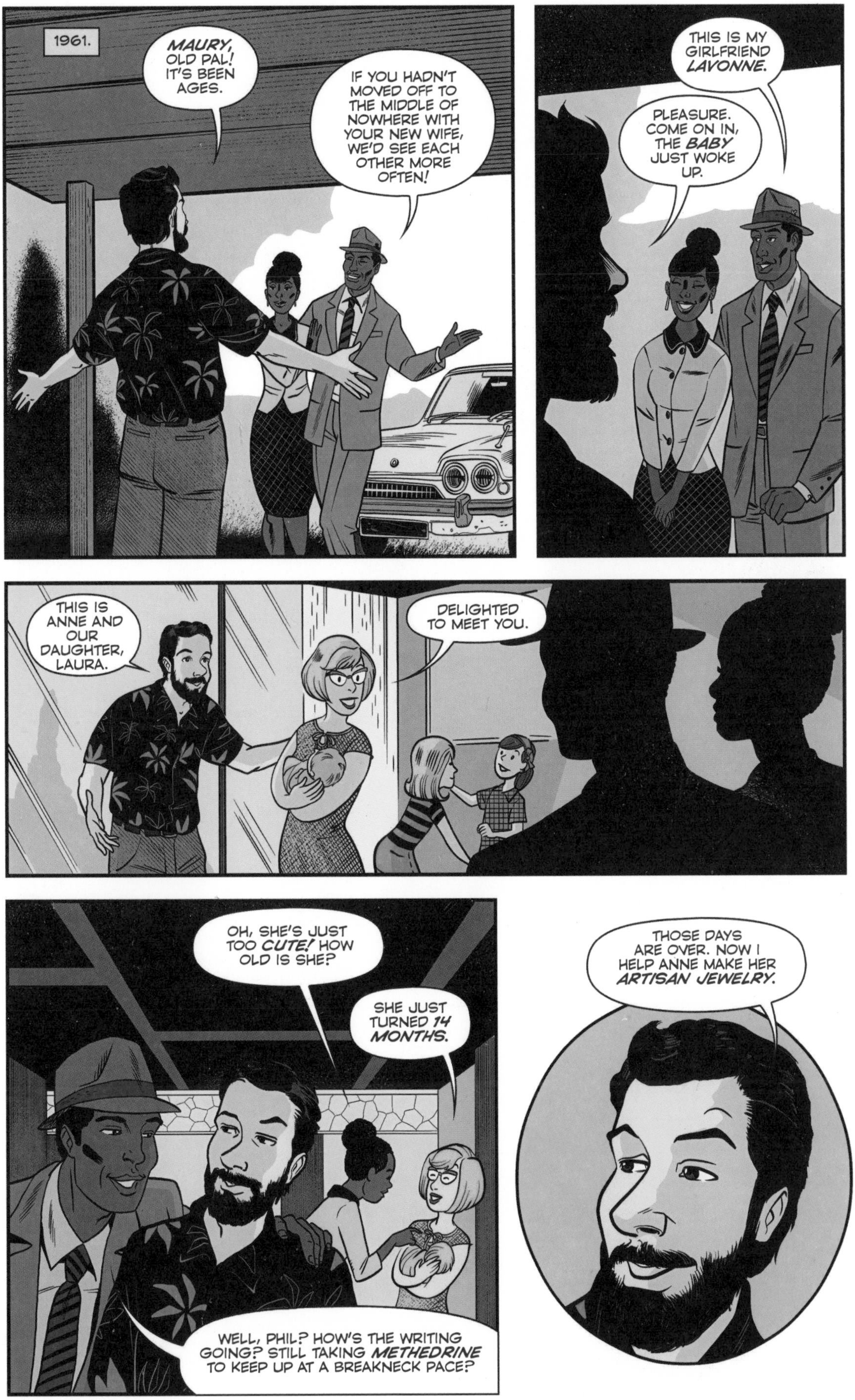
1961.
MAURY, OLD PAL! IT'S BEEN AGES.
IF YOU HADN'T MOVED OFF TO THE MIDDLE OF NOWHERE WITH YOUR NEW WIFE, WE'D SEE EACH OTHER MORE OFTEN!
THIS IS MY GIRLFRIEND LAVONNE.
PLEASURE. COME ON IN, THE BABY JUST WOKE UP.
THIS IS ANNE AND OUR DAUGHTER, LAURA.
DELIGHTED TO MEET YOU.
OH, SHE'S JUST TOO CUTE! HOW OLD IS SHE?
SHE JUST TURNED 14 MONTHS.
WELL, PHIL? HOW'S THE WRITING GOING? STILL TAKING METHEDRINE TO KEEP UP AT A BREAKNECK PACE?
THOSE DAYS ARE OVER. NOW I HELP ANNE MAKE HER ARTISAN JEWELRY.

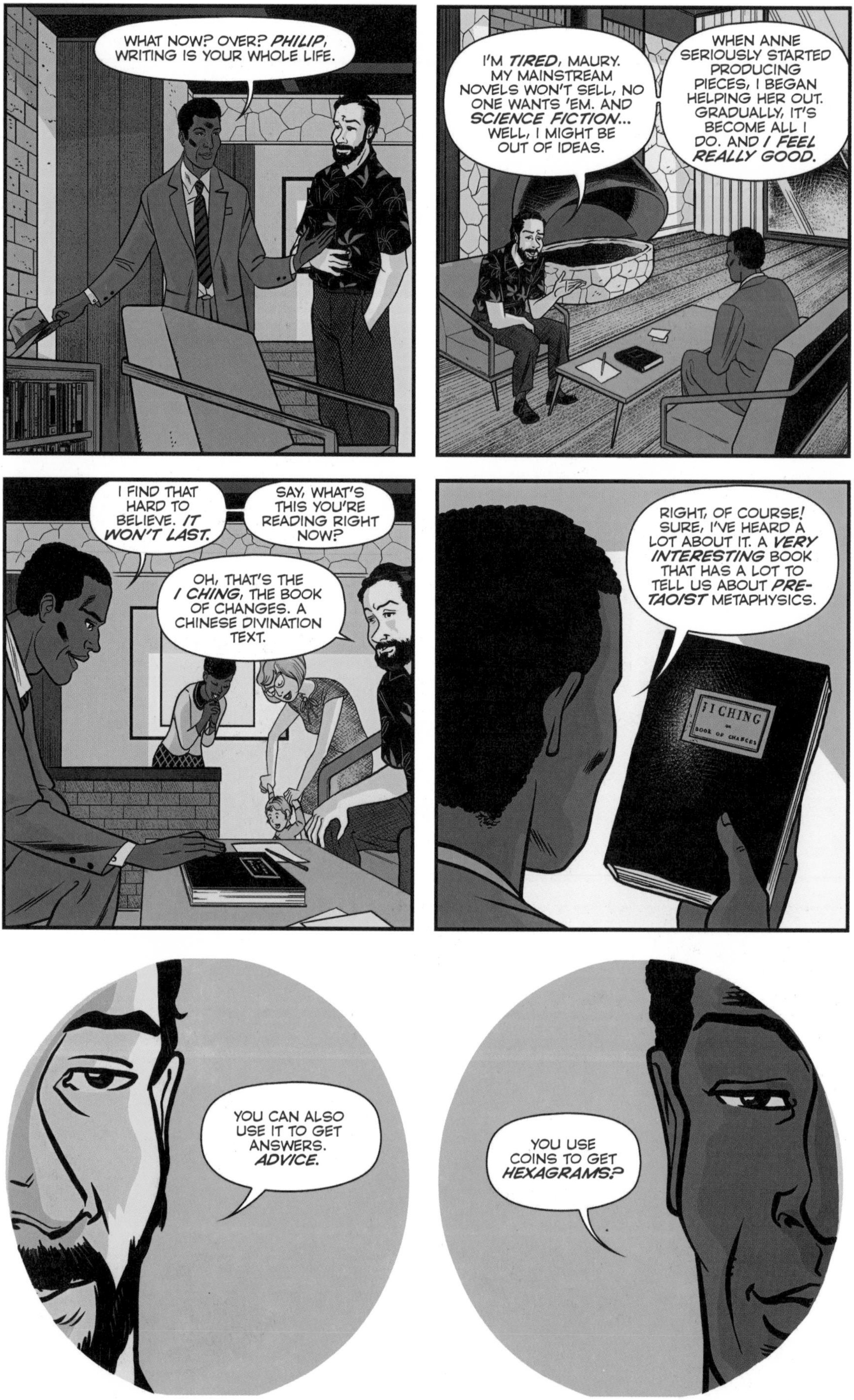
WHAT NOW? OVER? PHILIP, WRITING IS YOUR WHOLE LIFE.
I'M TIRED, MAURY. MY MAINSTREAM NOVELS WON'T SELL, NO ONE WANTS 'EM. AND SCIENCE FICTION... WELL, I MIGHT BE OUT OF IDEAS.
WHEN ANNE SERIOUSLY STARTED PRODUCING PIECES, I BEGAN HELPING HER OUT. GRADUALLY, IT'S BECOME ALL I DO. AND I FEEL REALLY GOOD.
I FIND THAT HARD TO BELIEVE. IT WON'T LAST.
SAY, WHAT'S THIS YOU'RE READING RIGHT NOW?
OH, THAT'S THE I CHING, THE BOOK OF CHANGES. A CHINESE DIVINATION TEXT.
RIGHT, OF COURSE! SURE, I'VE HEARD A LOT ABOUT IT. A VERY INTERESTING BOOK THAT HAS A LOT TO TELL US ABOUT PRE-TAOIST METAPHYSICS.
I CHING
BOOK OF CHANGES
YOU CAN ALSO USE IT TO GET ANSWERS. ADVICE.
YOU USE COINS TO GET HEXAGRAMS?

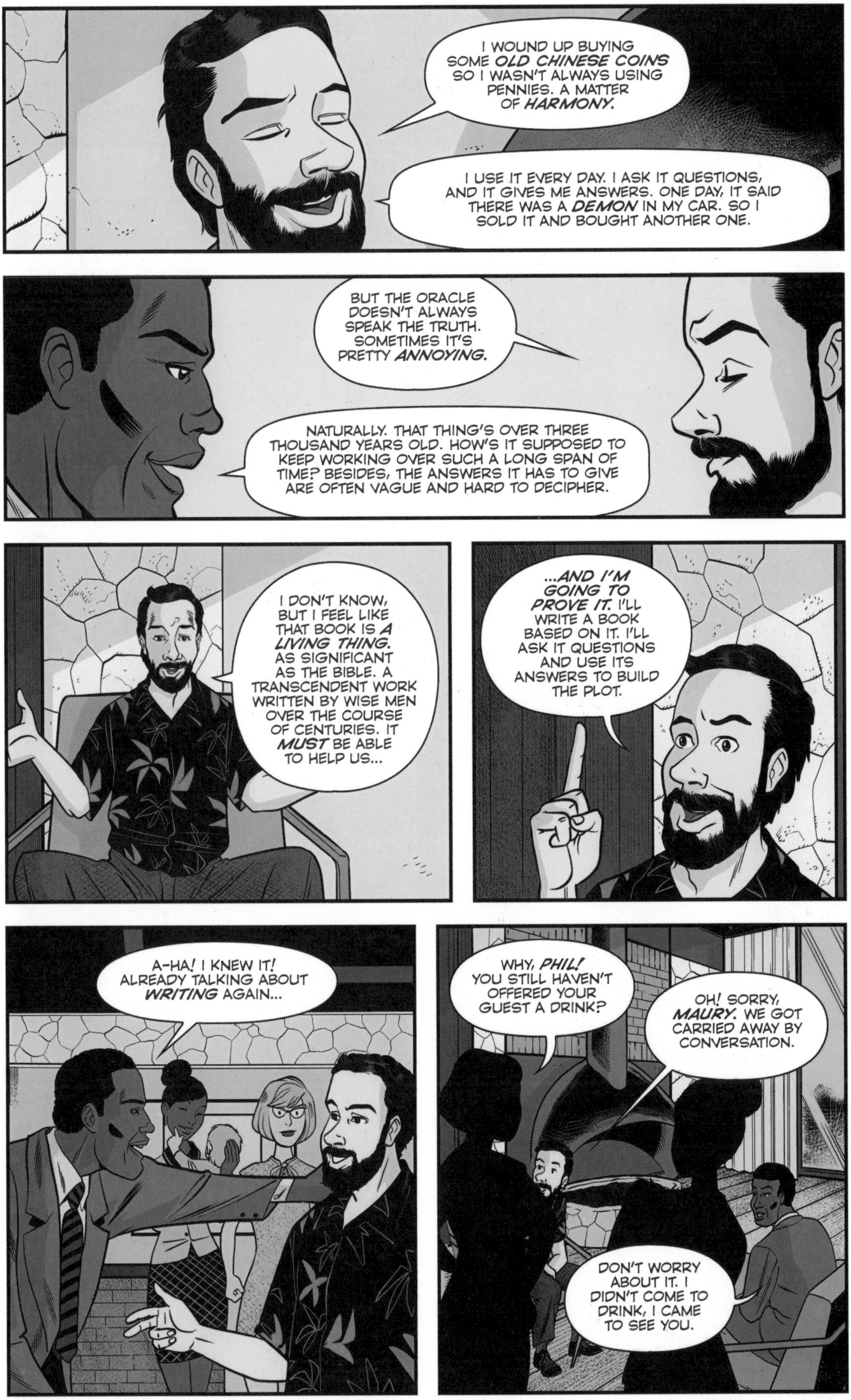
I WOUND UP BUYING SOME OLD CHINESE COINS SO I WASN'T ALWAYS USING PENNIES. A MATTER OF HARMONY.
I USE IT EVERY DAY. I ASK IT QUESTIONS, AND IT GIVES ME ANSWERS. ONE DAY, IT SAID THERE WAS A DEMON IN MY CAR. SO I SOLD IT AND BOUGHT ANOTHER ONE.
BUT THE ORACLE DOESN'T ALWAYS SPEAK THE TRUTH. SOMETIMES IT'S PRETTY ANNOYING.
NATURALLY. THAT THING'S OVER THREE THOUSAND YEARS OLD. HOW'S IT SUPPOSED TO KEEP WORKING OVER SUCH A LONG SPAN OF TIME? BESIDES, THE ANSWERS IT HAS TO GIVE ARE OFTEN VAGUE AND HARD TO DECIPHER.
I DON'T KNOW, BUT I FEEL LIKE THAT BOOK IS A LIVING THING. AS SIGNIFICANT AS THE BIBLE. A TRANSCENDENT WORK WRITTEN BY WISE MEN OVER THE COURSE OF CENTURIES. IT MUST BE ABLE TO HELP US...
...AND I'M GOING TO PROVE IT. I'LL WRITE A BOOK BASED ON IT. I'LL ASK IT QUESTIONS AND USE ITS ANSWERS TO BUILD THE PLOT.
A-HA! I KNEW IT! ALREADY TALKING ABOUT WRITING AGAIN...
WHY, PHIL! YOU STILL HAVEN'T OFFERED YOUR GUEST A DRINK?
OH! SORRY, MAURY. WE GOT CARRIED AWAY BY CONVERSATION.
DON'T WORRY ABOUT IT. I DIDN'T COME TO DRINK, I CAME TO SEE YOU.

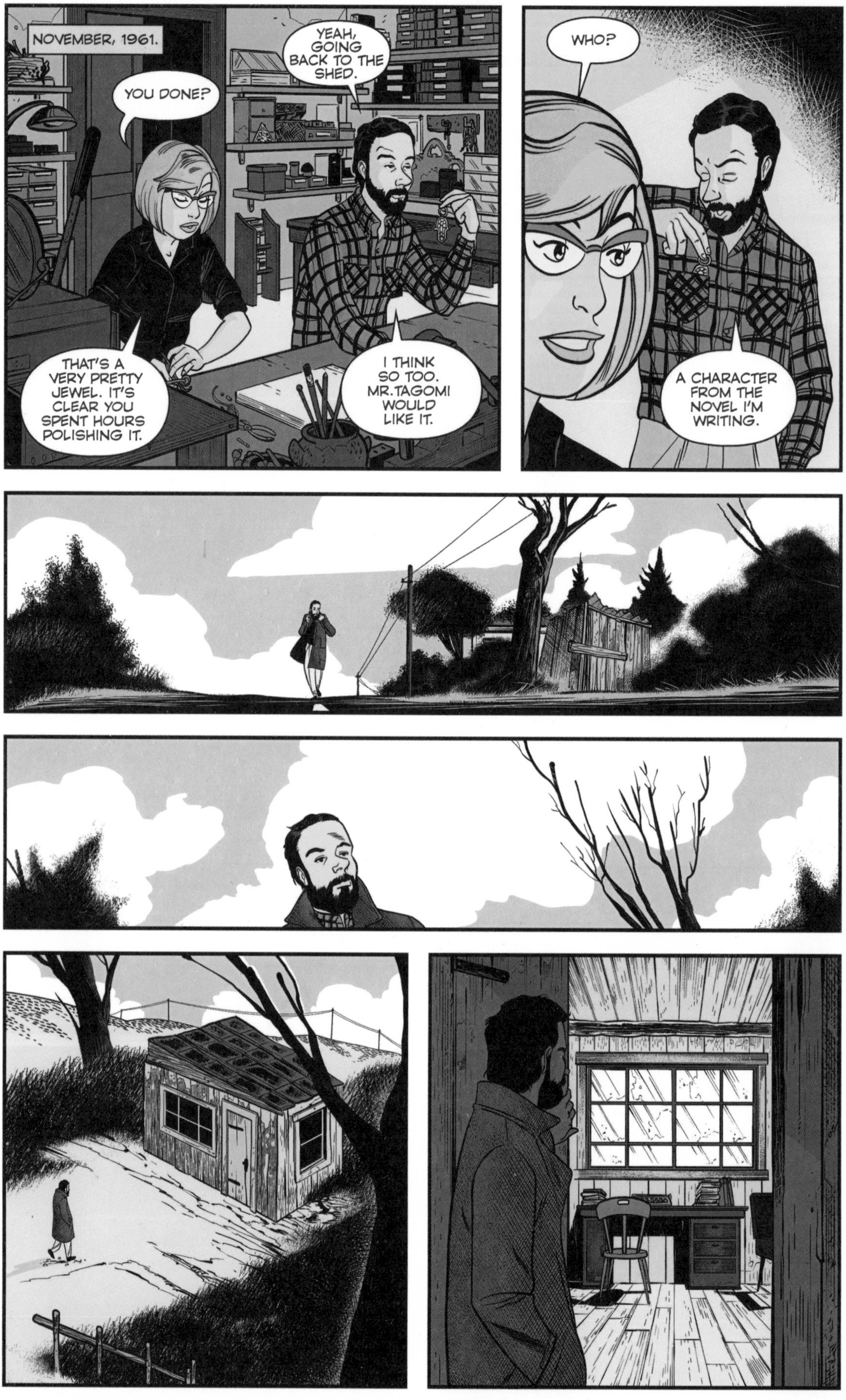
NOVEMBER, 1961.
YOU DONE?
YEAH, GOING BACK TO THE SHED.
THAT'S A VERY PRETTY JEWEL. IT'S CLEAR YOU SPENT HOURS POLISHING IT.
I THINK SO TOO. MR.TAGOMI WOULD LIKE IT.
WHO?
A CHARACTER FROM THE NOVEL I'M WRITING.

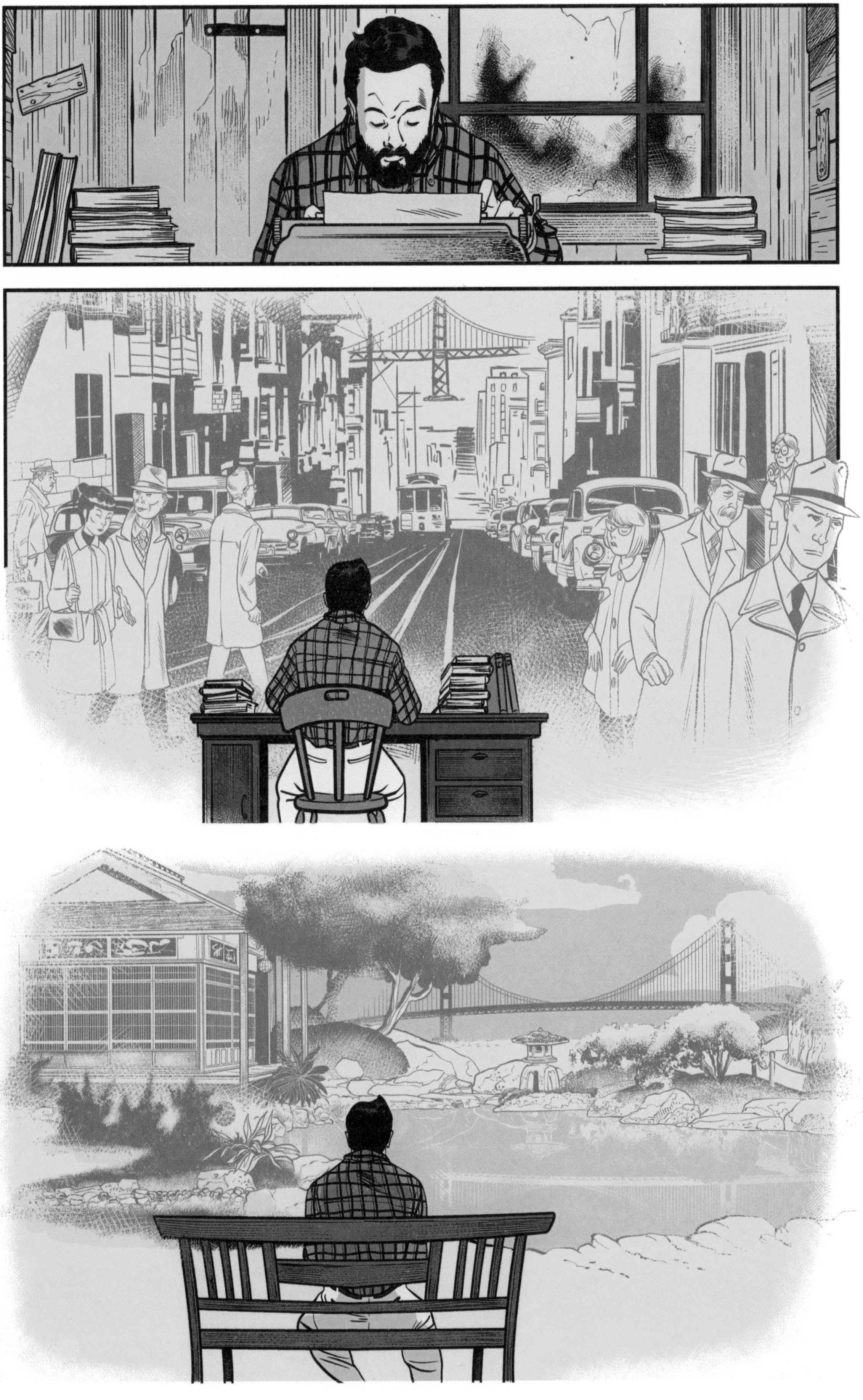

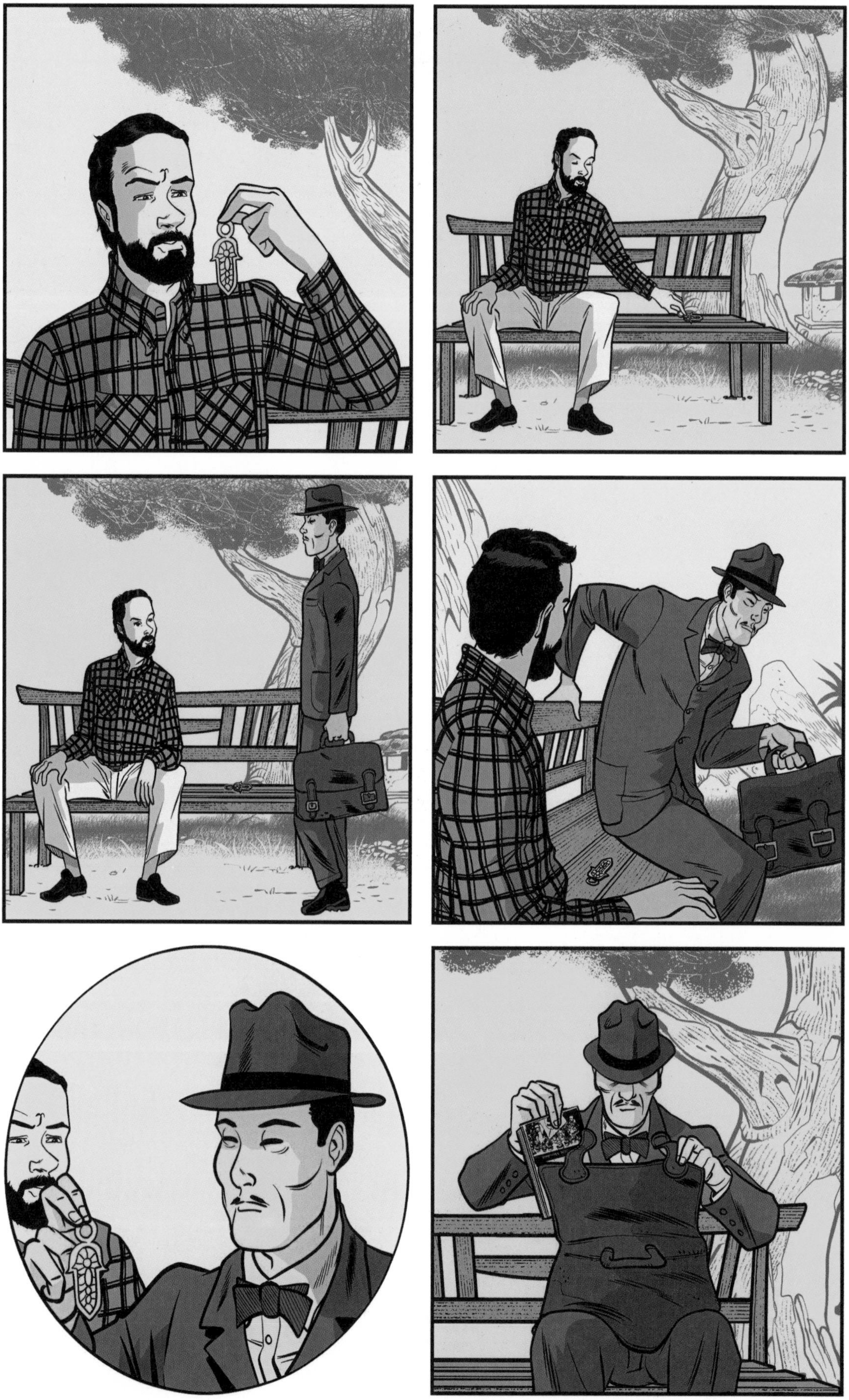

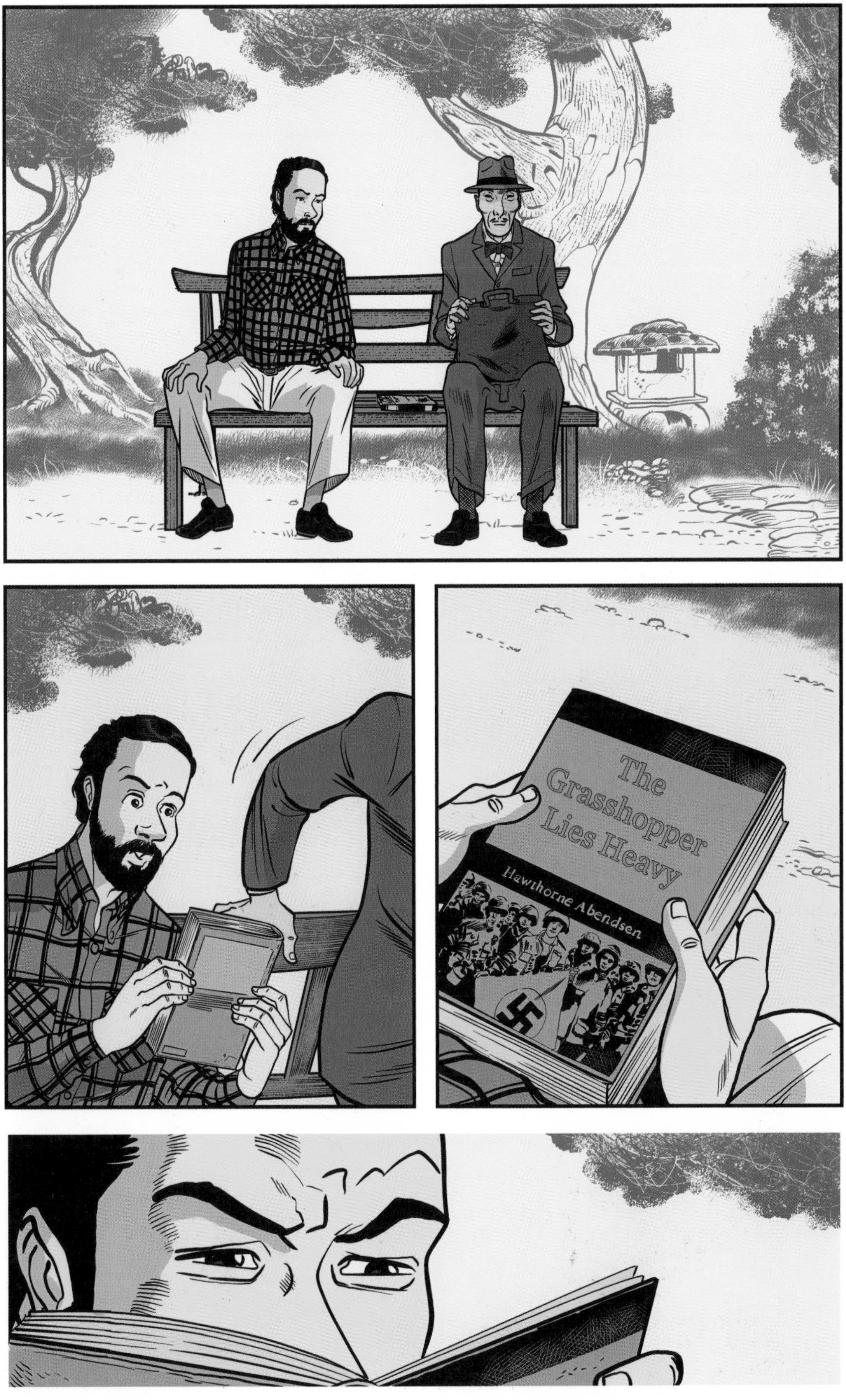
The Grasshopper Lies Heavy
Hawthorne Abendsen

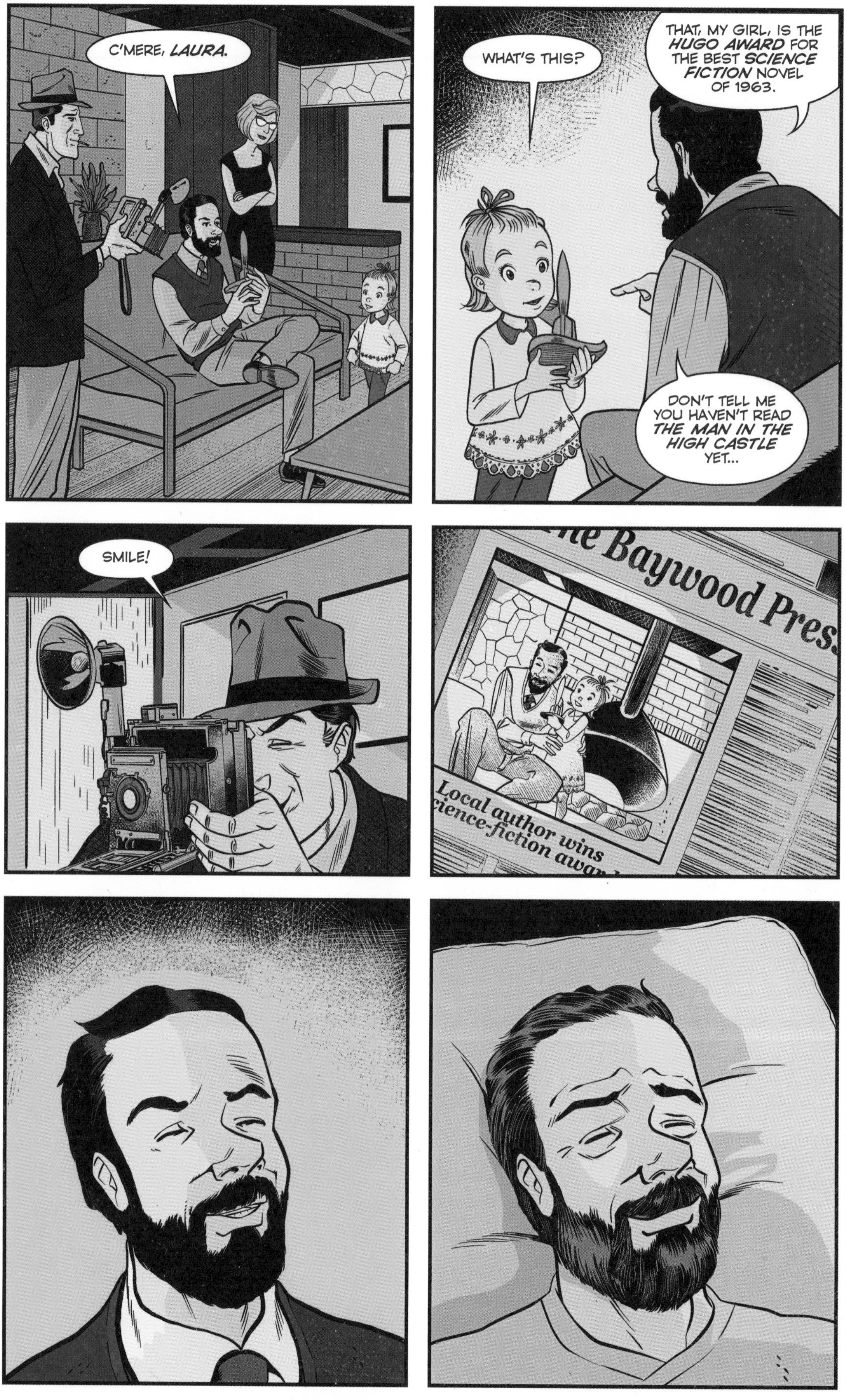
C'MERE, LAURA.
WHAT'S THIS?
THAT, MY GIRL, IS THE HUGO AWARD FOR THE BEST SCIENCE FICTION NOVEL OF 1963.
DON'T TELL ME YOU HAVEN'T READ THE MAN IN THE HIGH CASTLE YET...
SMILE!
The Baywood Press
Local author wins science-fiction award

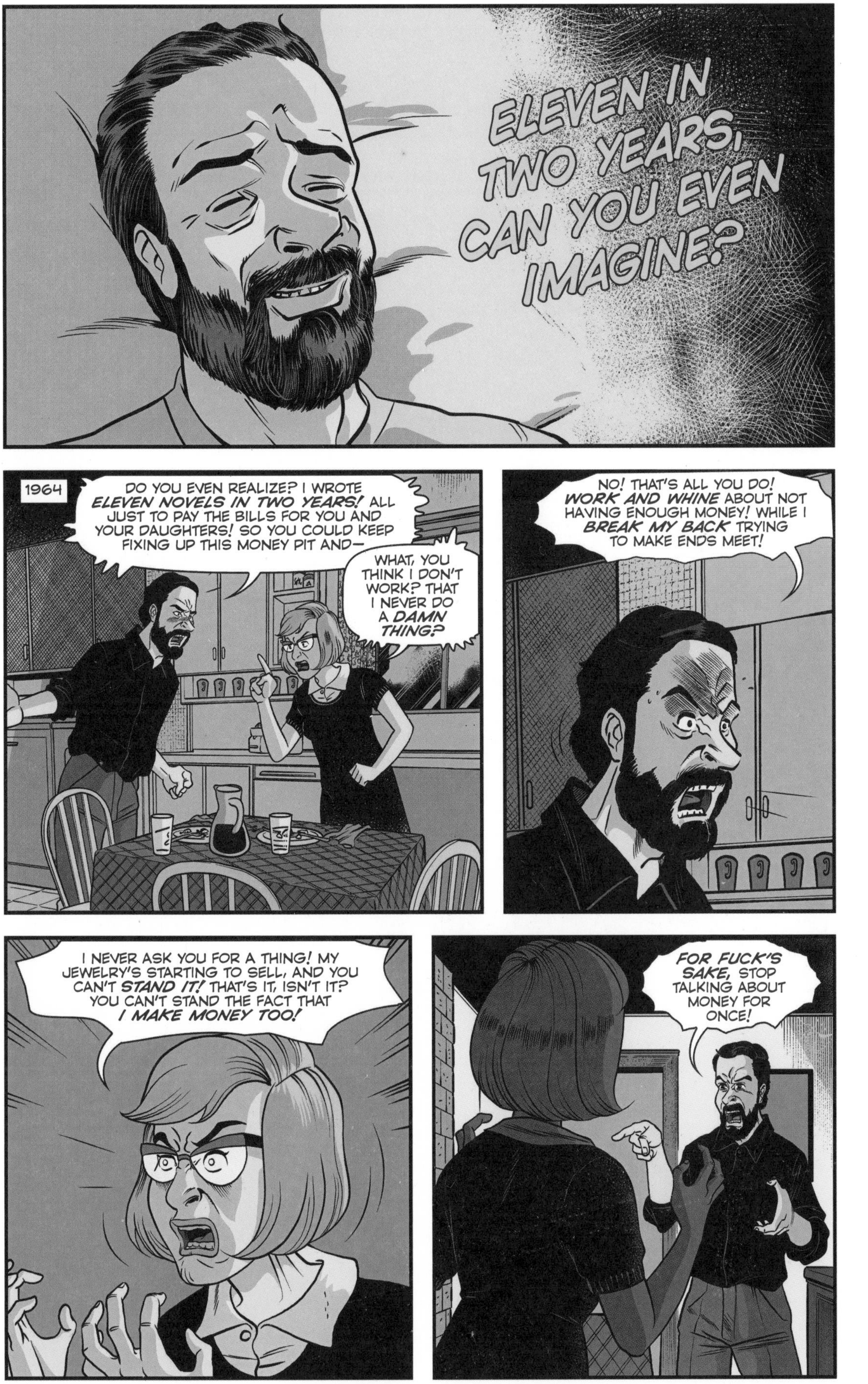
ELEVEN IN TWO YEARS, CAN YOU EVEN IMAGINE?
1964
DO YOU EVEN REALIZE? I WROTE ELEVEN NOVELS IN TWO YEARS! ALL JUST TO PAY THE BILLS FOR YOU AND YOUR DAUGHTERS! SO YOU COULD KEEP FIXING UP THIS MONEY PIT AND—
WHAT, YOU THINK I DON'T WORK? THAT I NEVER DO A DAMN THING?
NO! THAT'S ALL YOU DO! WORK AND WHINE ABOUT NOT HAVING ENOUGH MONEY! WHILE I BREAK MY BACK TRYING TO MAKE ENDS MEET!
I NEVER ASK YOU FOR A THING! MY JEWELRY'S STARTING TO SELL, AND YOU CAN'T STAND IT! THAT'S IT, ISN'T IT? YOU CAN'T STAND THE FACT THAT I MAKE MONEY TOO!
FOR FUCK'S SAKE, STOP TALKING ABOUT MONEY FOR ONCE!

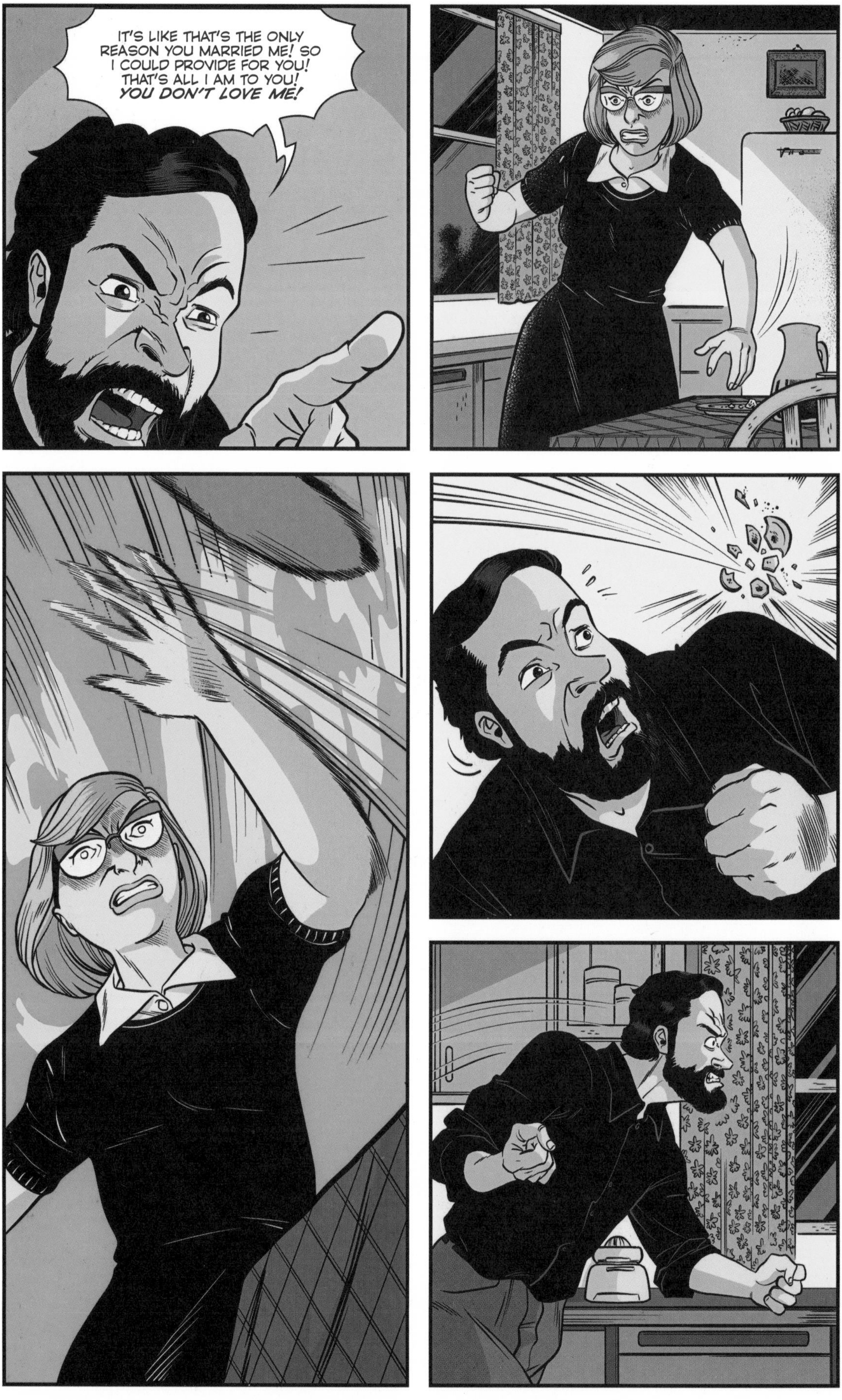
IT'S LIKE THAT'S THE ONLY REASON YOU MARRIED ME! SO I COULD PROVIDE FOR YOU! THAT'S ALL I AM TO YOU! *YOU DON'T LOVE ME!*

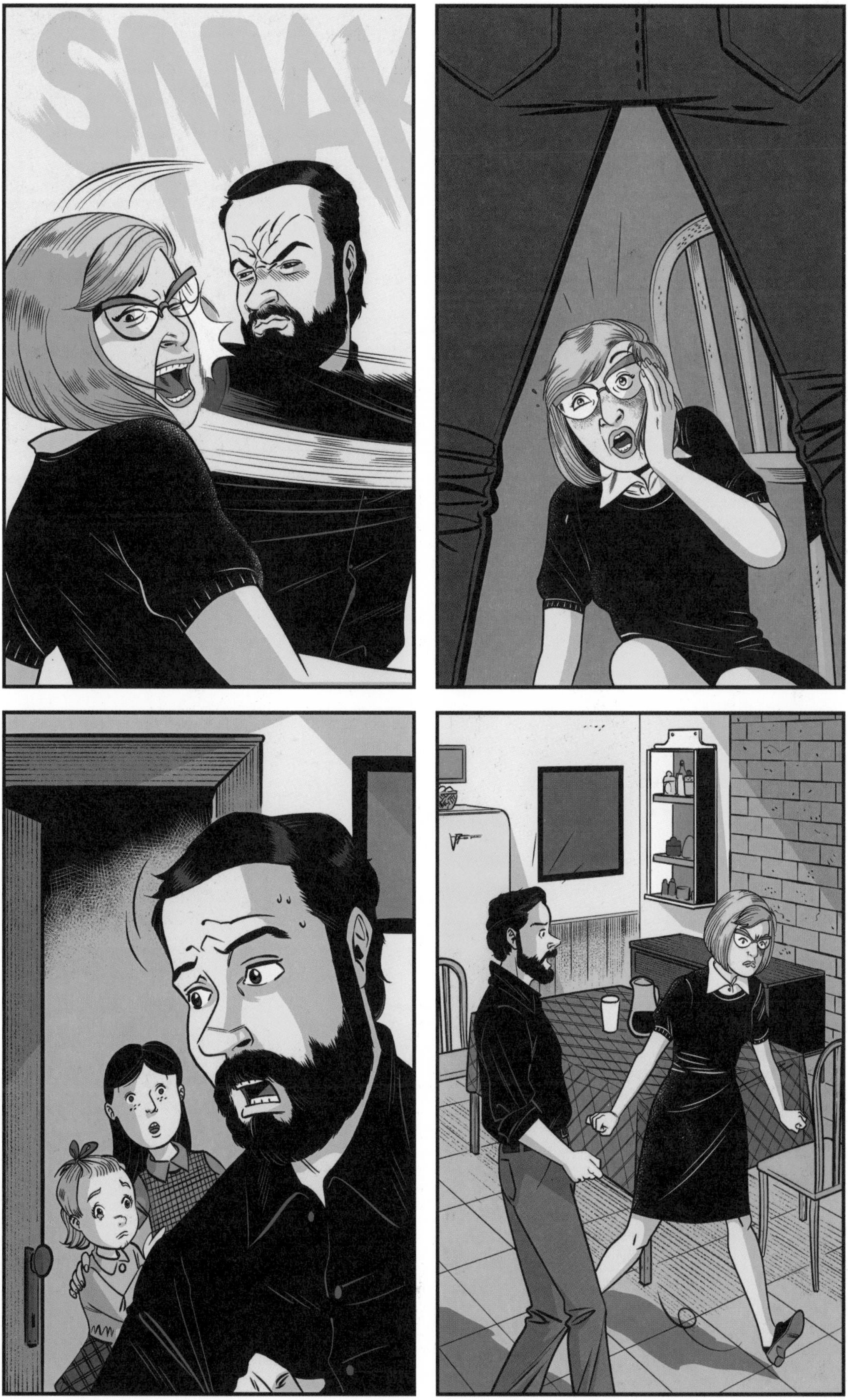
SMAK

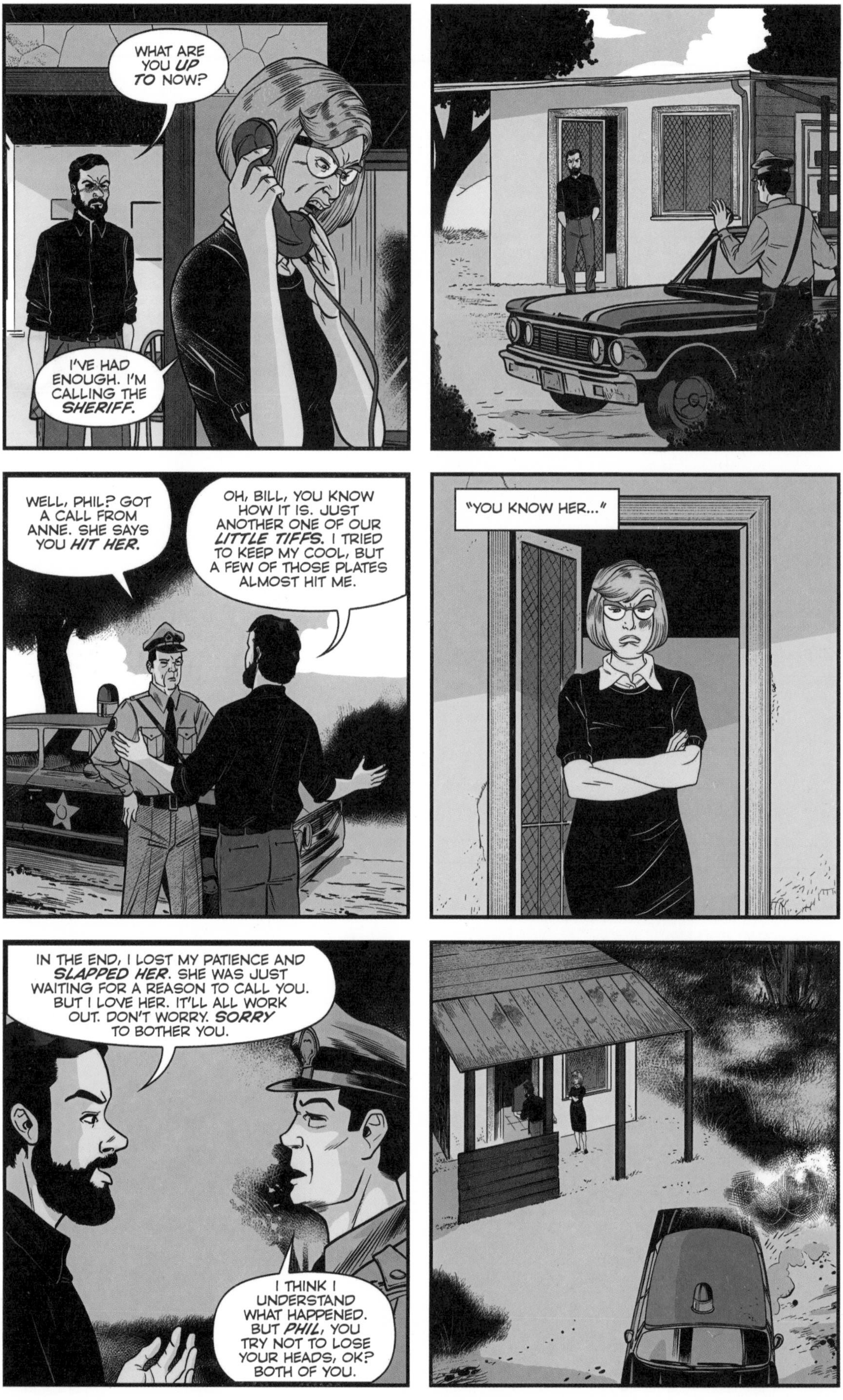
WHAT ARE YOU UP TO NOW?
I'VE HAD ENOUGH. I'M CALLING THE SHERIFF.
WELL, PHIL? GOT A CALL FROM ANNE. SHE SAYS YOU HIT HER.
OH, BILL, YOU KNOW HOW IT IS. JUST ANOTHER ONE OF OUR LITTLE TIFFS. I TRIED TO KEEP MY COOL, BUT A FEW OF THOSE PLATES ALMOST HIT ME.
"YOU KNOW HER..."
IN THE END, I LOST MY PATIENCE AND SLAPPED HER. SHE WAS JUST WAITING FOR A REASON TO CALL YOU. BUT I LOVE HER. IT'LL ALL WORK OUT. DON'T WORRY. SORRY TO BOTHER YOU.
I THINK I UNDERSTAND WHAT HAPPENED. BUT PHIL, YOU TRY NOT TO LOSE YOUR HEADS, OK? BOTH OF YOU.

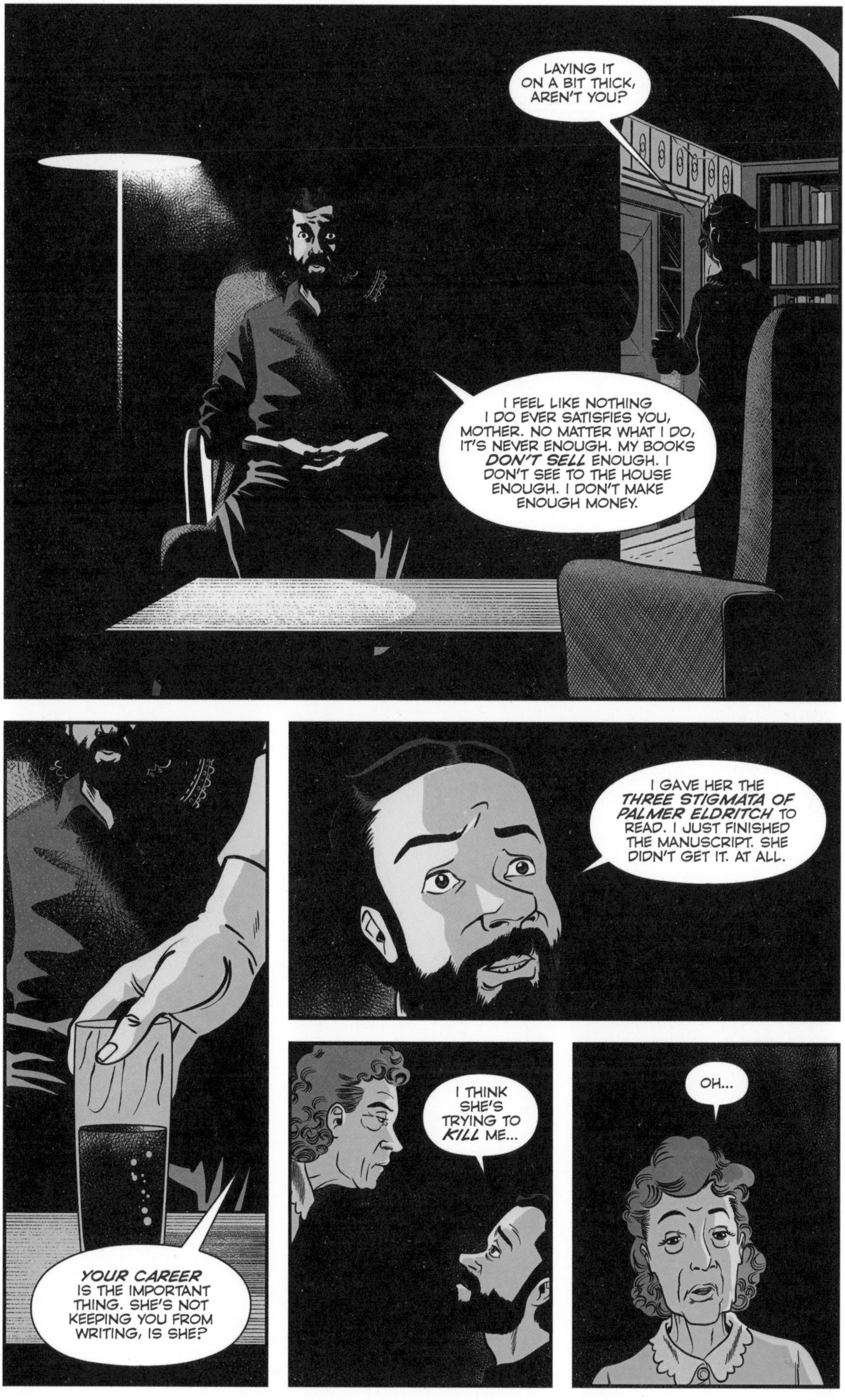
LAYING IT ON A BIT THICK, AREN'T YOU?
I FEEL LIKE NOTHING I DO EVER SATISFIES YOU, MOTHER. NO MATTER WHAT I DO, IT'S NEVER ENOUGH. MY BOOKS DON'T SELL ENOUGH. I DON'T SEE TO THE HOUSE ENOUGH. I DON'T MAKE ENOUGH MONEY.
YOUR CAREER IS THE IMPORTANT THING. SHE'S NOT KEEPING YOU FROM WRITING, IS SHE?
I GAVE HER THE THREE STIGMATA OF PALMER ELDRITCH TO READ. I JUST FINISHED THE MANUSCRIPT. SHE DIDN'T GET IT. AT ALL.
I THINK SHE'S TRYING TO KILL ME...
OH...

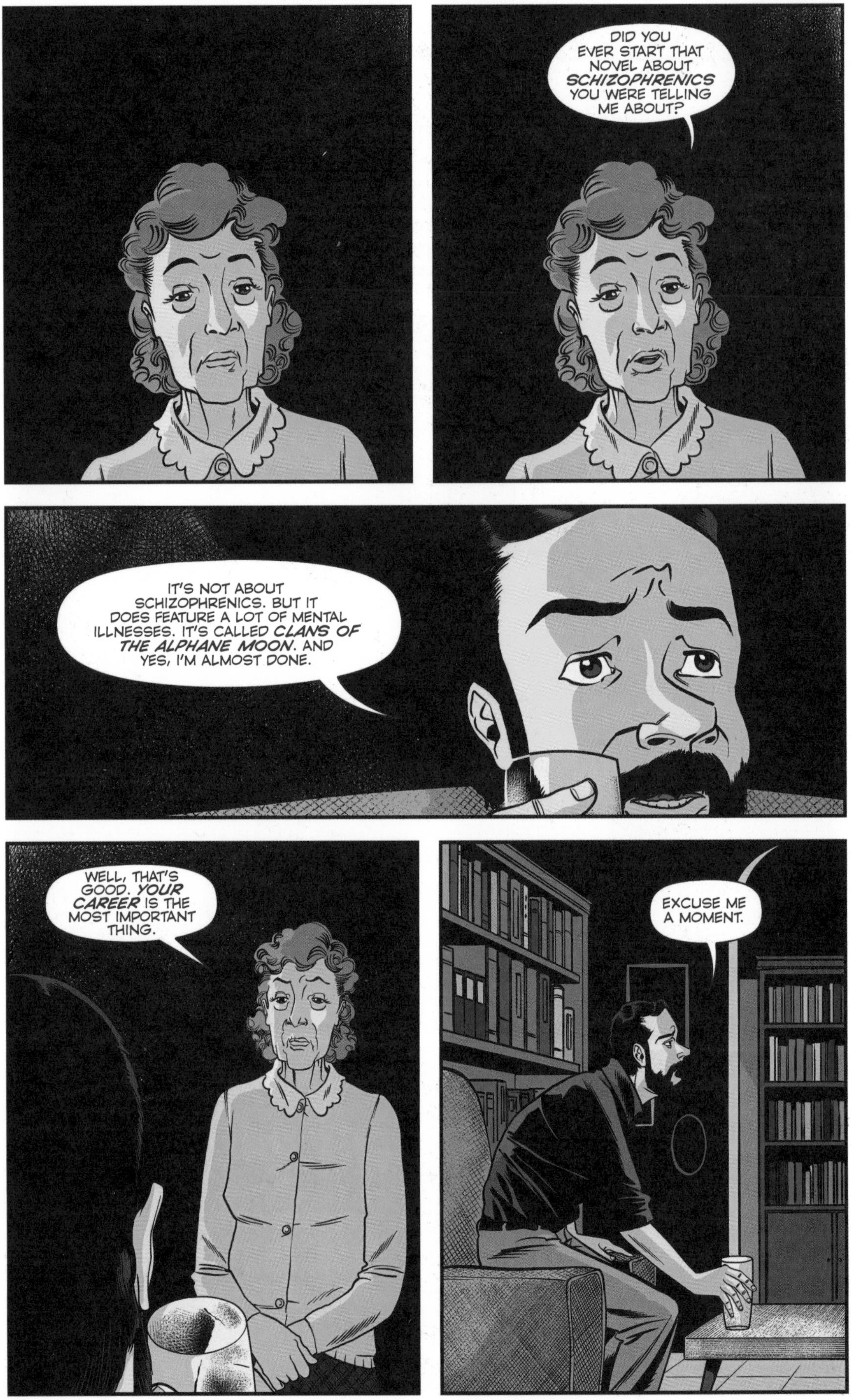
DID YOU EVER START THAT NOVEL ABOUT SCHIZOPHRENICS YOU WERE TELLING ME ABOUT?
IT'S NOT ABOUT SCHIZOPHRENICS. BUT IT DOES FEATURE A LOT OF MENTAL ILLNESSES. IT'S CALLED CLANS OF THE ALPHANE MOON. AND YES, I'M ALMOST DONE.
WELL, THAT'S GOOD. YOUR CAREER IS THE MOST IMPORTANT THING.
EXCUSE ME A MOMENT.

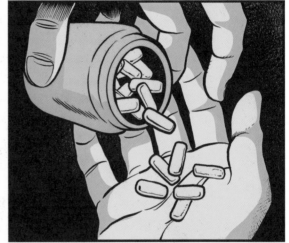

YOU KNOW, PHIL, SOMEDAY I'M GOING TO PUT A PADLOCK ON THAT *MEDICINE CABINET*.

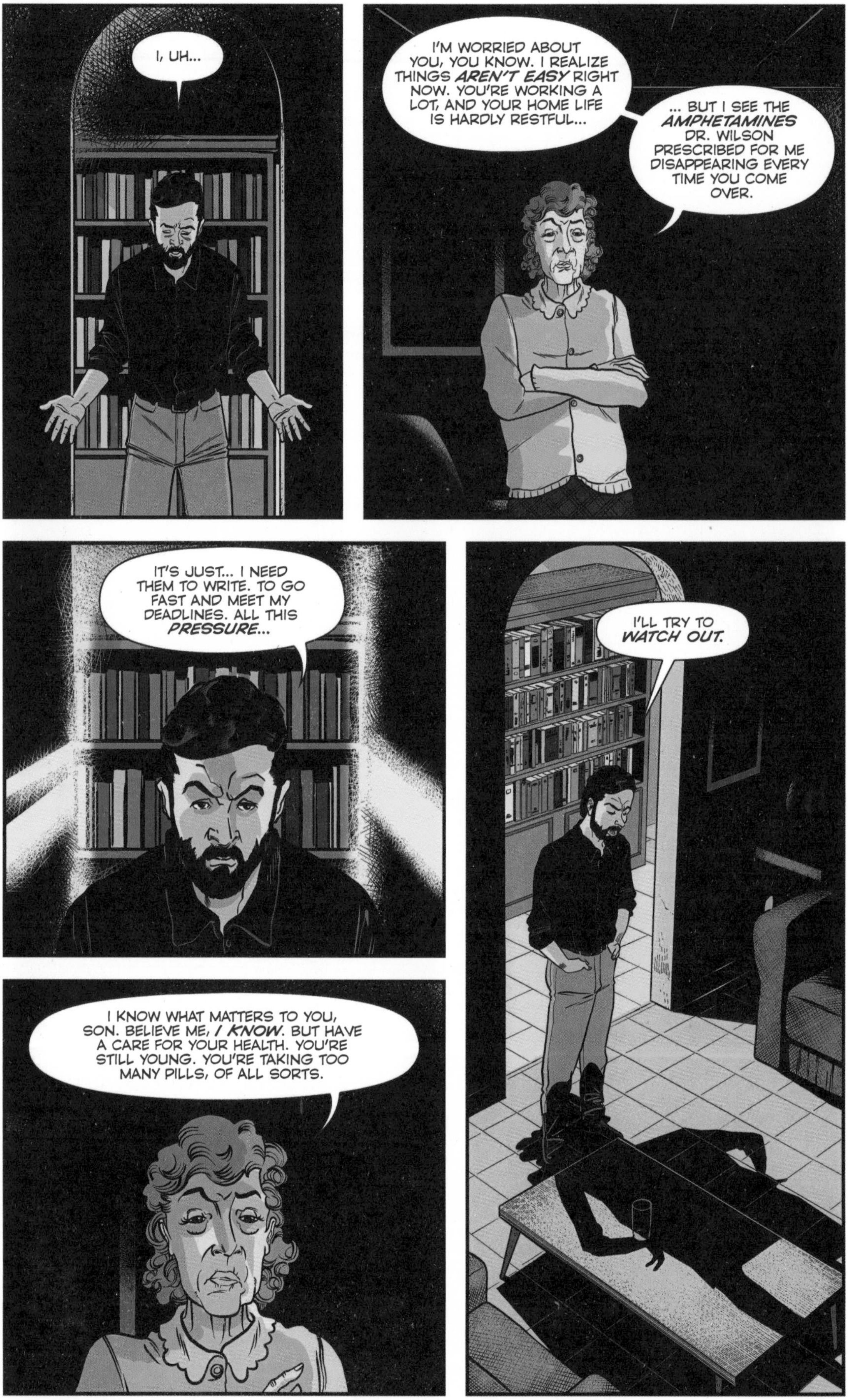
I, UH...
I'M WORRIED ABOUT YOU, YOU KNOW. I REALIZE THINGS AREN'T EASY RIGHT NOW. YOU'RE WORKING A LOT, AND YOUR HOME LIFE IS HARDLY RESTFUL...
... BUT I SEE THE AMPHETAMINES DR. WILSON PRESCRIBED FOR ME DISAPPEARING EVERY TIME YOU COME OVER.
IT'S JUST... I NEED THEM TO WRITE. TO GO FAST AND MEET MY DEADLINES. ALL THIS PRESSURE...
I KNOW WHAT MATTERS TO YOU, SON. BELIEVE ME, I KNOW. BUT HAVE A CARE FOR YOUR HEALTH. YOU'RE STILL YOUNG. YOU'RE TAKING TOO MANY PILLS, OF ALL SORTS.
I'LL TRY TO WATCH OUT.

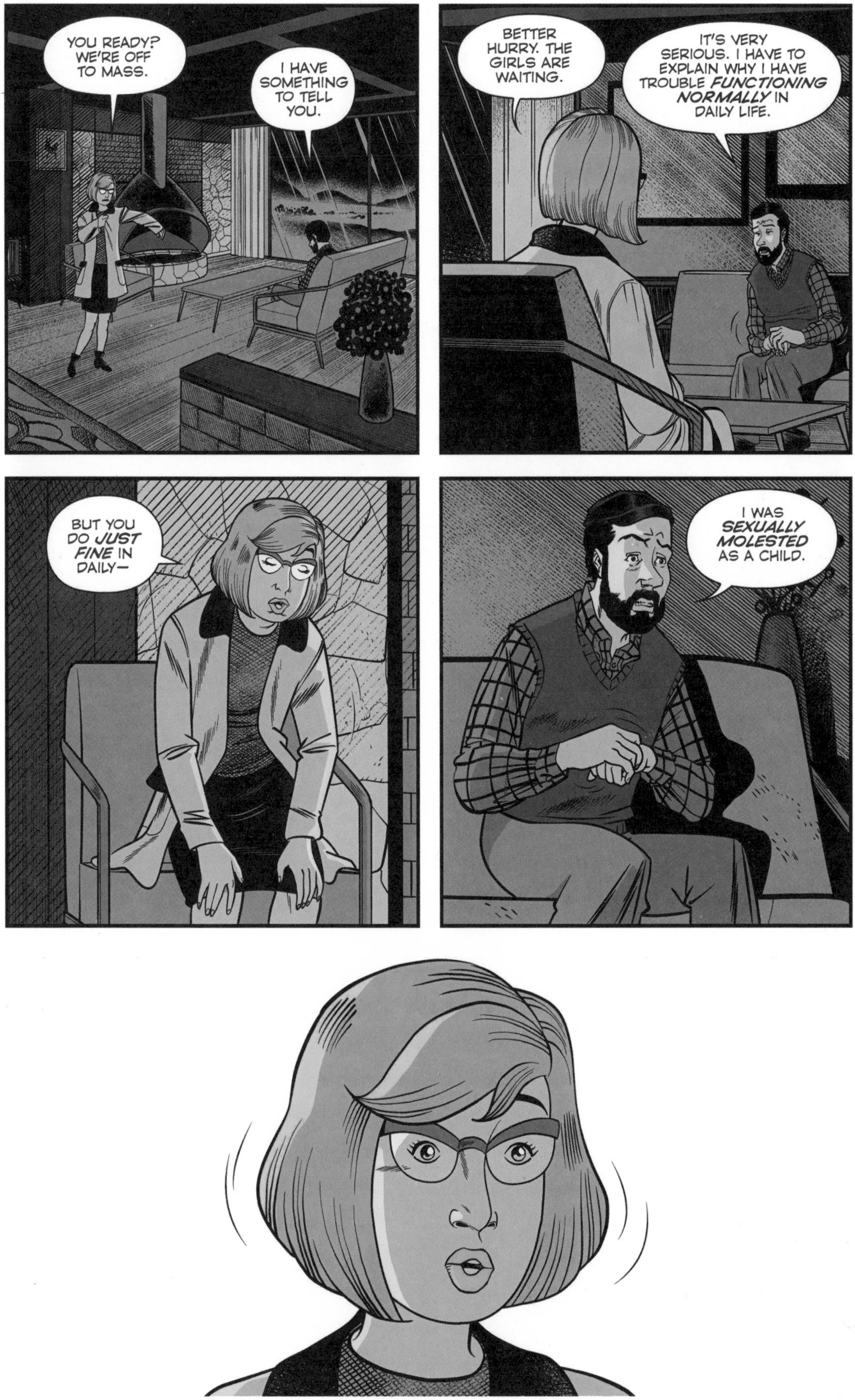
YOU READY? WE'RE OFF TO MASS.
I HAVE SOMETHING TO TELL YOU.
BETTER HURRY. THE GIRLS ARE WAITING.
IT'S VERY SERIOUS. I HAVE TO EXPLAIN WHY I HAVE TROUBLE *FUNCTIONING NORMALLY* IN DAILY LIFE.
BUT YOU DO *JUST FINE* IN DAILY—
I WAS *SEXUALLY MOLESTED* AS A CHILD.

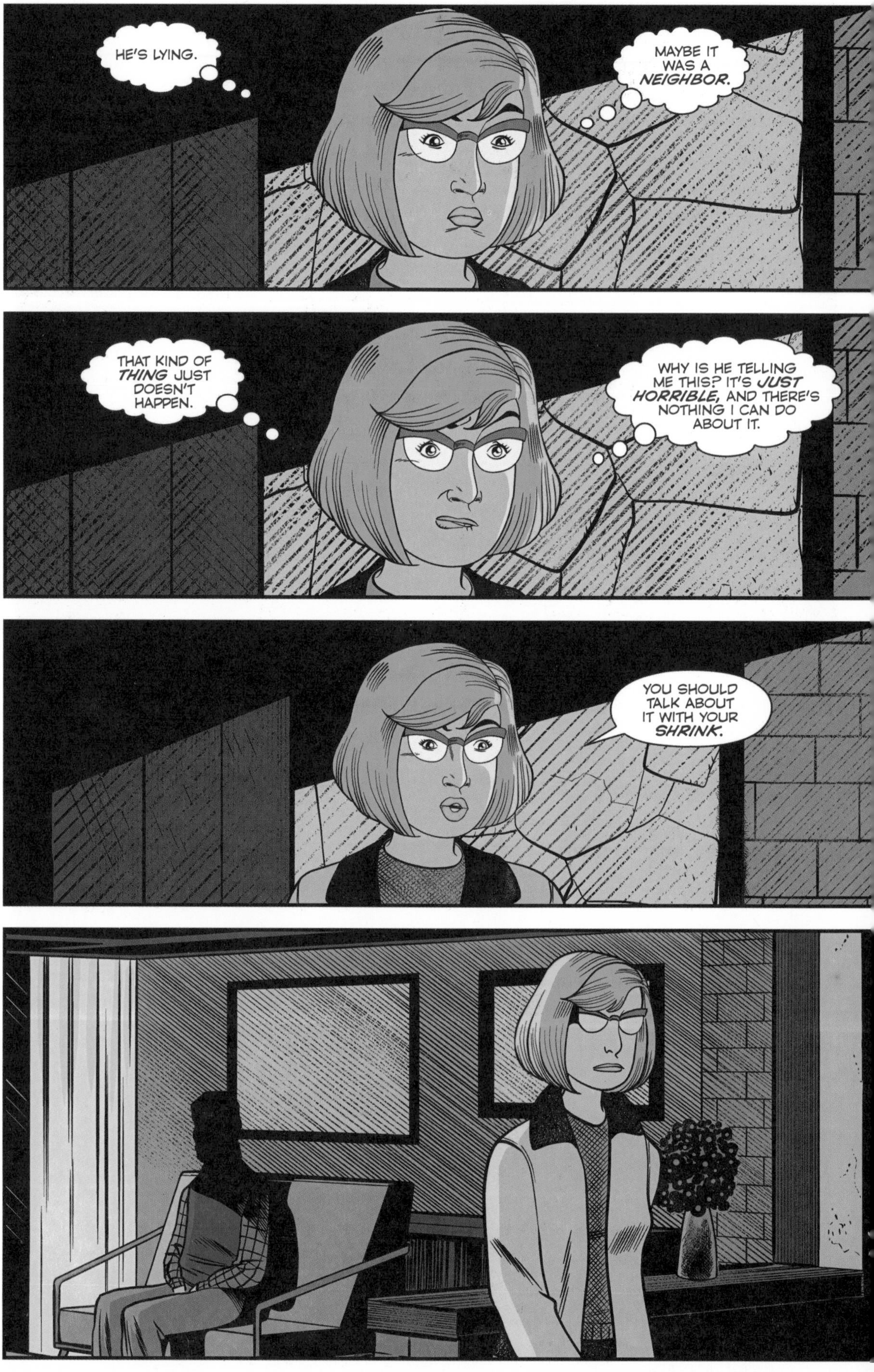
HE'S LYING.
MAYBE IT WAS A NEIGHBOR.
THAT KIND OF THING JUST DOESN'T HAPPEN.
WHY IS HE TELLING ME THIS? IT'S JUST HORRIBLE, AND THERE'S NOTHING I CAN DO ABOUT IT.
YOU SHOULD TALK ABOUT IT WITH YOUR SHRINK.

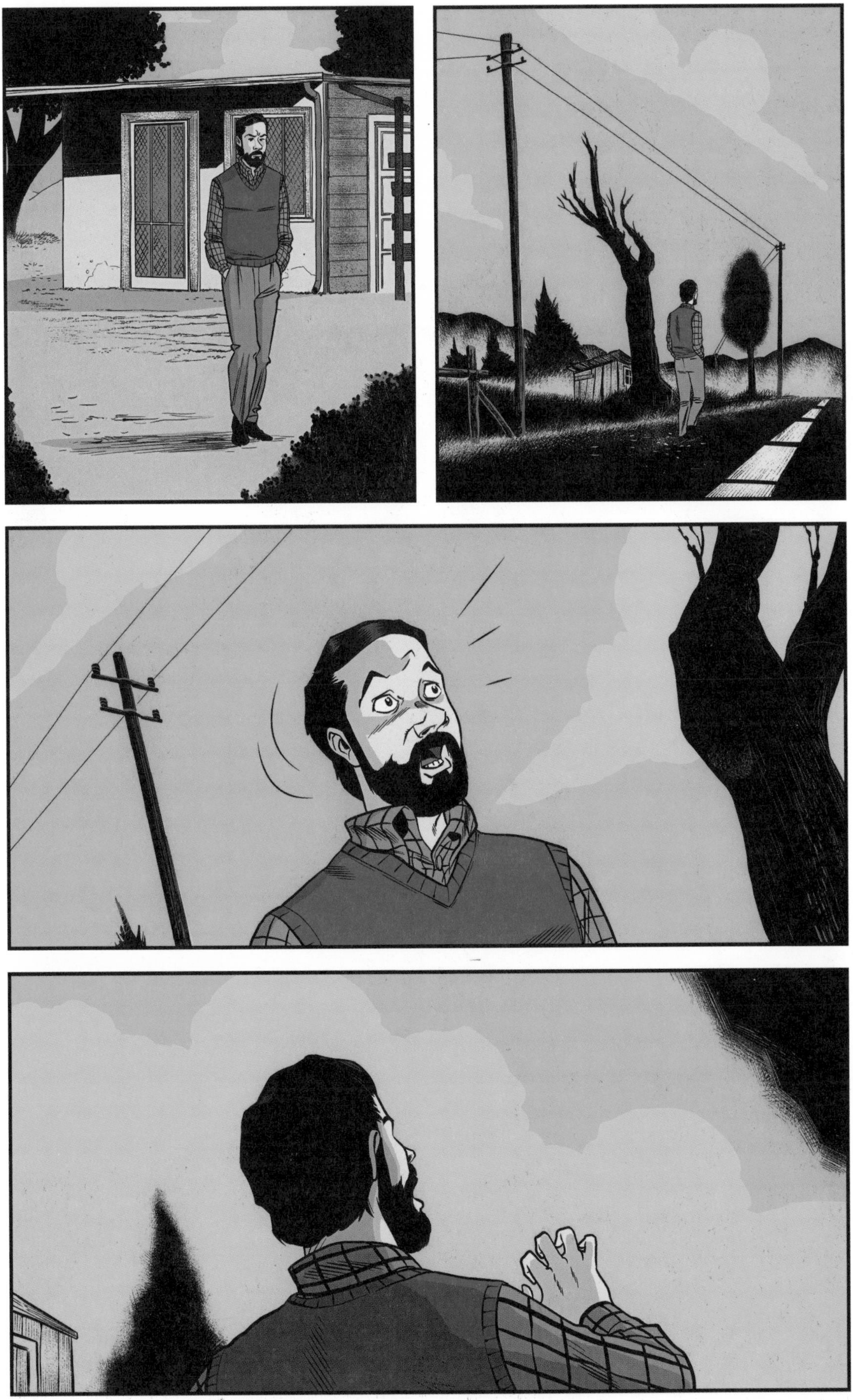

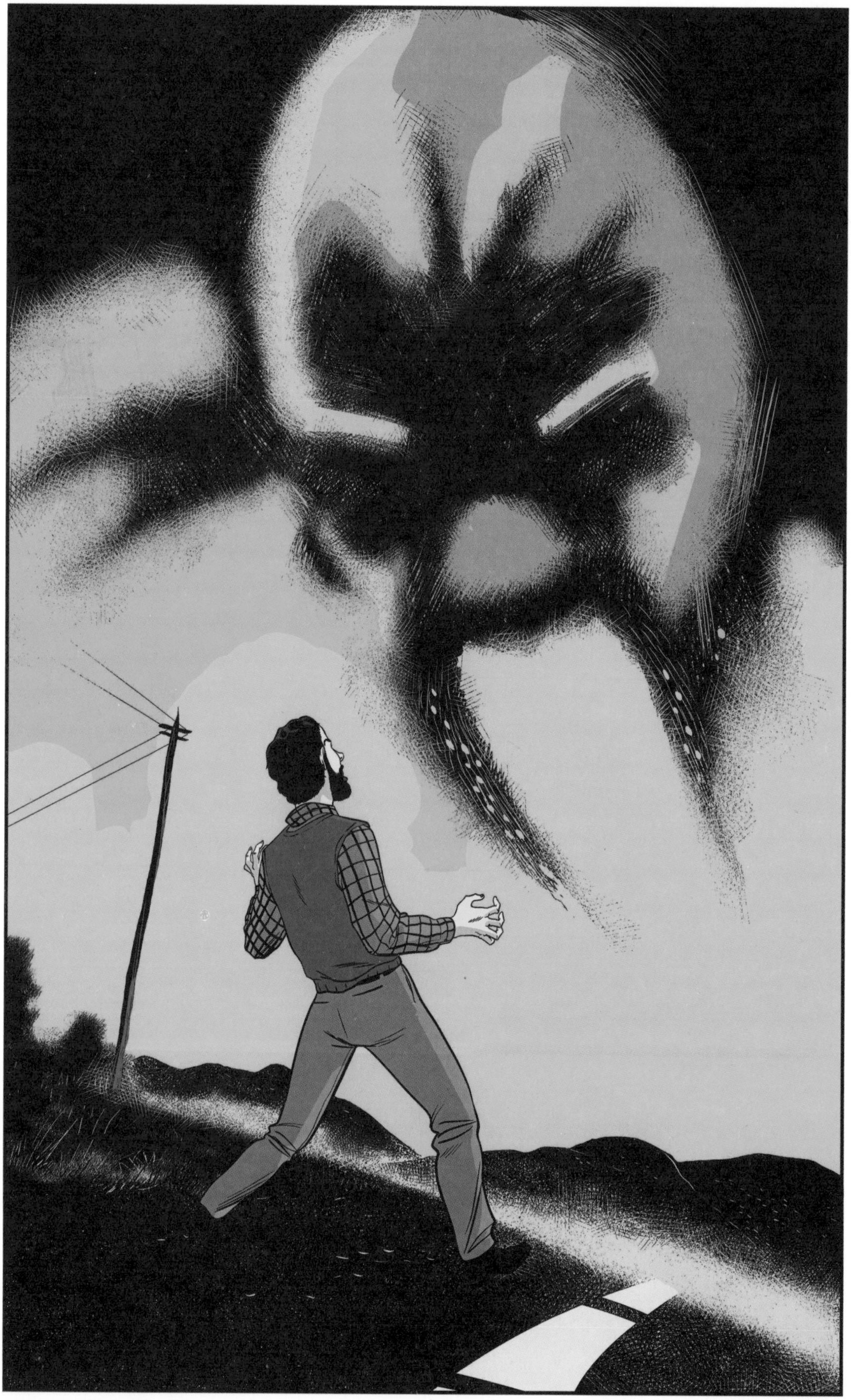

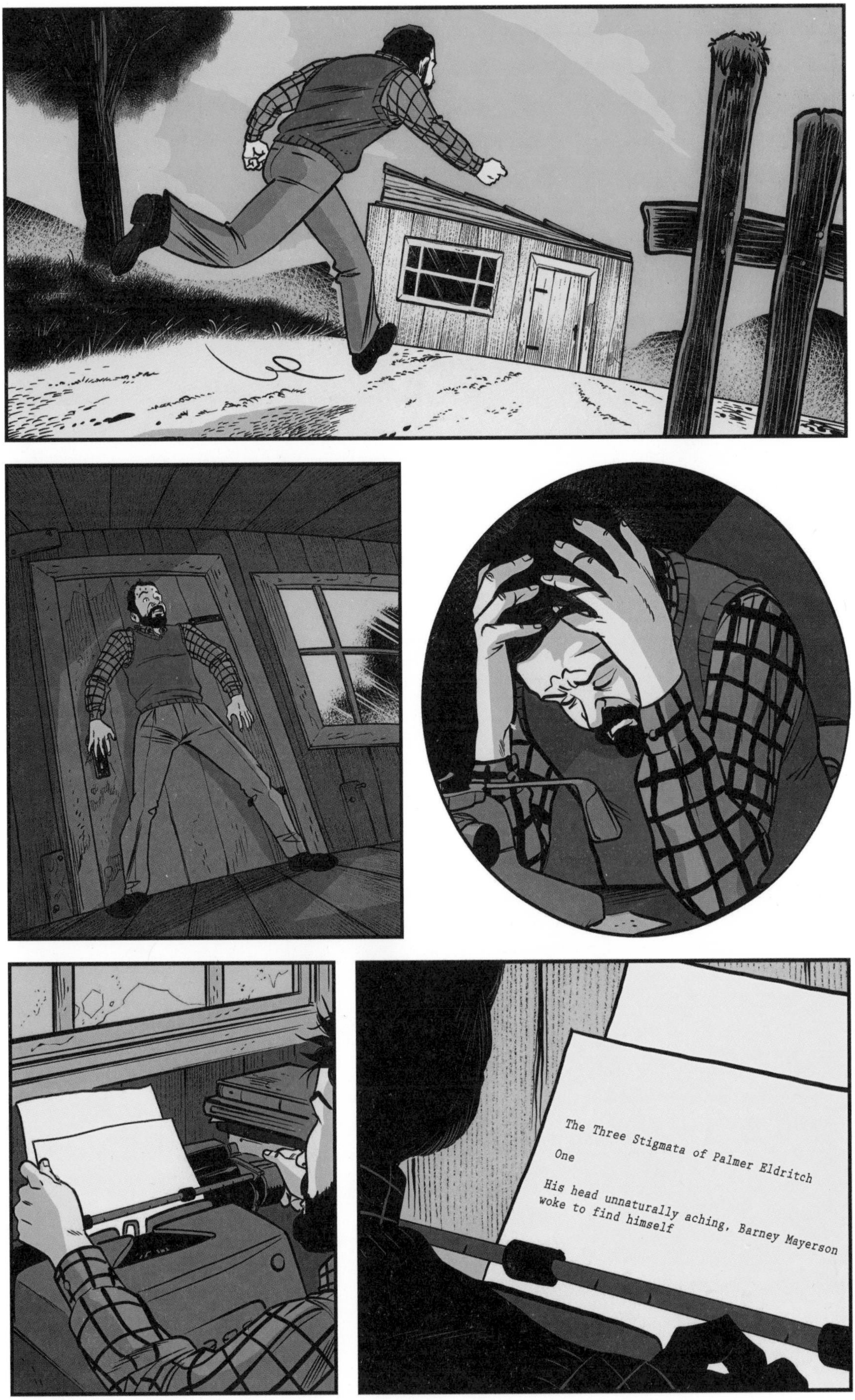
The Three Stigmata of Palmer Eldritch
One
His head unnaturally aching, Barney Mayerson woke to find himself

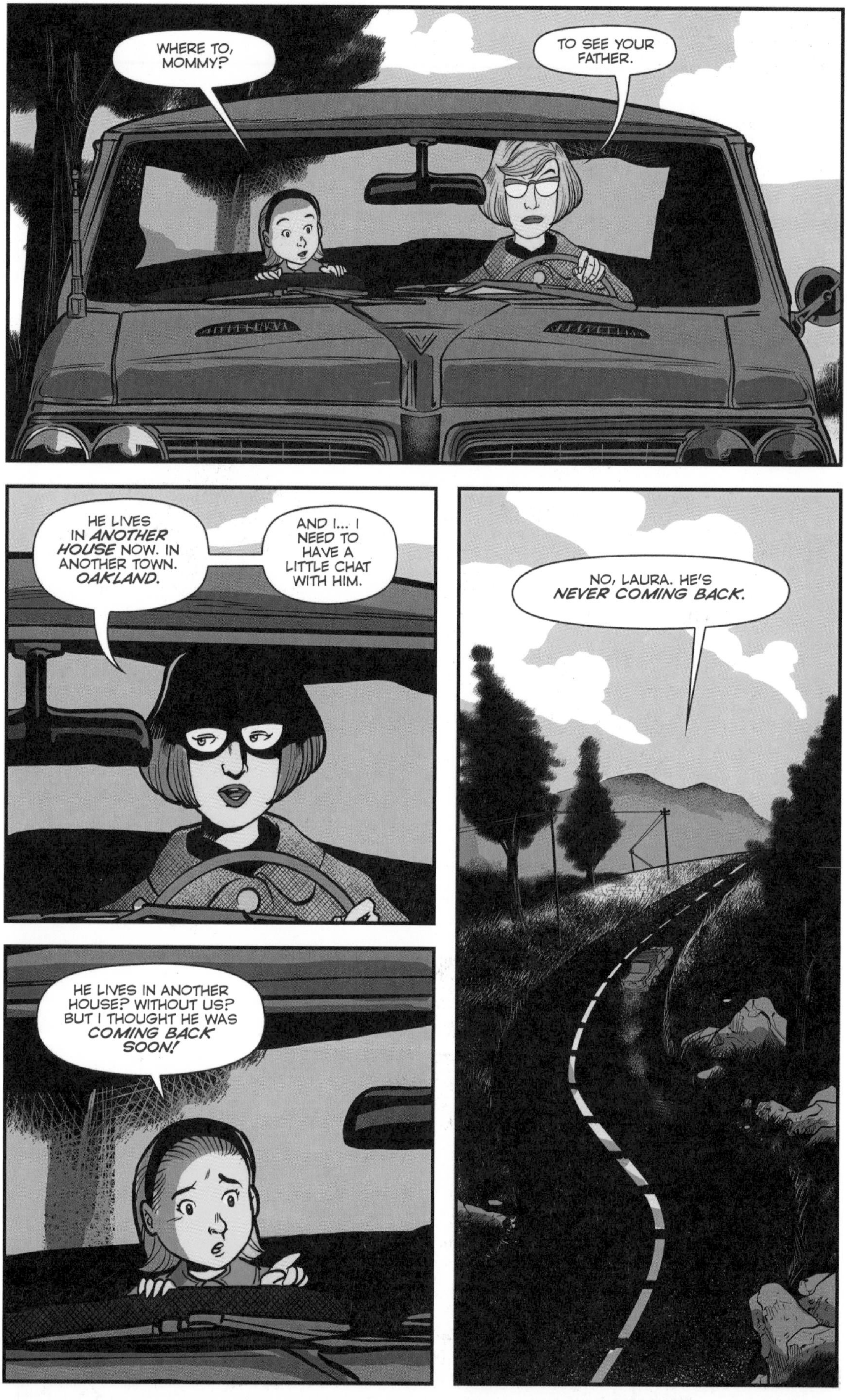
WHERE TO, MOMMY?
TO SEE YOUR FATHER.
HE LIVES IN ANOTHER HOUSE NOW. IN ANOTHER TOWN. OAKLAND.
AND I... I NEED TO HAVE A LITTLE CHAT WITH HIM.
HE LIVES IN ANOTHER HOUSE? WITHOUT US? BUT I THOUGHT HE WAS COMING BACK SOON!
NO, LAURA. HE'S NEVER COMING BACK.

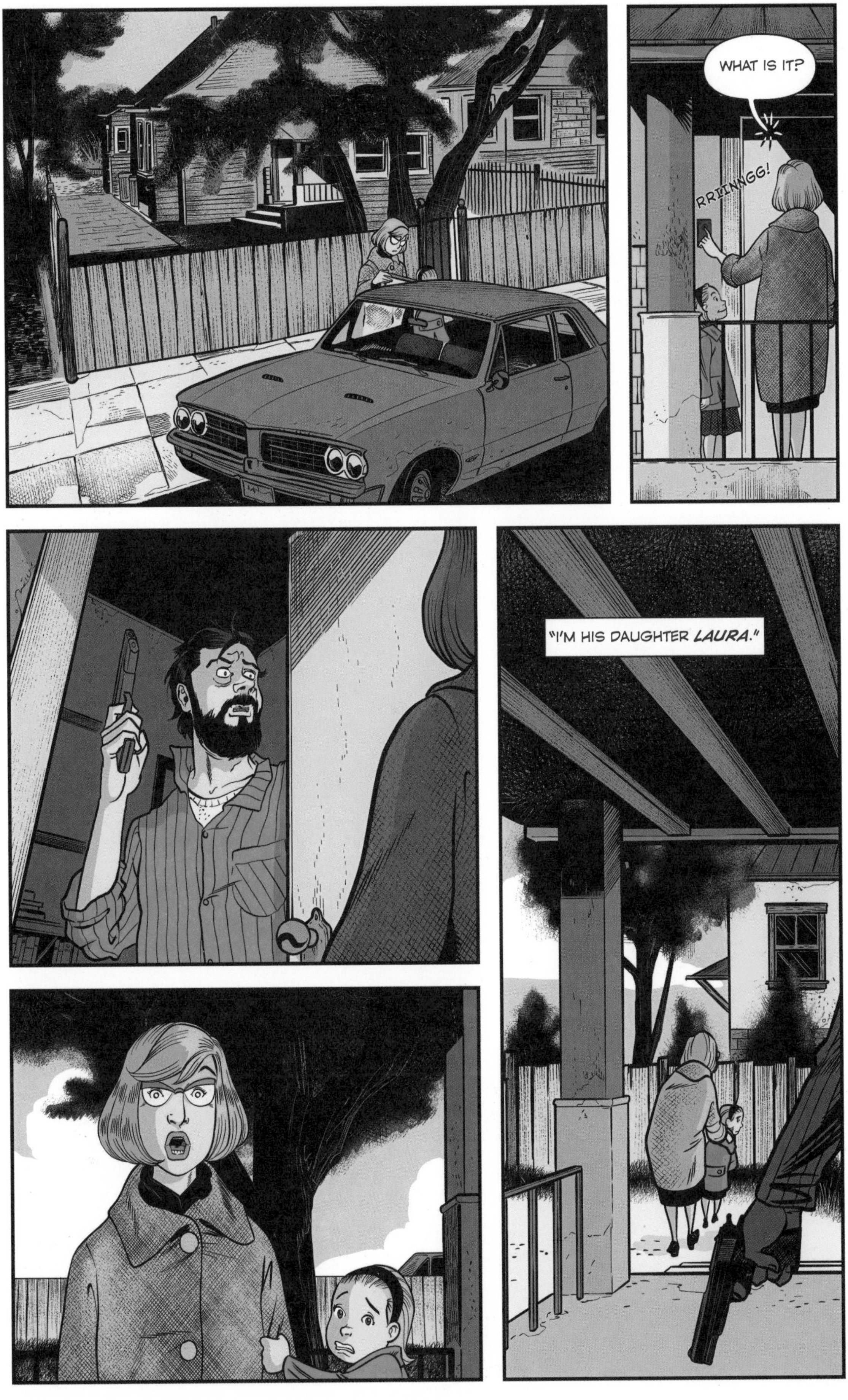
WHAT IS IT?
RRIIINNGG!
"I'M HIS DAUGHTER LAURA."

YOUR FATHER HAD HIS FIRST STROKE AT HIS HOME ON THURSDAY. WHEN HE WAS ADMITTED, WE THOUGHT HE WAS ON THE MEND.

BUT THIS MORNING, HE HAD A SECOND ONE, MUCH WORSE. WE HAD TO RESUSCITATE HIM, AND HE'S BEEN IN INTENSIVE CARE EVER SINCE.

DO YOU THINK HE'LL GET BETTER?

ANYTHING'S POSSIBLE, BUT I DON'T WANT TO GIVE YOU ANY FALSE HOPE.

IT DOESN'T SEEM LIKELY.

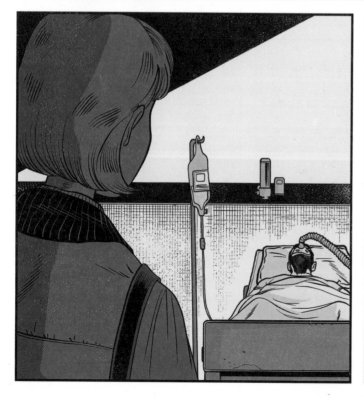

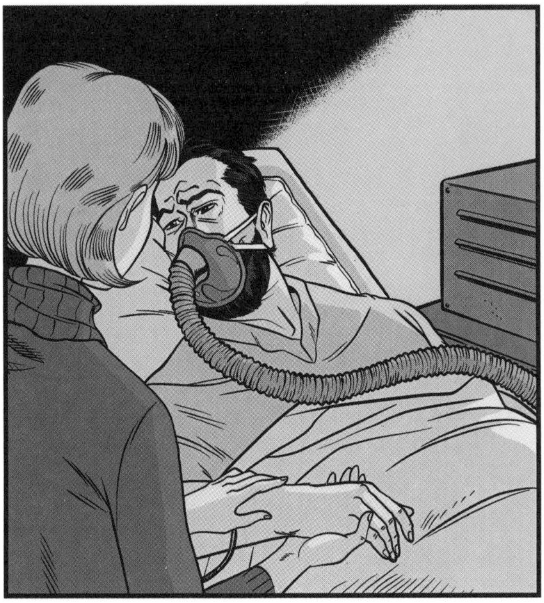

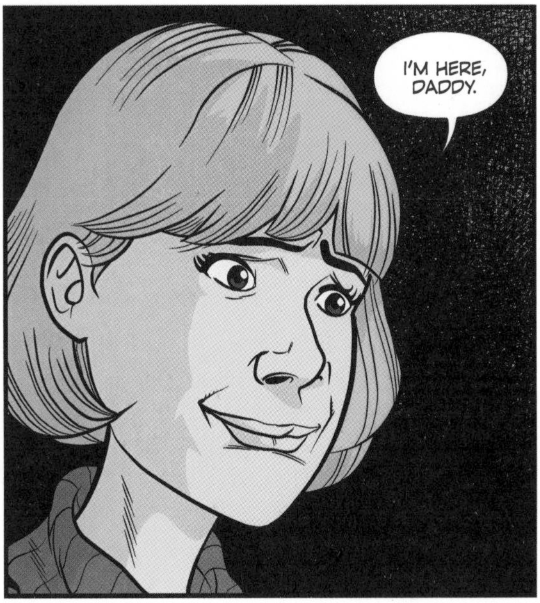
I'M HERE, DADDY.

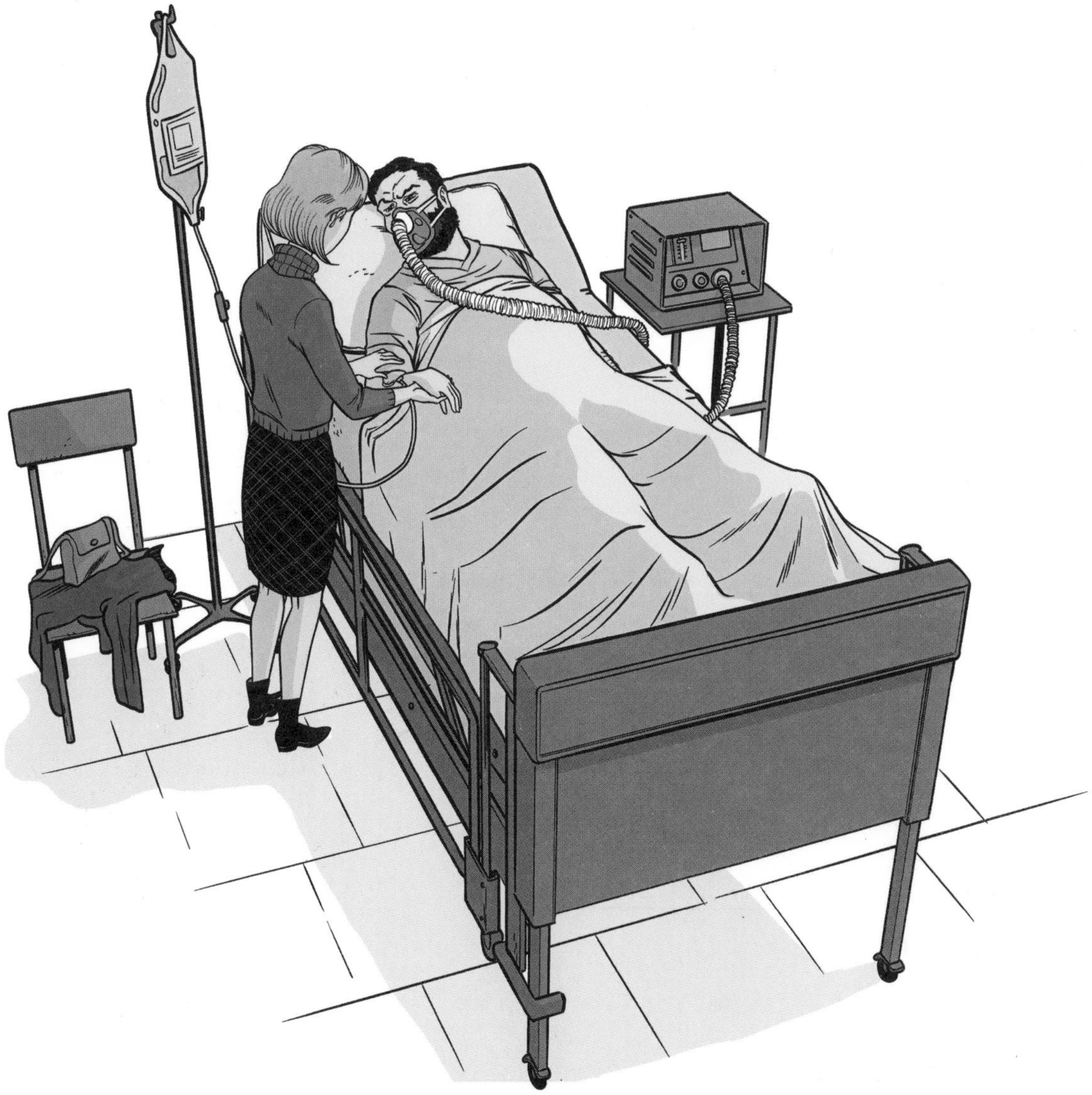

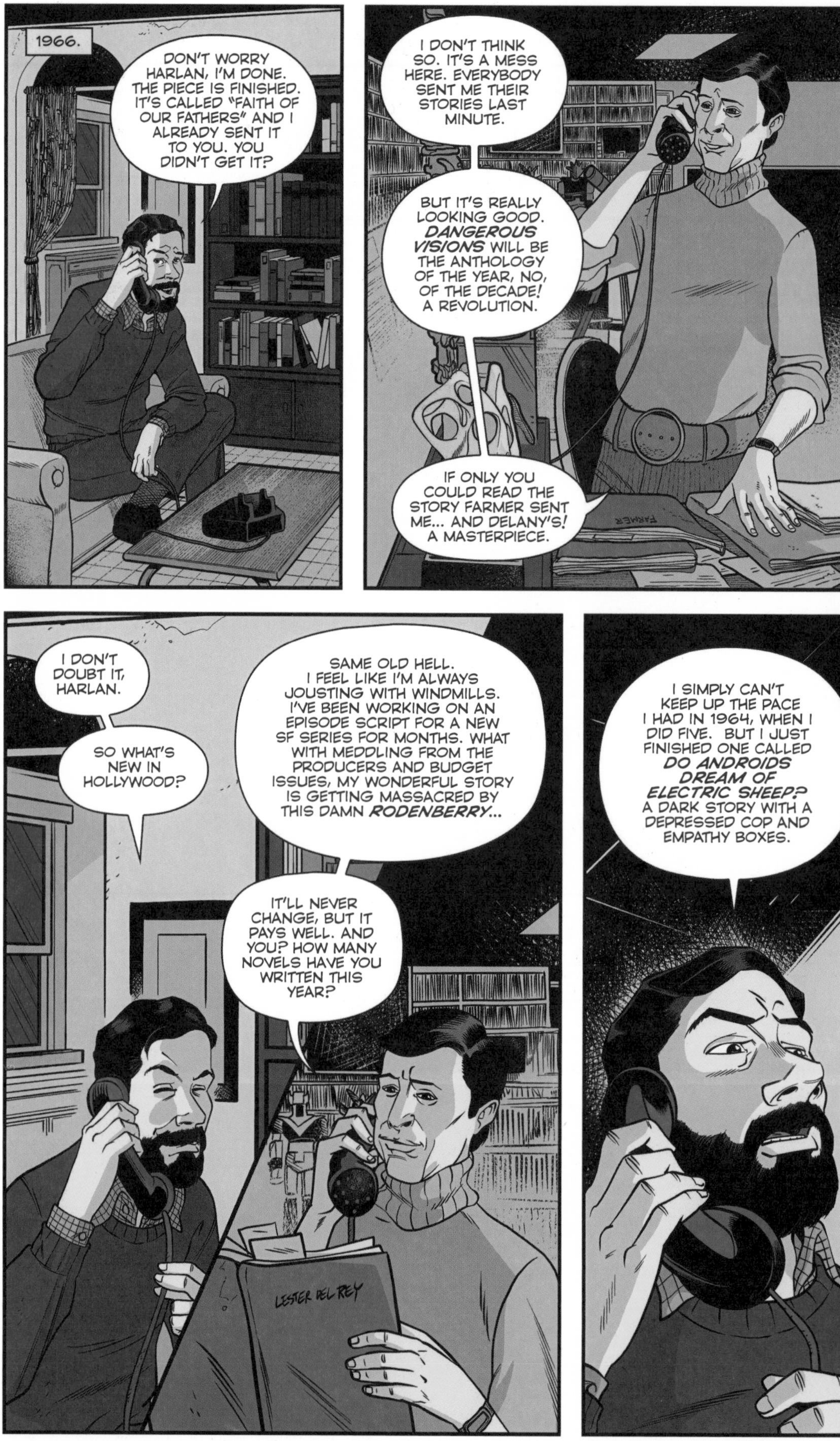

1966.
DON'T WORRY HARLAN, I'M DONE. THE PIECE IS FINISHED. IT'S CALLED "FAITH OF OUR FATHERS" AND I ALREADY SENT IT TO YOU. YOU DIDN'T GET IT?
I DON'T THINK SO. IT'S A MESS HERE. EVERYBODY SENT ME THEIR STORIES LAST MINUTE.
BUT IT'S REALLY LOOKING GOOD. DANGEROUS VISIONS WILL BE THE ANTHOLOGY OF THE YEAR, NO, OF THE DECADE! A REVOLUTION.
IF ONLY YOU COULD READ THE STORY FARMER SENT ME... AND DELANY'S! A MASTERPIECE.
FARMER
I DON'T DOUBT IT, HARLAN.
SO WHAT'S NEW IN HOLLYWOOD?
SAME OLD HELL. I FEEL LIKE I'M ALWAYS JOUSTING WITH WINDMILLS. I'VE BEEN WORKING ON AN EPISODE SCRIPT FOR A NEW SF SERIES FOR MONTHS. WHAT WITH MEDDLING FROM THE PRODUCERS AND BUDGET ISSUES, MY WONDERFUL STORY IS GETTING MASSACRED BY THIS DAMN RODENBERRY...
IT'LL NEVER CHANGE, BUT IT PAYS WELL. AND YOU? HOW MANY NOVELS HAVE YOU WRITTEN THIS YEAR?
LESTER DEL REY
I SIMPLY CAN'T KEEP UP THE PACE I HAD IN 1964, WHEN I DID FIVE. BUT I JUST FINISHED ONE CALLED DO ANDROIDS DREAM OF ELECTRIC SHEEP? A DARK STORY WITH A DEPRESSED COP AND EMPATHY BOXES.

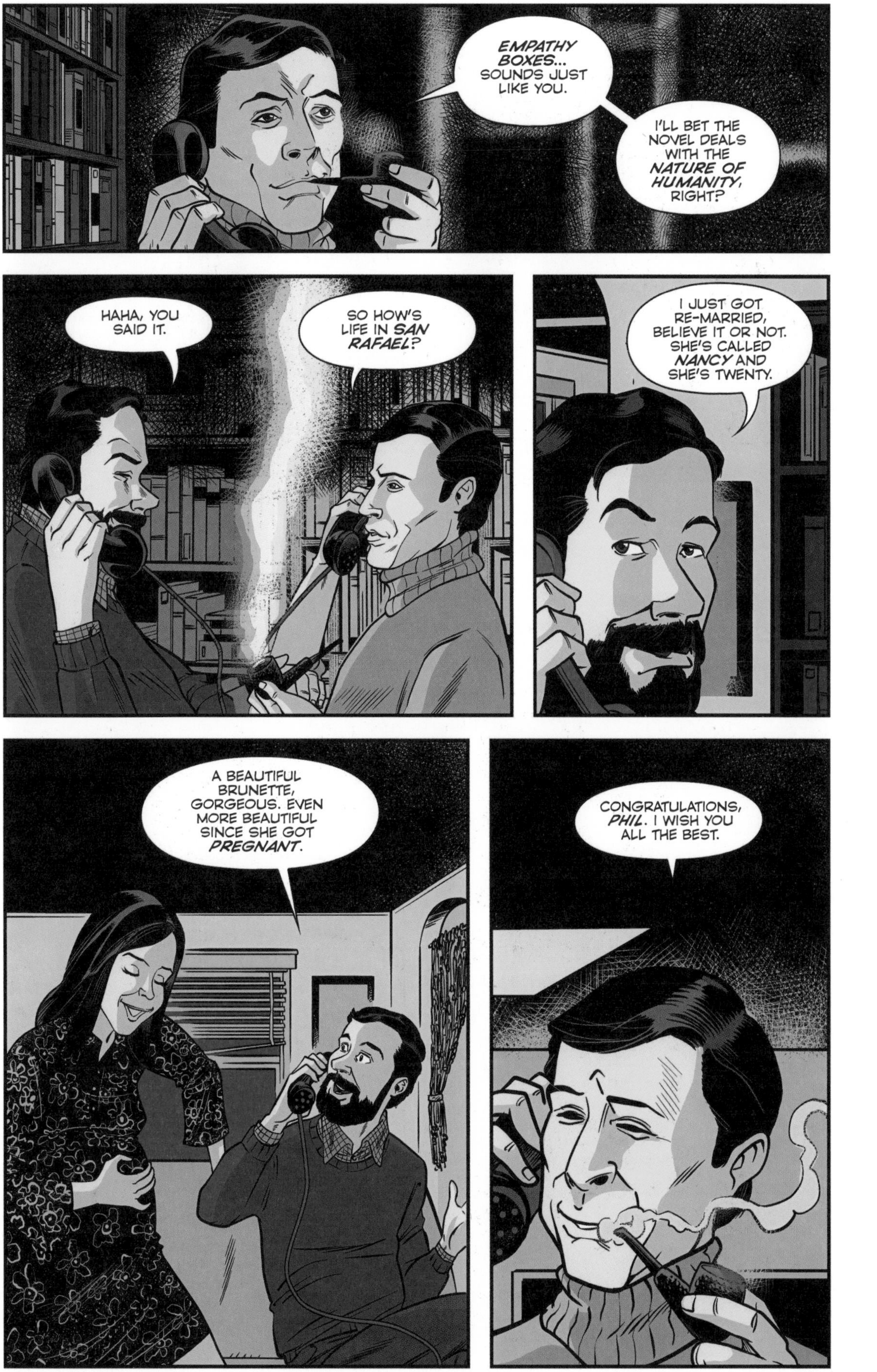
EMPATHY BOXES... SOUNDS JUST LIKE YOU.
I'LL BET THE NOVEL DEALS WITH THE NATURE OF HUMANITY, RIGHT?
HAHA, YOU SAID IT.
SO HOW'S LIFE IN SAN RAFAEL?
I JUST GOT RE-MARRIED, BELIEVE IT OR NOT. SHE'S CALLED NANCY AND SHE'S TWENTY.
A BEAUTIFUL BRUNETTE, GORGEOUS. EVEN MORE BEAUTIFUL SINCE SHE GOT PREGNANT.
CONGRATULATIONS, PHIL. I WISH YOU ALL THE BEST.

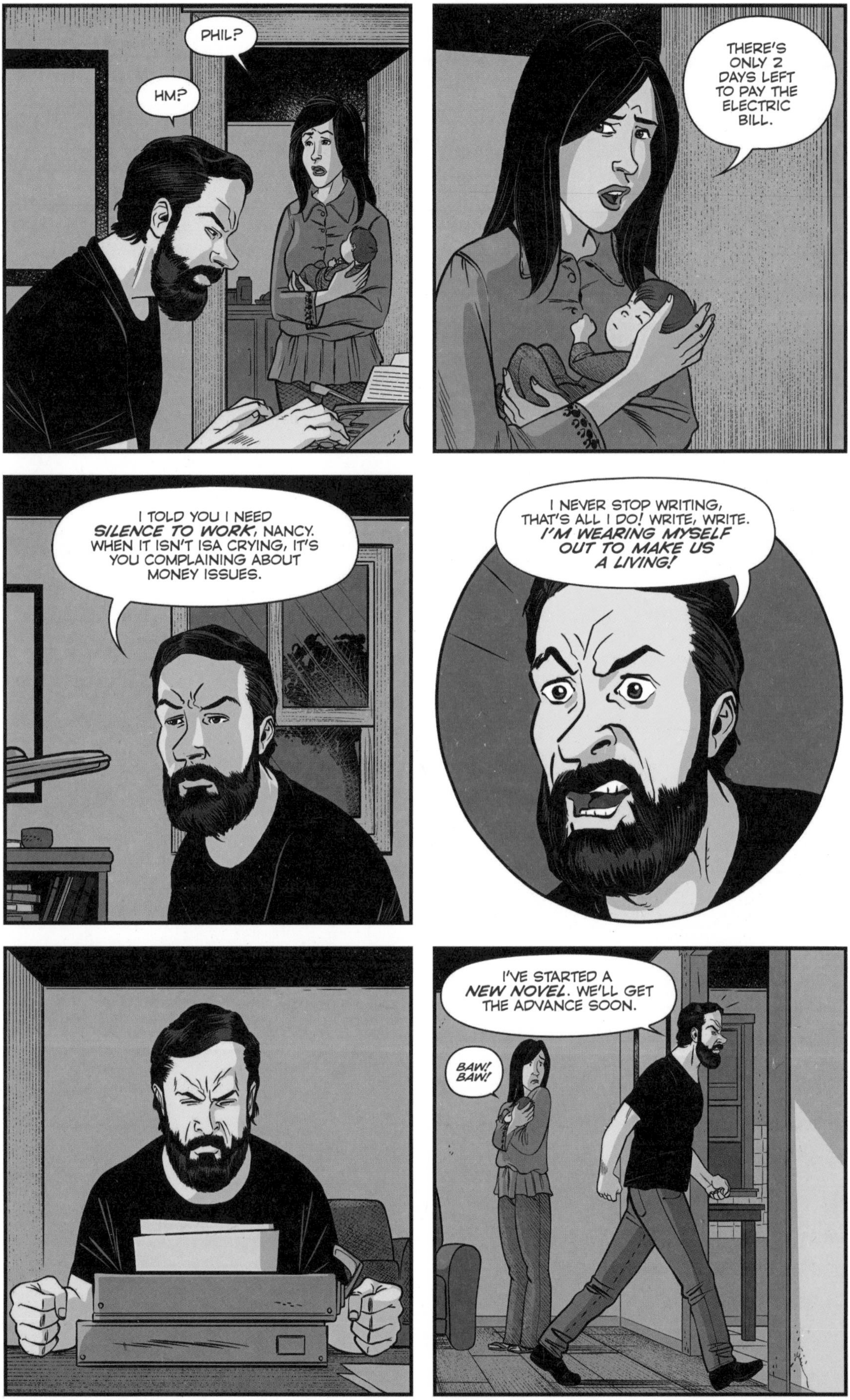
PHIL?
HM?
THERE'S ONLY 2 DAYS LEFT TO PAY THE ELECTRIC BILL.
I TOLD YOU I NEED *SILENCE TO WORK*, NANCY. WHEN IT ISN'T ISA CRYING, IT'S YOU COMPLAINING ABOUT MONEY ISSUES.
I NEVER STOP WRITING, THAT'S ALL I DO! WRITE, WRITE. *I'M WEARING MYSELF OUT TO MAKE US A LIVING!*
I'VE STARTED A *NEW NOVEL*. WE'LL GET THE ADVANCE SOON.
BAW! BAW!

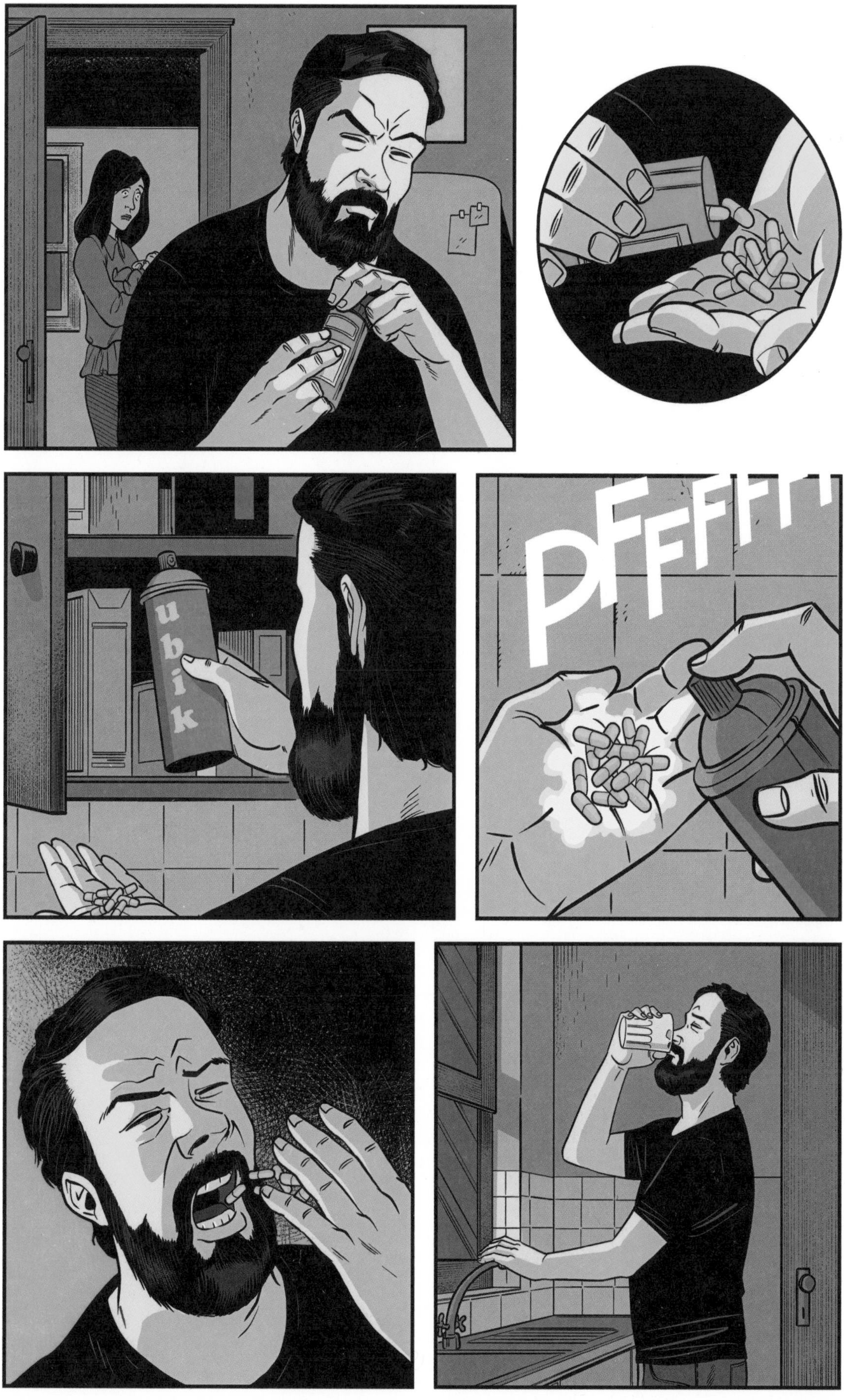
ubik
PFFF

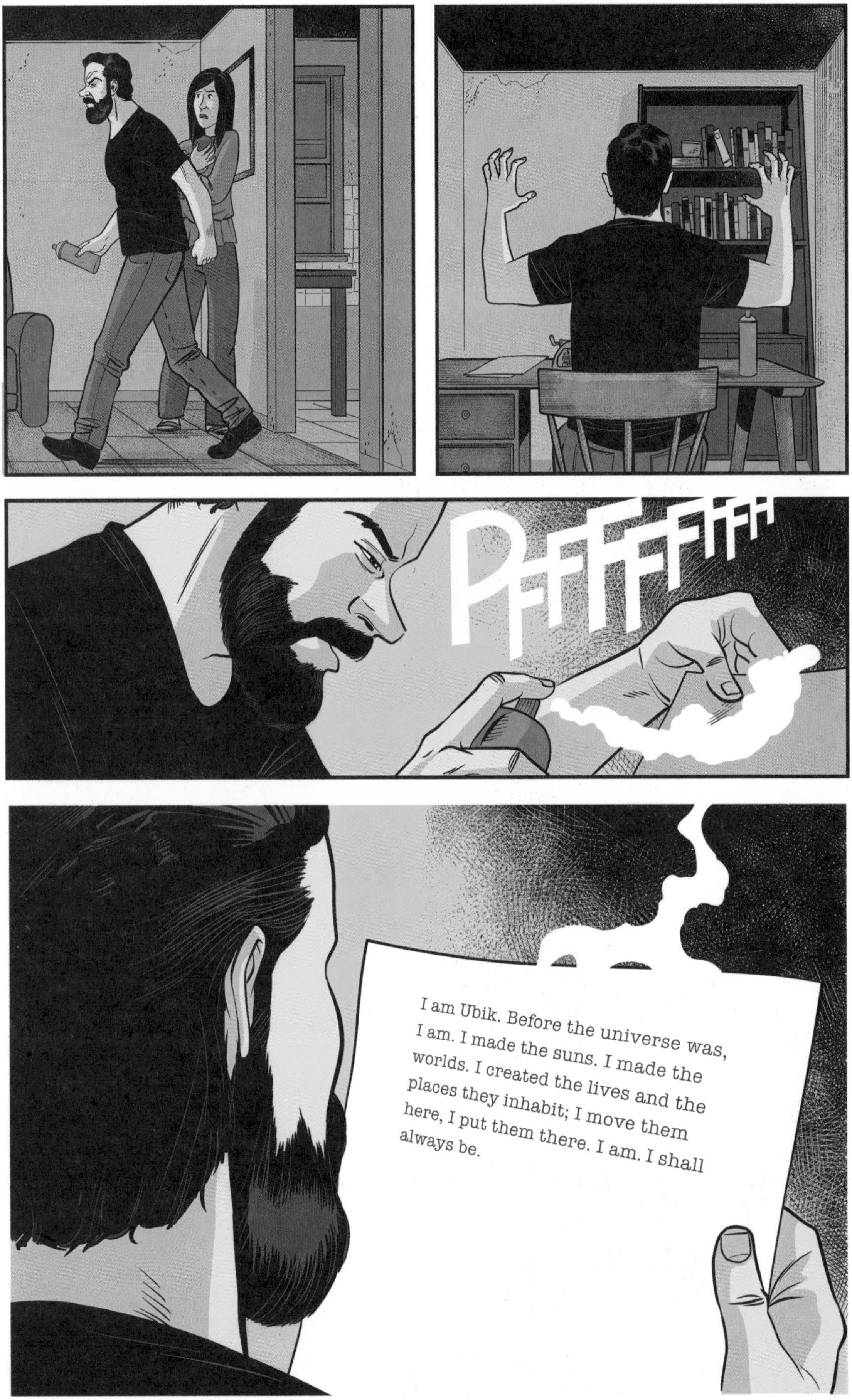

PFFFFFFFFF
I am Ubik. Before the universe was, I am. I made the suns. I made the worlds. I created the lives and the places they inhabit; I move them here, I put them there. I am. I shall always be.

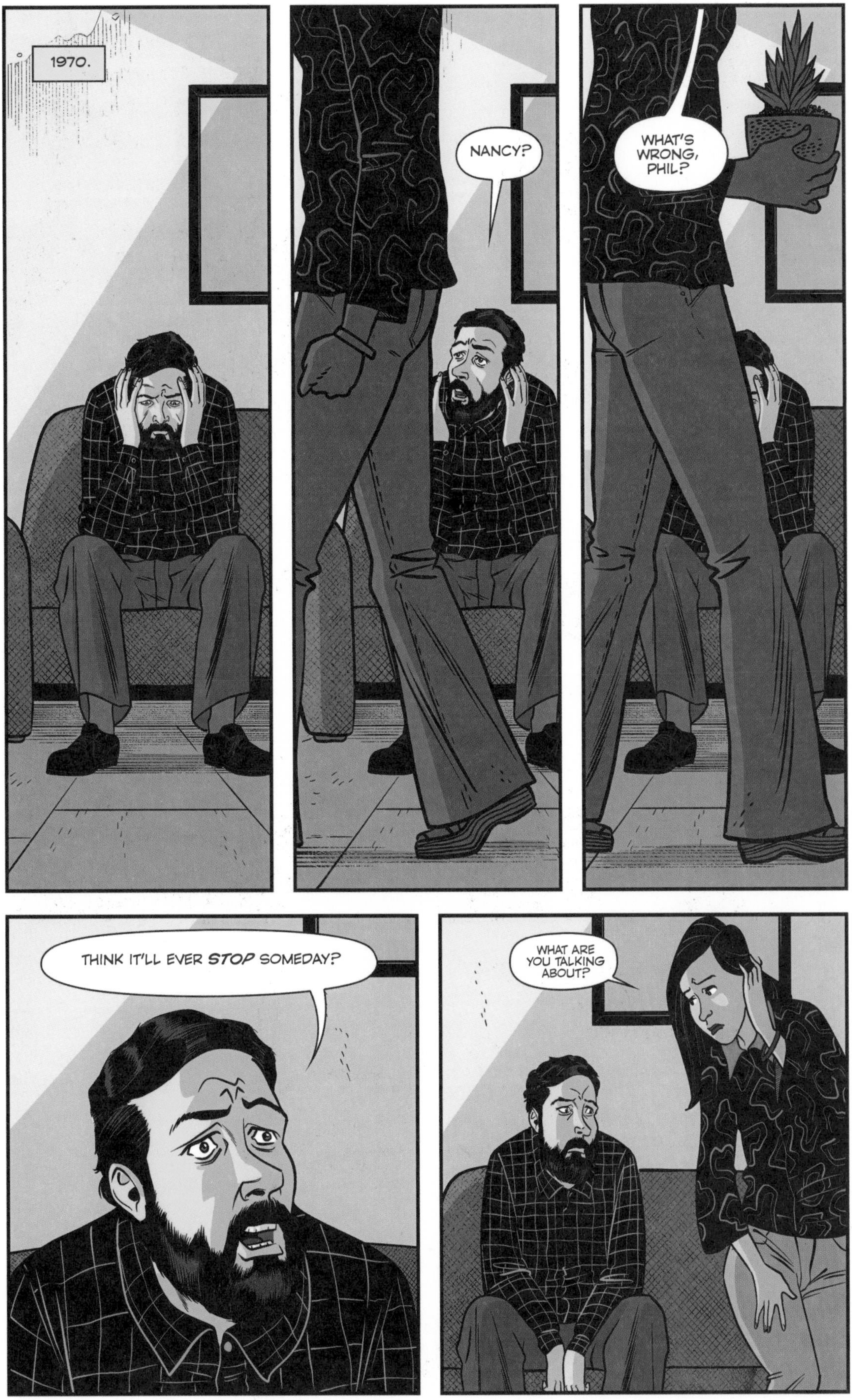
1970.
NANCY?
WHAT'S WRONG, PHIL?
THINK IT'LL EVER STOP SOMEDAY?
WHAT ARE YOU TALKING ABOUT?

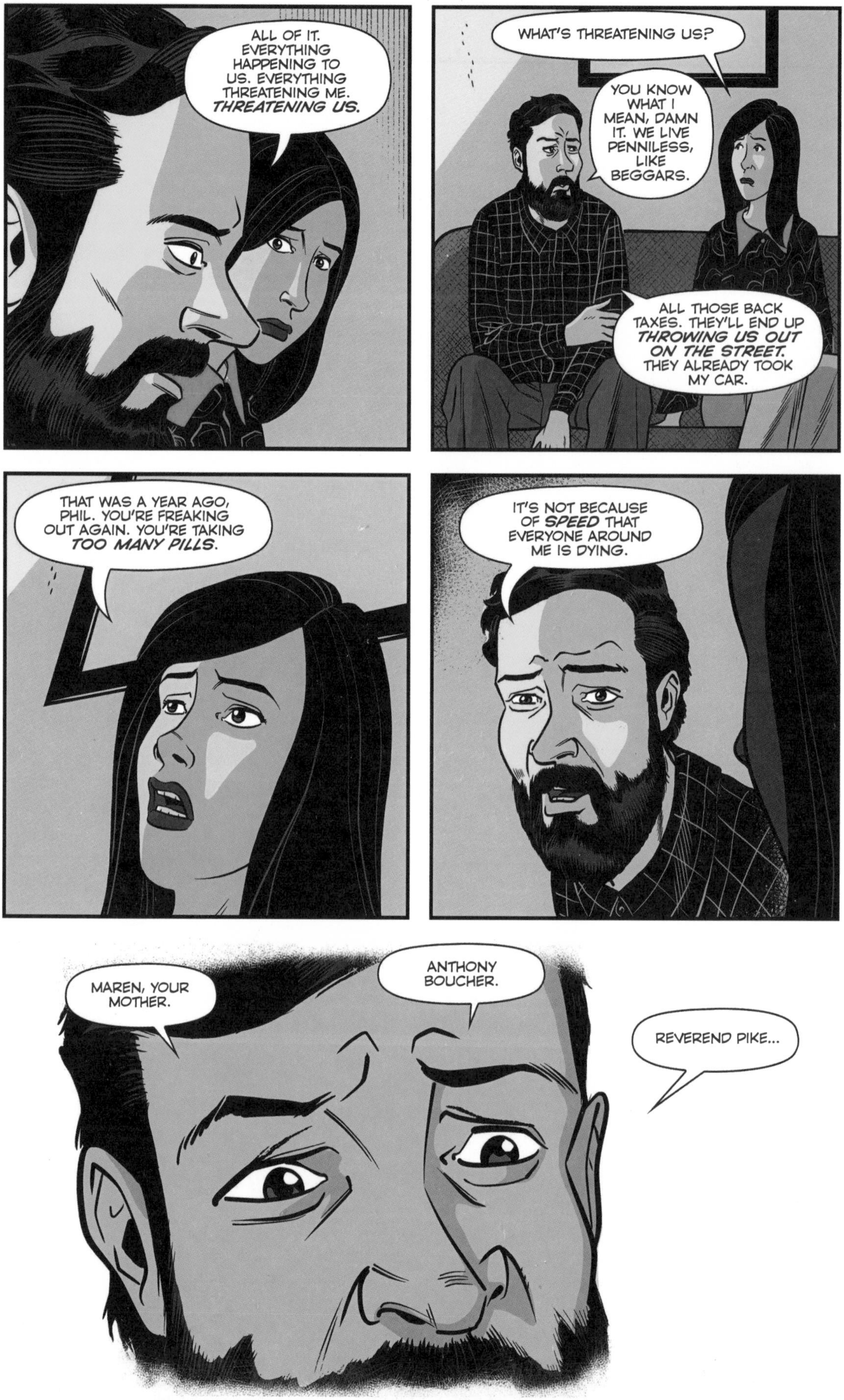
ALL OF IT. EVERYTHING HAPPENING TO US. EVERYTHING THREATENING ME. *THREATENING US.*
WHAT'S THREATENING US?
YOU KNOW WHAT I MEAN, DAMN IT. WE LIVE PENNILESS, LIKE BEGGARS.
ALL THOSE BACK TAXES. THEY'LL END UP *THROWING US OUT ON THE STREET.* THEY ALREADY TOOK MY CAR.
THAT WAS A YEAR AGO, PHIL. YOU'RE FREAKING OUT AGAIN. YOU'RE TAKING *TOO MANY PILLS*.
IT'S NOT BECAUSE OF *SPEED* THAT EVERYONE AROUND ME IS DYING.
MAREN, YOUR MOTHER.
ANTHONY BOUCHER.
REVEREND PIKE...

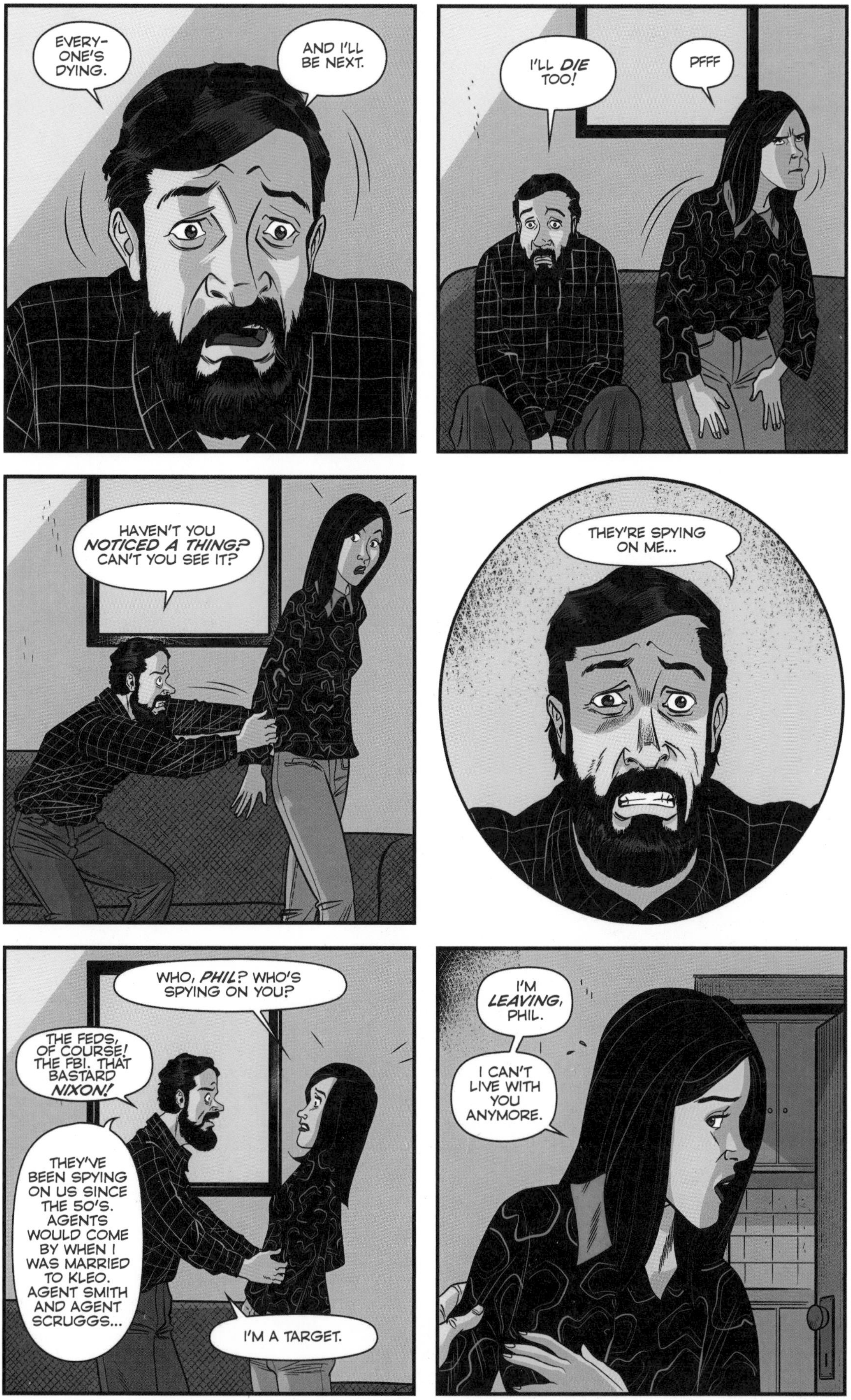
EVERY-ONE'S DYING.
AND I'LL BE NEXT.
I'LL *DIE* TOO!
PFFF
HAVEN'T YOU *NOTICED A THING?* CAN'T YOU SEE IT?
THEY'RE SPYING ON ME...
WHO, *PHIL?* WHO'S SPYING ON YOU?
THE FEDS, OF COURSE! THE FBI. THAT BASTARD *NIXON!*
THEY'VE BEEN SPYING ON US SINCE THE 50'S. AGENTS WOULD COME BY WHEN I WAS MARRIED TO KLEO. AGENT SMITH AND AGENT SCRUGGS...
I'M A TARGET.
I'M *LEAVING*, PHIL.
I CAN'T LIVE WITH YOU ANYMORE.

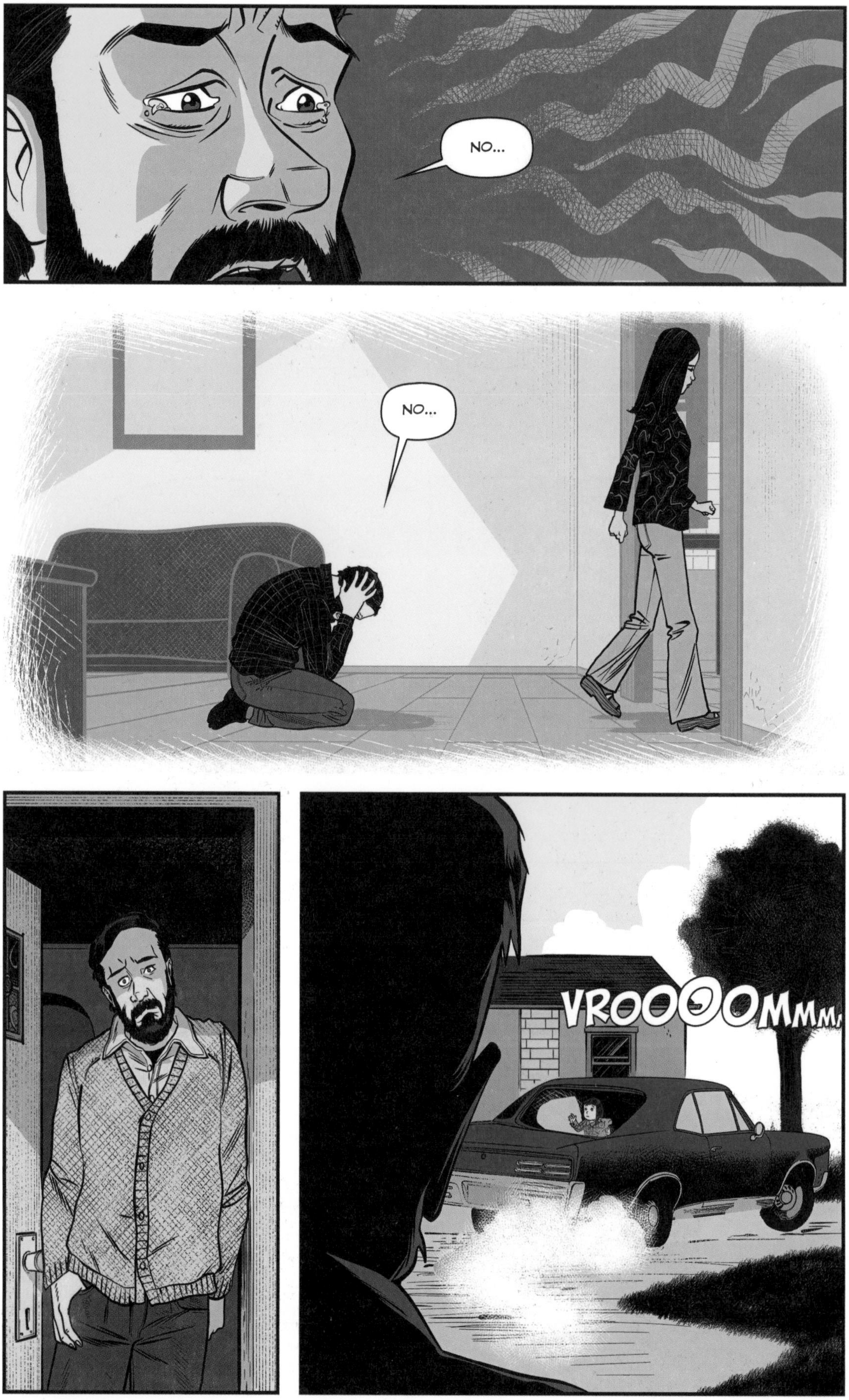
NO...
NO...
VROOOOOMMM

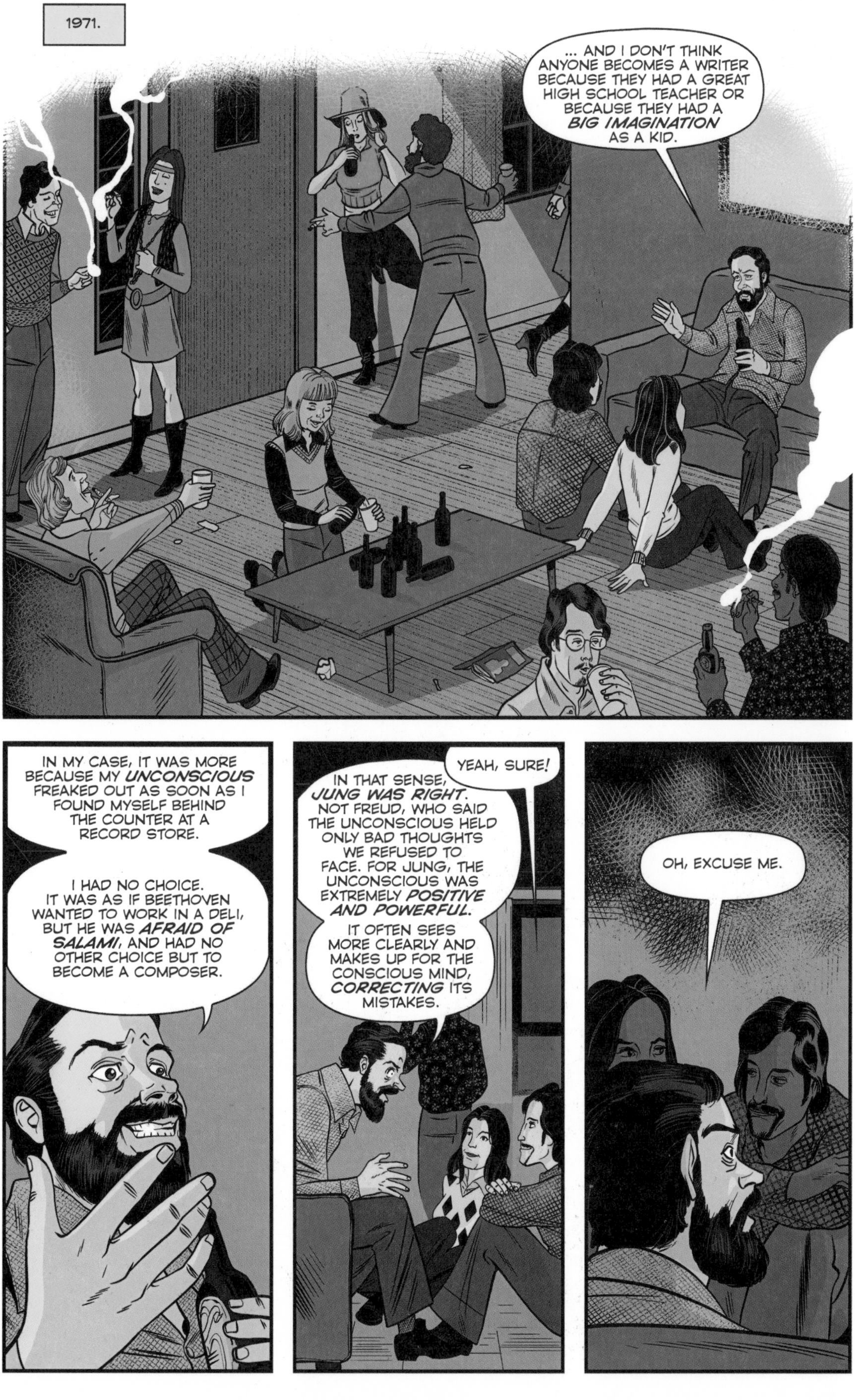
1971.
... AND I DON'T THINK ANYONE BECOMES A WRITER BECAUSE THEY HAD A GREAT HIGH SCHOOL TEACHER OR BECAUSE THEY HAD A *BIG IMAGINATION* AS A KID.
IN MY CASE, IT WAS MORE BECAUSE MY *UNCONSCIOUS* FREAKED OUT AS SOON AS I FOUND MYSELF BEHIND THE COUNTER AT A RECORD STORE.
I HAD NO CHOICE. IT WAS AS IF BEETHOVEN WANTED TO WORK IN A DELI, BUT HE WAS *AFRAID OF SALAMI*, AND HAD NO OTHER CHOICE BUT TO BECOME A COMPOSER.
YEAH, SURE!
IN THAT SENSE, *JUNG WAS RIGHT*. NOT FREUD, WHO SAID THE UNCONSCIOUS HELD ONLY BAD THOUGHTS WE REFUSED TO FACE. FOR JUNG, THE UNCONSCIOUS WAS EXTREMELY *POSITIVE AND POWERFUL*.
IT OFTEN SEES MORE CLEARLY AND MAKES UP FOR THE CONSCIOUS MIND, *CORRECTING* ITS MISTAKES.
OH, EXCUSE ME.

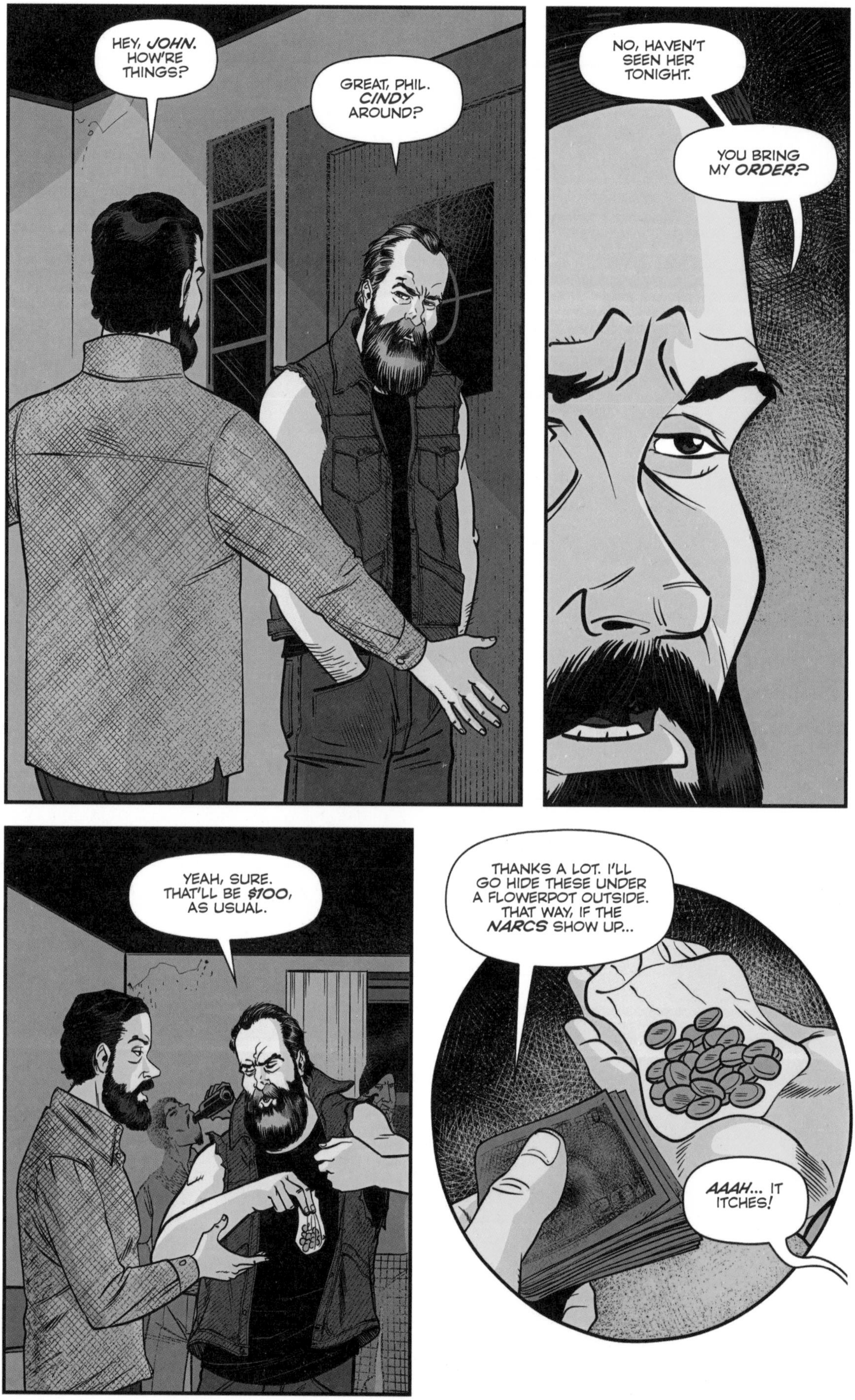
HEY, JOHN. HOW'RE THINGS?
GREAT, PHIL. CINDY AROUND?
NO, HAVEN'T SEEN HER TONIGHT.
YOU BRING MY ORDER?
YEAH, SURE. THAT'LL BE $100, AS USUAL.
THANKS A LOT. I'LL GO HIDE THESE UNDER A FLOWERPOT OUTSIDE. THAT WAY, IF THE NARCS SHOW UP...
AAAH... IT ITCHES!

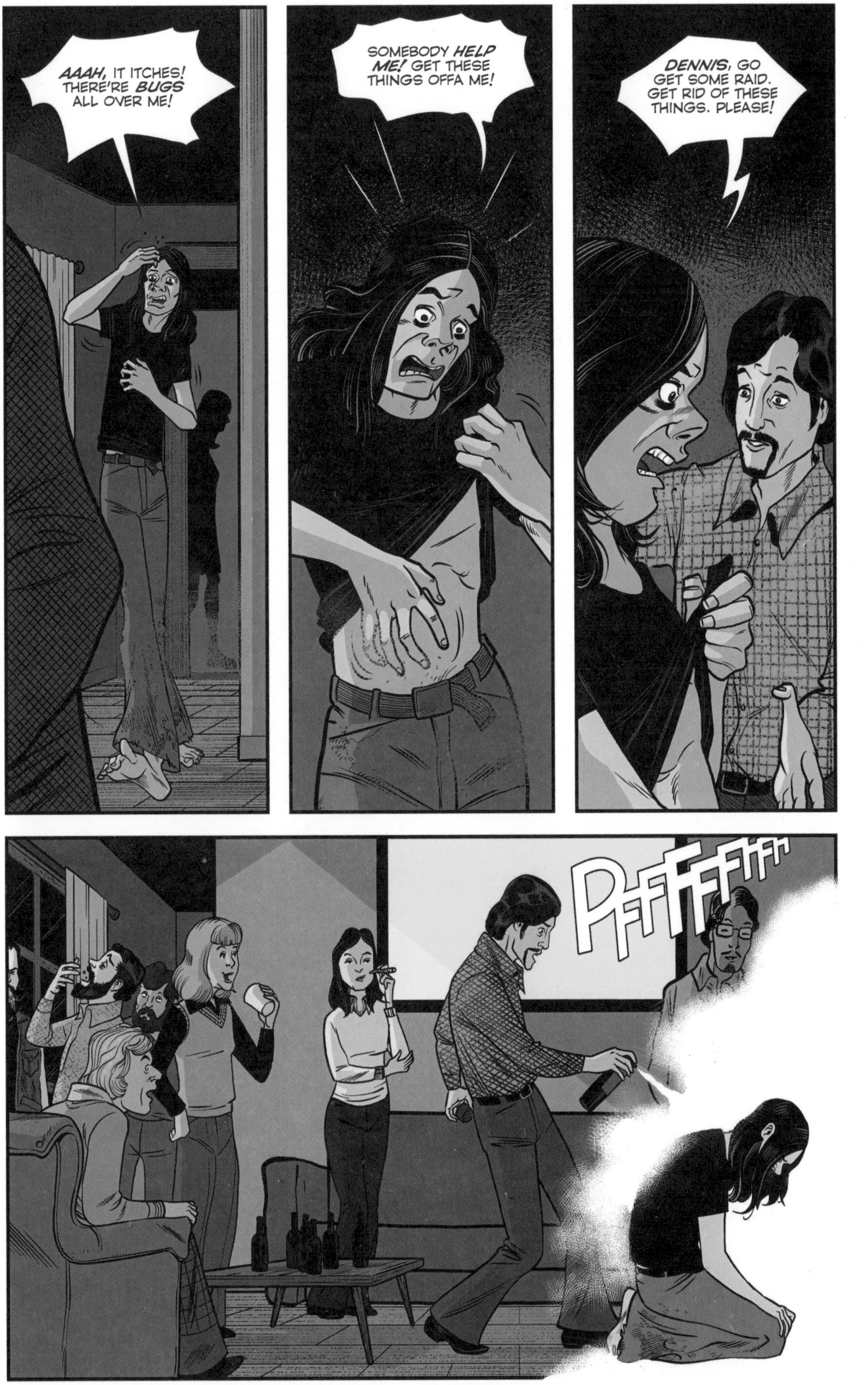
AAAH, IT ITCHES! THERE'RE BUGS ALL OVER ME!
SOMEBODY HELP ME! GET THESE THINGS OFFA ME!
DENNIS, GO GET SOME RAID. GET RID OF THESE THINGS. PLEASE!
PFFFFFfffr

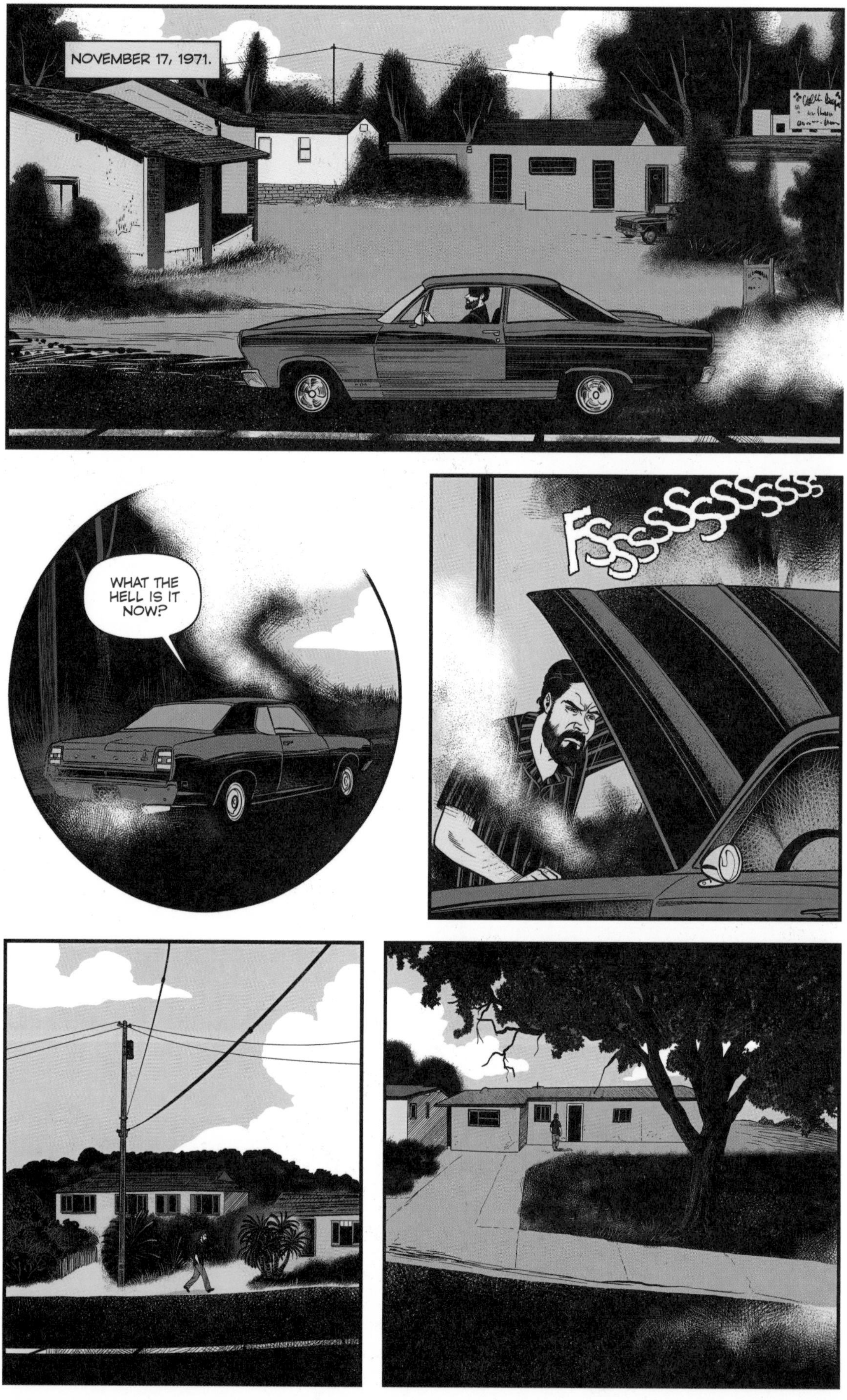
NOVEMBER 17, 1971.
WHAT THE HELL IS IT NOW?
FSSSSSSSSSSSS

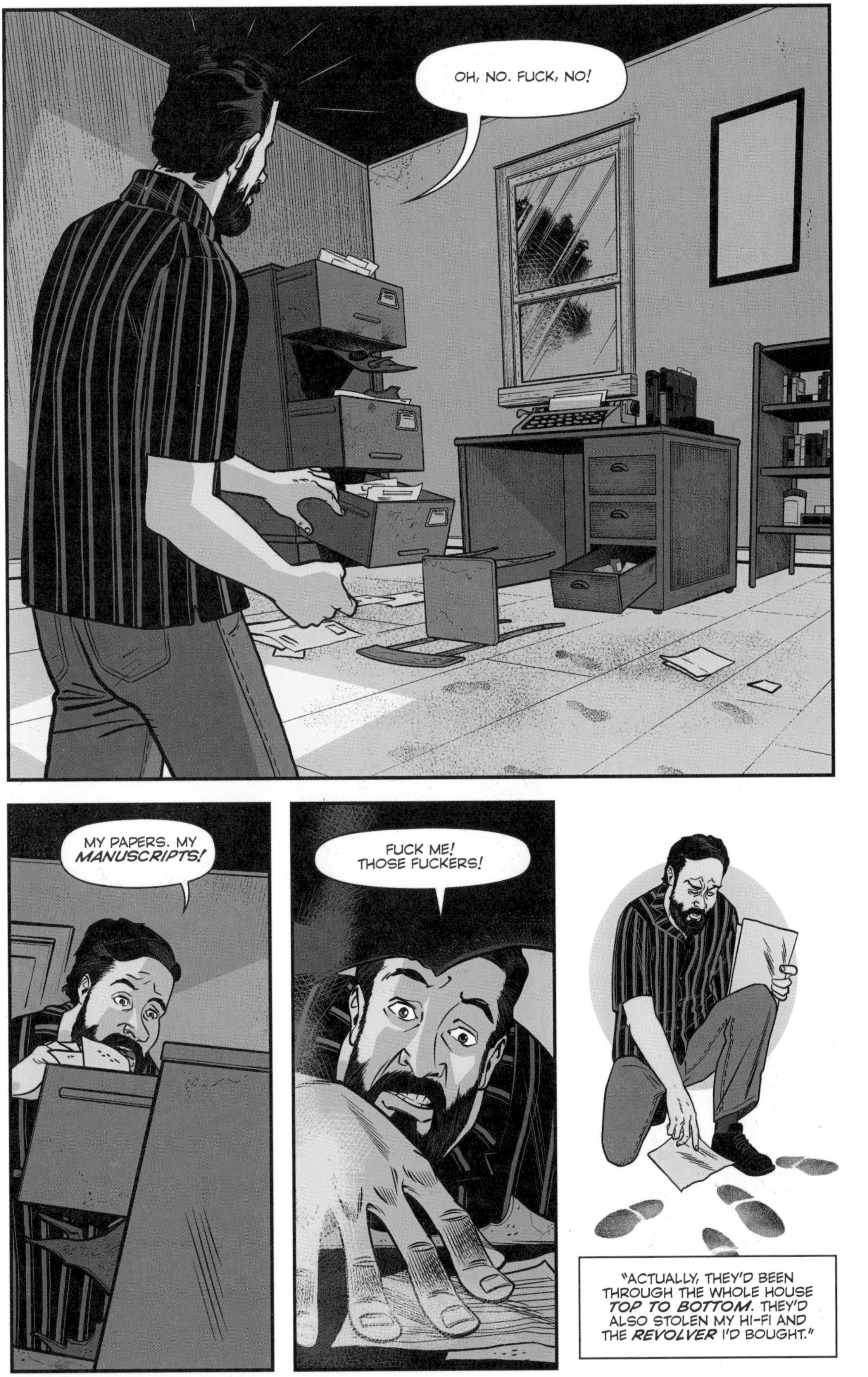
OH, NO. FUCK, NO!
MY PAPERS. MY MANUSCRIPTS!
FUCK ME! THOSE FUCKERS!
"ACTUALLY, THEY'D BEEN THROUGH THE WHOLE HOUSE TOP TO BOTTOM. THEY'D ALSO STOLEN MY HI-FI AND THE REVOLVER I'D BOUGHT."

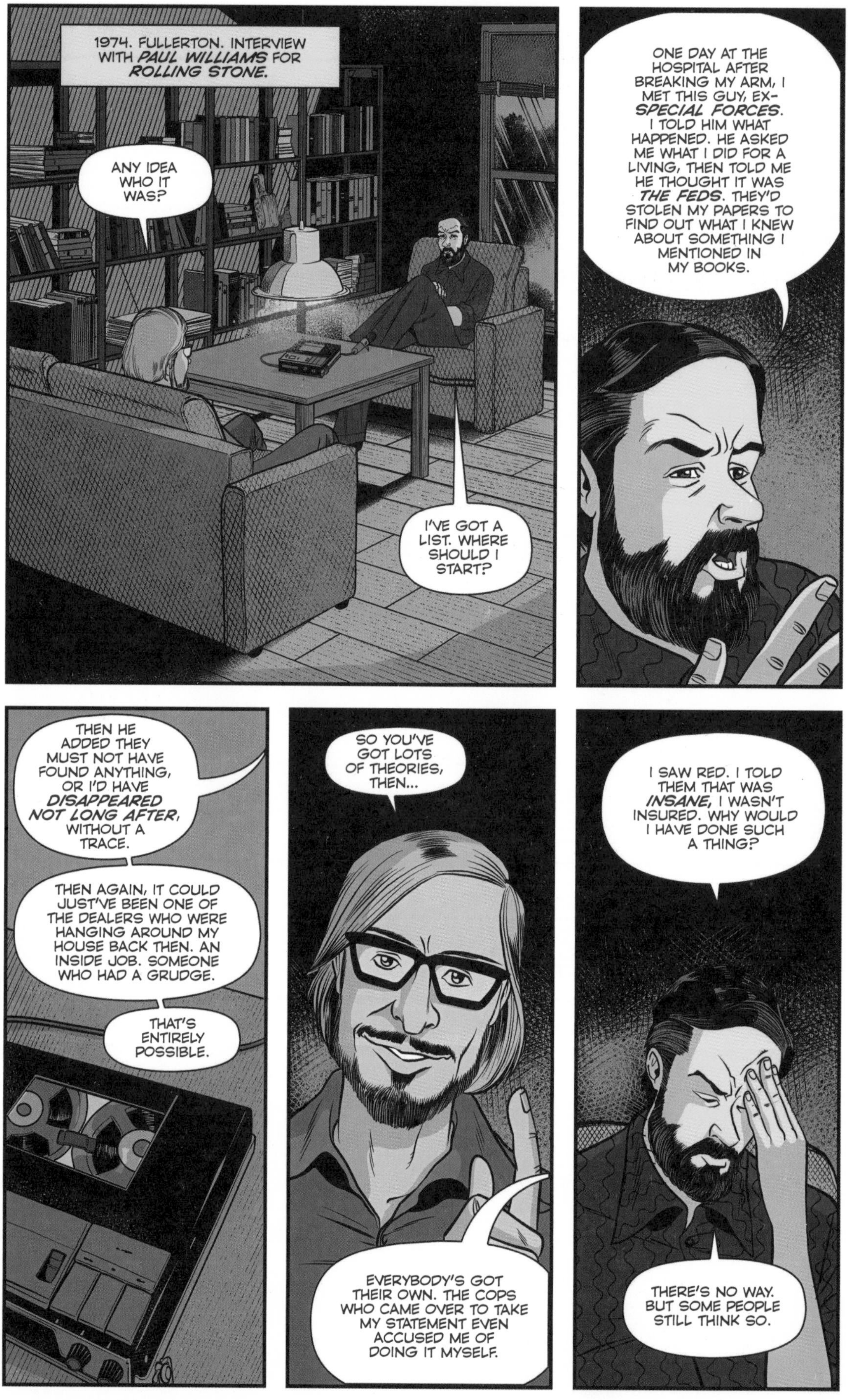
1974. FULLERTON. INTERVIEW WITH PAUL WILLIAMS FOR ROLLING STONE.
ANY IDEA WHO IT WAS?
I'VE GOT A LIST. WHERE SHOULD I START?
ONE DAY AT THE HOSPITAL AFTER BREAKING MY ARM, I MET THIS GUY, EX-SPECIAL FORCES. I TOLD HIM WHAT HAPPENED. HE ASKED ME WHAT I DID FOR A LIVING, THEN TOLD ME HE THOUGHT IT WAS THE FEDS. THEY'D STOLEN MY PAPERS TO FIND OUT WHAT I KNEW ABOUT SOMETHING I MENTIONED IN MY BOOKS.
THEN HE ADDED THEY MUST NOT HAVE FOUND ANYTHING, OR I'D HAVE DISAPPEARED NOT LONG AFTER, WITHOUT A TRACE.
THEN AGAIN, IT COULD JUST'VE BEEN ONE OF THE DEALERS WHO WERE HANGING AROUND MY HOUSE BACK THEN. AN INSIDE JOB. SOMEONE WHO HAD A GRUDGE.
THAT'S ENTIRELY POSSIBLE.
SO YOU'VE GOT LOTS OF THEORIES, THEN...
EVERYBODY'S GOT THEIR OWN. THE COPS WHO CAME OVER TO TAKE MY STATEMENT EVEN ACCUSED ME OF DOING IT MYSELF.
I SAW RED. I TOLD THEM THAT WAS INSANE, I WASN'T INSURED. WHY WOULD I HAVE DONE SUCH A THING?
THERE'S NO WAY. BUT SOME PEOPLE STILL THINK SO.

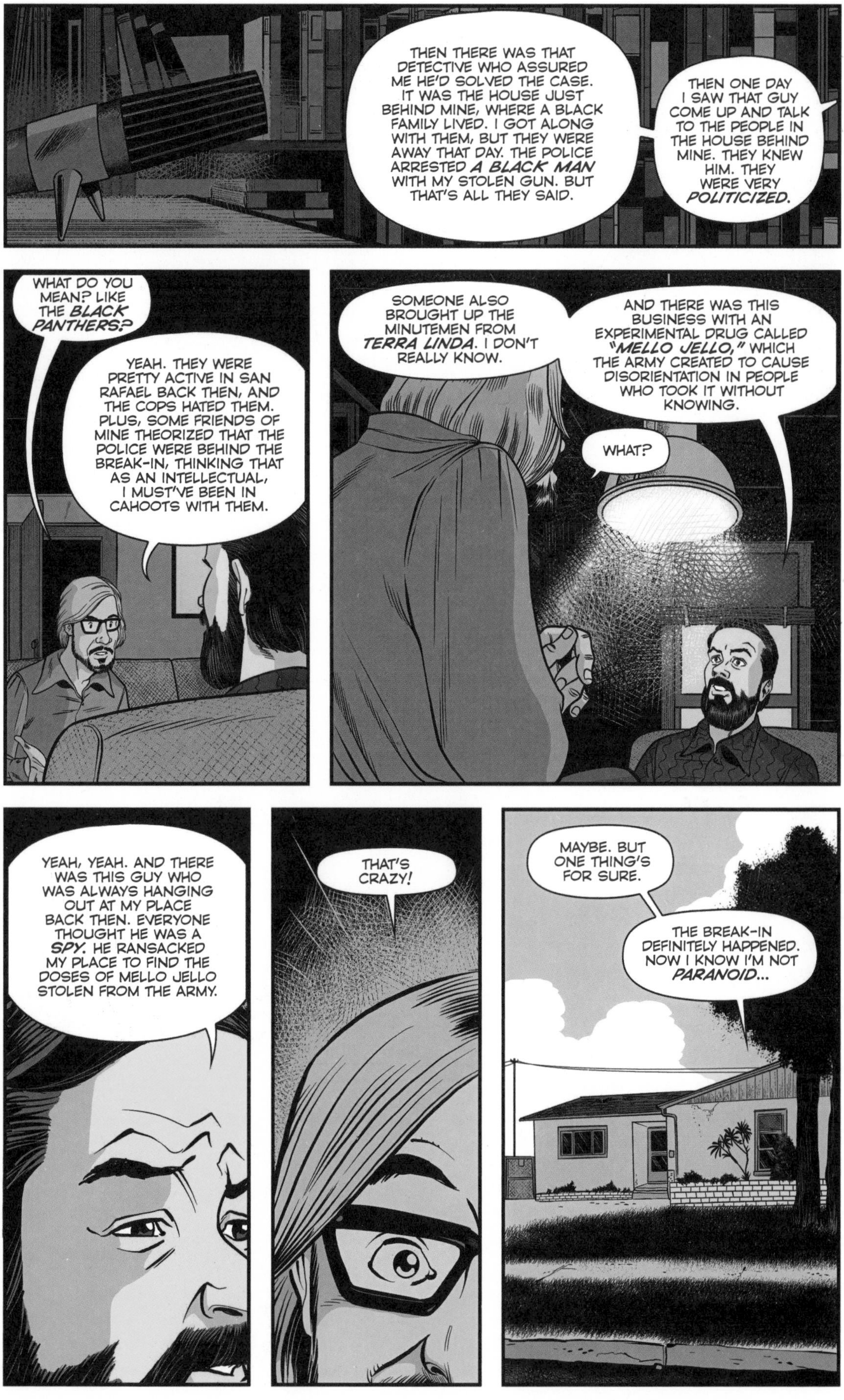
THEN THERE WAS THAT DETECTIVE WHO ASSURED ME HE'D SOLVED THE CASE. IT WAS THE HOUSE JUST BEHIND MINE, WHERE A BLACK FAMILY LIVED. I GOT ALONG WITH THEM, BUT THEY WERE AWAY THAT DAY. THE POLICE ARRESTED *A BLACK MAN* WITH MY STOLEN GUN. BUT THAT'S ALL THEY SAID.
THEN ONE DAY I SAW THAT GUY COME UP AND TALK TO THE PEOPLE IN THE HOUSE BEHIND MINE. THEY KNEW HIM. THEY WERE VERY *POLITICIZED*.
WHAT DO YOU MEAN? LIKE THE *BLACK PANTHERS?*
YEAH. THEY WERE PRETTY ACTIVE IN SAN RAFAEL BACK THEN, AND THE COPS HATED THEM. PLUS, SOME FRIENDS OF MINE THEORIZED THAT THE POLICE WERE BEHIND THE BREAK-IN, THINKING THAT AS AN INTELLECTUAL, I MUST'VE BEEN IN CAHOOTS WITH THEM.
SOMEONE ALSO BROUGHT UP THE MINUTEMEN FROM *TERRA LINDA*. I DON'T REALLY KNOW.
AND THERE WAS THIS BUSINESS WITH AN EXPERIMENTAL DRUG CALLED *"MELLO JELLO,"* WHICH THE ARMY CREATED TO CAUSE DISORIENTATION IN PEOPLE WHO TOOK IT WITHOUT KNOWING.
WHAT?
YEAH, YEAH. AND THERE WAS THIS GUY WHO WAS ALWAYS HANGING OUT AT MY PLACE BACK THEN. EVERYONE THOUGHT HE WAS A *SPY*. HE RANSACKED MY PLACE TO FIND THE DOSES OF MELLO JELLO STOLEN FROM THE ARMY.
THAT'S CRAZY!
MAYBE. BUT ONE THING'S FOR SURE.
THE BREAK-IN DEFINITELY HAPPENED. NOW I KNOW I'M NOT *PARANOID*...

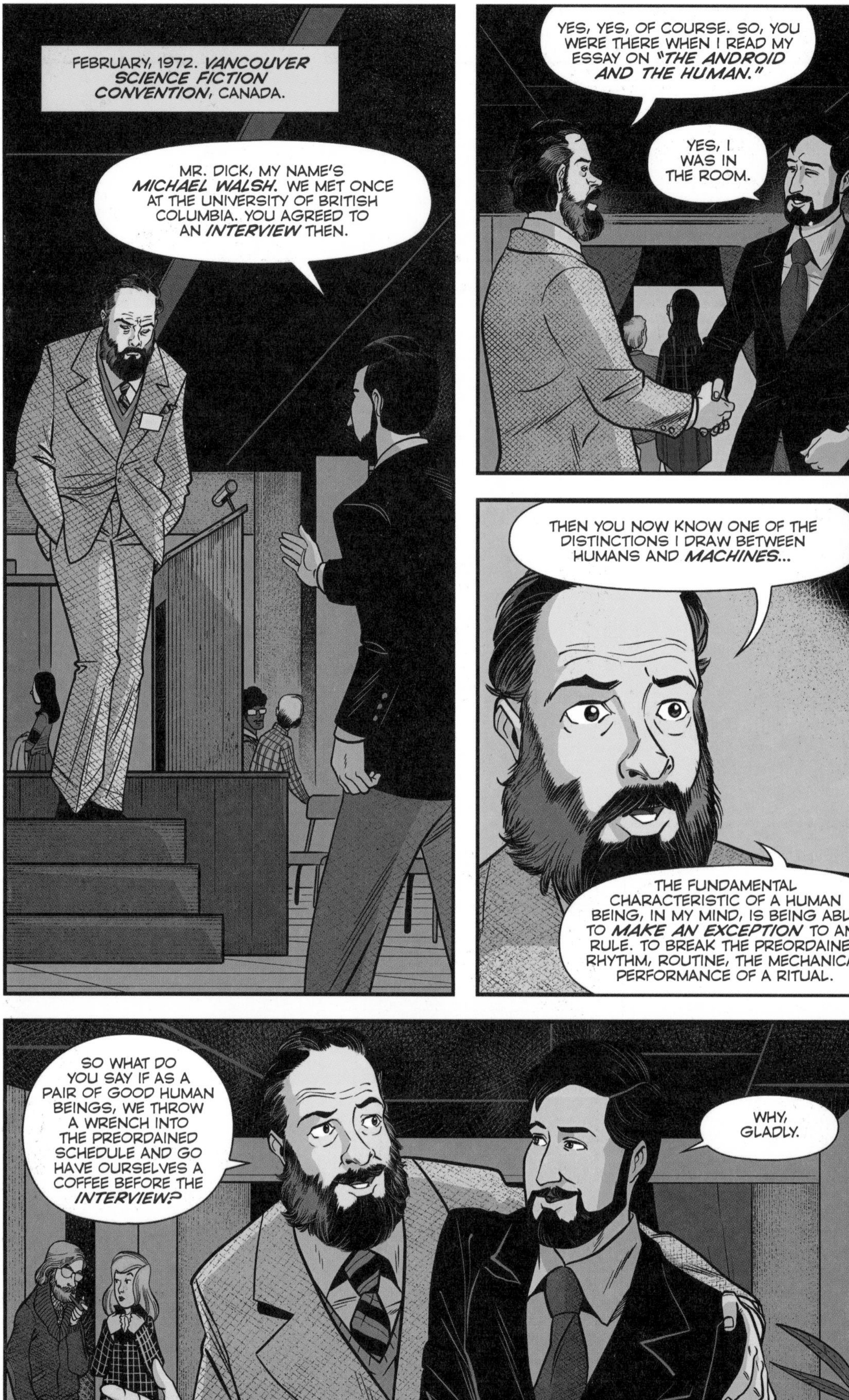
FEBRUARY, 1972. VANCOUVER SCIENCE FICTION CONVENTION, CANADA.
MR. DICK, MY NAME'S MICHAEL WALSH. WE MET ONCE AT THE UNIVERSITY OF BRITISH COLUMBIA. YOU AGREED TO AN INTERVIEW THEN.
YES, YES, OF COURSE. SO, YOU WERE THERE WHEN I READ MY ESSAY ON "THE ANDROID AND THE HUMAN."
YES, I WAS IN THE ROOM.
THEN YOU NOW KNOW ONE OF THE DISTINCTIONS I DRAW BETWEEN HUMANS AND MACHINES...
THE FUNDAMENTAL CHARACTERISTIC OF A HUMAN BEING, IN MY MIND, IS BEING ABLE TO MAKE AN EXCEPTION TO ANY RULE. TO BREAK THE PREORDAINED RHYTHM, ROUTINE, THE MECHANICAL PERFORMANCE OF A RITUAL.
SO WHAT DO YOU SAY IF AS A PAIR OF GOOD HUMAN BEINGS, WE THROW A WRENCH INTO THE PREORDAINED SCHEDULE AND GO HAVE OURSELVES A COFFEE BEFORE THE INTERVIEW?
WHY, GLADLY.

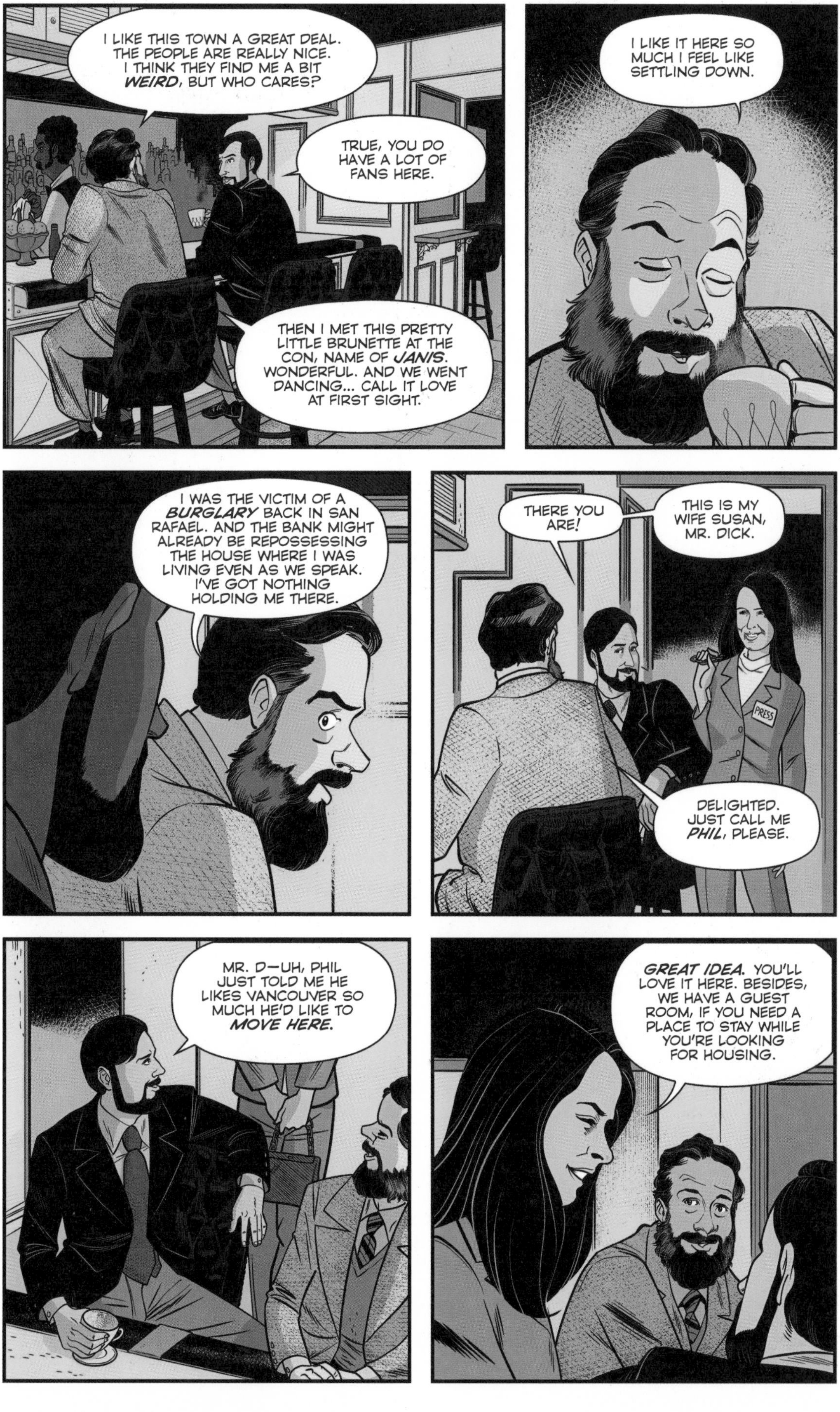

I LIKE THIS TOWN A GREAT DEAL. THE PEOPLE ARE REALLY NICE. I THINK THEY FIND ME A BIT *WEIRD*, BUT WHO CARES?
TRUE, YOU DO HAVE A LOT OF FANS HERE.
THEN I MET THIS PRETTY LITTLE BRUNETTE AT THE CON, NAME OF *JANIS*. WONDERFUL. AND WE WENT DANCING... CALL IT LOVE AT FIRST SIGHT.
I LIKE IT HERE SO MUCH I FEEL LIKE SETTLING DOWN.
I WAS THE VICTIM OF A *BURGLARY* BACK IN SAN RAFAEL. AND THE BANK MIGHT ALREADY BE REPOSSESSING THE HOUSE WHERE I WAS LIVING EVEN AS WE SPEAK. I'VE GOT NOTHING HOLDING ME THERE.
THERE YOU ARE!
THIS IS MY WIFE SUSAN, MR. DICK.
PRESS
DELIGHTED. JUST CALL ME *PHIL*, PLEASE.
MR. D—UH, PHIL JUST TOLD ME HE LIKES VANCOUVER SO MUCH HE'D LIKE TO *MOVE HERE.*
GREAT IDEA. YOU'LL LOVE IT HERE. BESIDES, WE HAVE A GUEST ROOM, IF YOU NEED A PLACE TO STAY WHILE YOU'RE LOOKING FOR HOUSING.

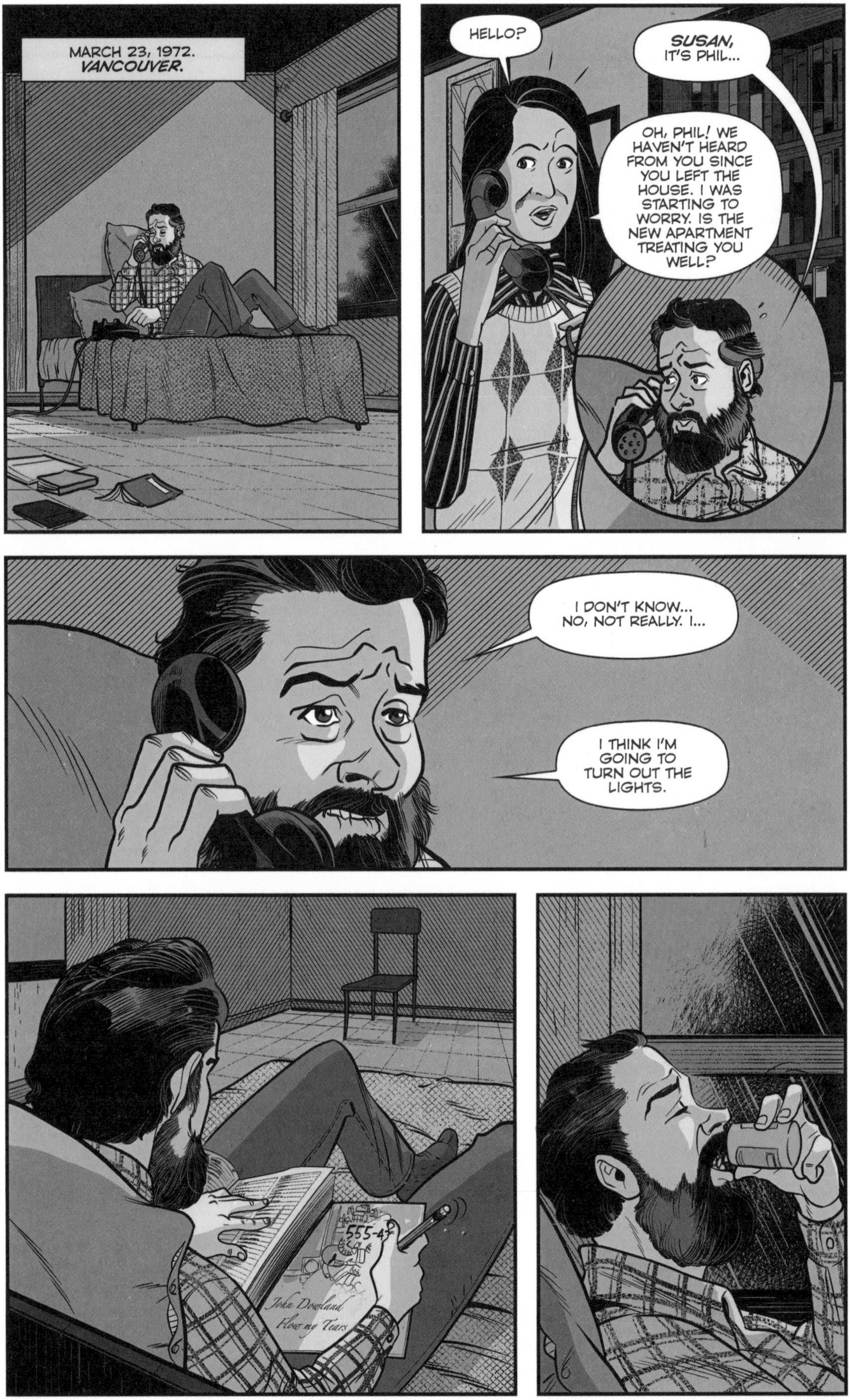
MARCH 23, 1972. *VANCOUVER.*
HELLO?
SUSAN, IT'S PHIL...
OH, PHIL! WE HAVEN'T HEARD FROM YOU SINCE YOU LEFT THE HOUSE. I WAS STARTING TO WORRY. IS THE NEW APARTMENT TREATING YOU WELL?
I DON'T KNOW... NO, NOT REALLY. I...
I THINK I'M GOING TO TURN OUT THE LIGHTS.
John Dowland
Flow my Tears

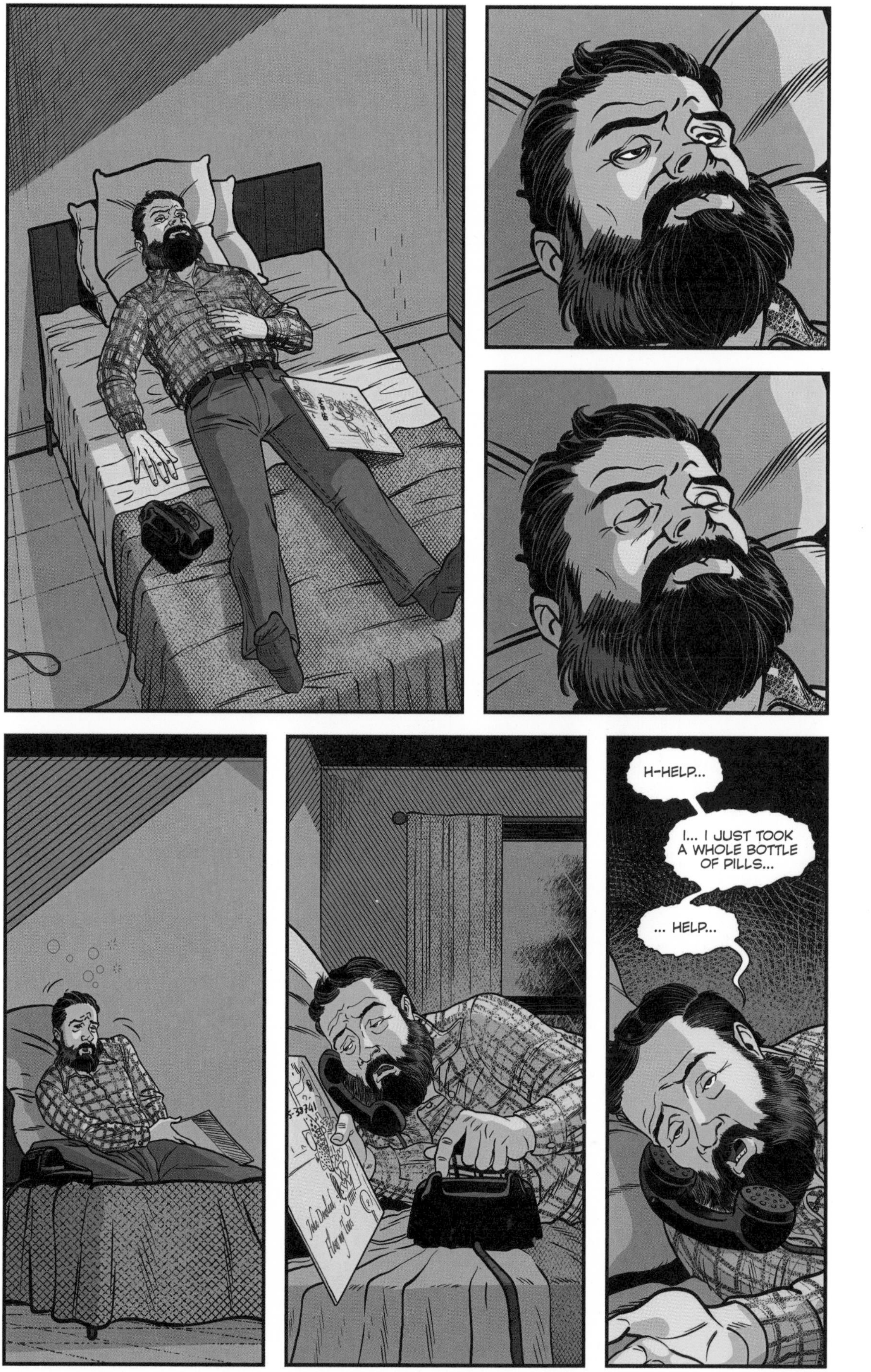
H-HELP...
I... I JUST TOOK A WHOLE BOTTLE OF PILLS...
... HELP...

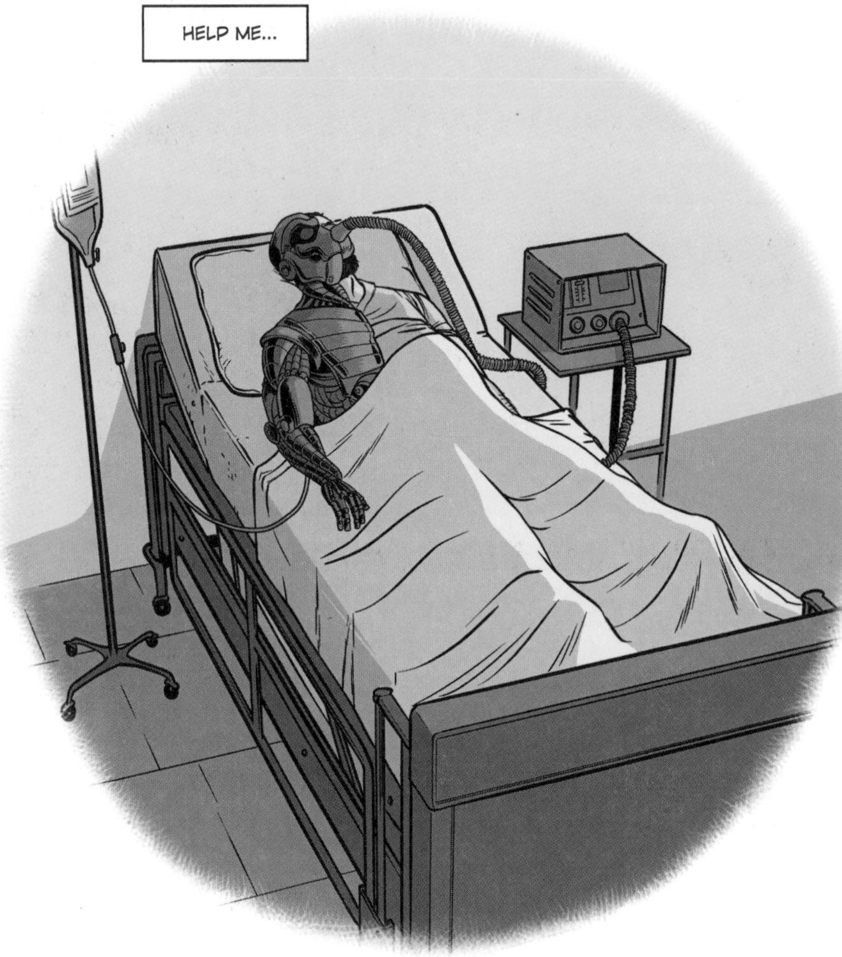
HELP ME...

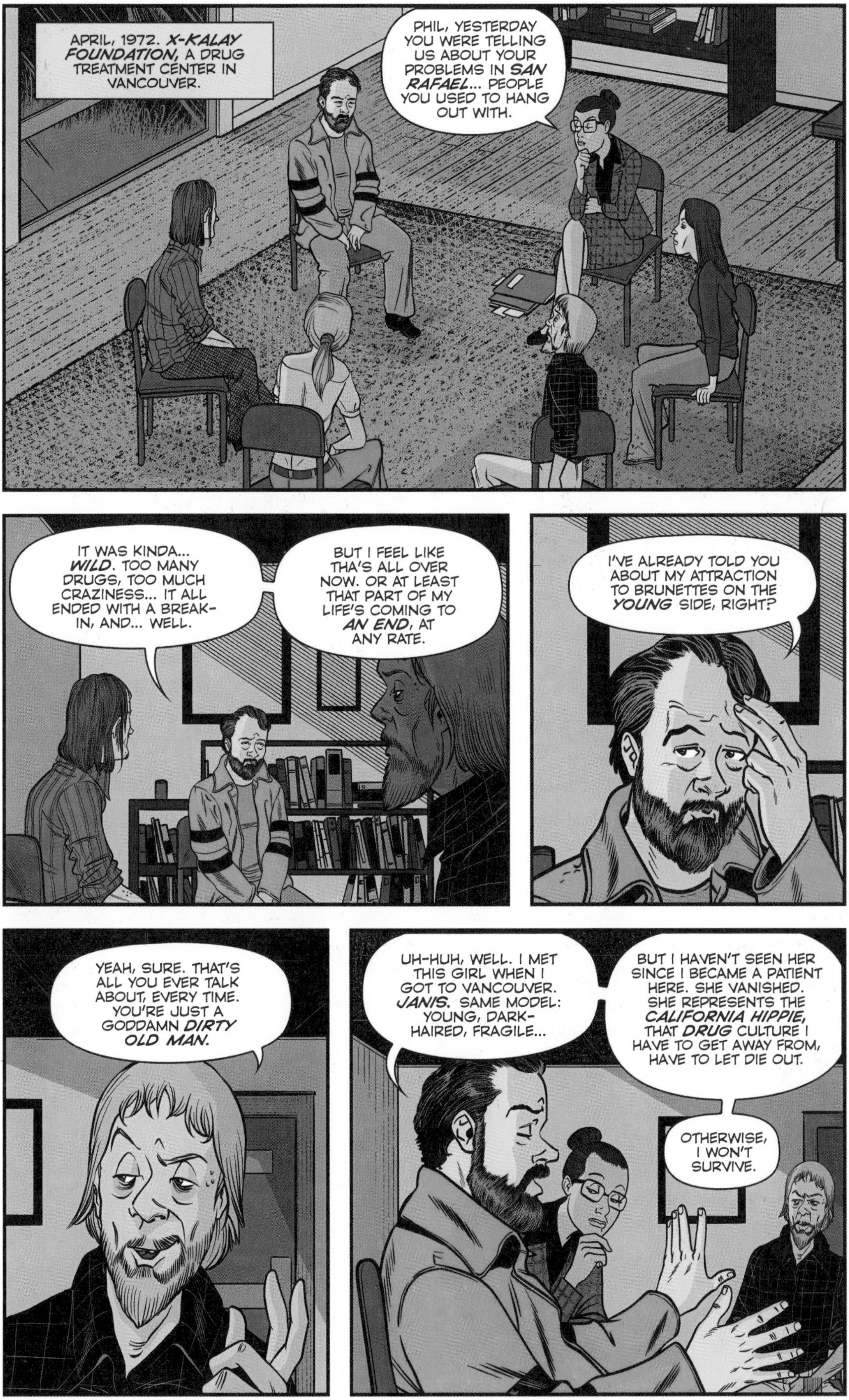
APRIL, 1972. X-KALAY FOUNDATION, A DRUG TREATMENT CENTER IN VANCOUVER.
PHIL, YESTERDAY YOU WERE TELLING US ABOUT YOUR PROBLEMS IN SAN RAFAEL... PEOPLE YOU USED TO HANG OUT WITH.
IT WAS KINDA... WILD. TOO MANY DRUGS, TOO MUCH CRAZINESS... IT ALL ENDED WITH A BREAK-IN, AND... WELL.
BUT I FEEL LIKE THA'S ALL OVER NOW. OR AT LEAST THAT PART OF MY LIFE'S COMING TO AN END, AT ANY RATE.
I'VE ALREADY TOLD YOU ABOUT MY ATTRACTION TO BRUNETTES ON THE YOUNG SIDE, RIGHT?
YEAH, SURE. THAT'S ALL YOU EVER TALK ABOUT, EVERY TIME. YOU'RE JUST A GODDAMN DIRTY OLD MAN.
UH-HUH, WELL. I MET THIS GIRL WHEN I GOT TO VANCOUVER. JANIS. SAME MODEL: YOUNG, DARK-HAIRED, FRAGILE...
BUT I HAVEN'T SEEN HER SINCE I BECAME A PATIENT HERE. SHE VANISHED. SHE REPRESENTS THE CALIFORNIA HIPPIE, THAT DRUG CULTURE I HAVE TO GET AWAY FROM, HAVE TO LET DIE OUT.
OTHERWISE, I WON'T SURVIVE.

I THINK I'VE BEEN DOING BETTER SINCE I GOT HERE. AND DEEP DOWN, I'D LIKE TO GO BACK TO *SAN RAFAEL*.

BUT THERE'S NO WAY. I'VE GOT NOTHING BACK THERE, NOT EVEN A HOUSE. WHEN SHE FOUND OUT I WAS STAYING IN CANADA, MY *SENILE OLD MOTHER* LET THE REAL ESTATE AGENT THROW OUT MY STUFF, OR PUT IT IN STORAGE SOME-WHERE.

MOTHERS! WE OUGHTA HAUL'EM OUT TO SEA AND LET'EM SINK. THEY'RE A *MENACE*, LIKE LEAD IN THE ATMOSPHERE.

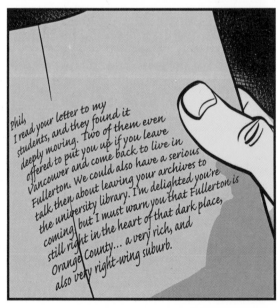

Phil,
I read your letter to my students, and they found it deeply moving. Two of them even offered to put you up if you leave Vancouver and come back to live in Fullerton. We could also have a serious talk then about leaving your archives to the university library. I'm delighted you're coming, but I must warn you that Fullerton is still right in the heart of that dark place, Orange County... a very rich, and also very right-wing suburb.

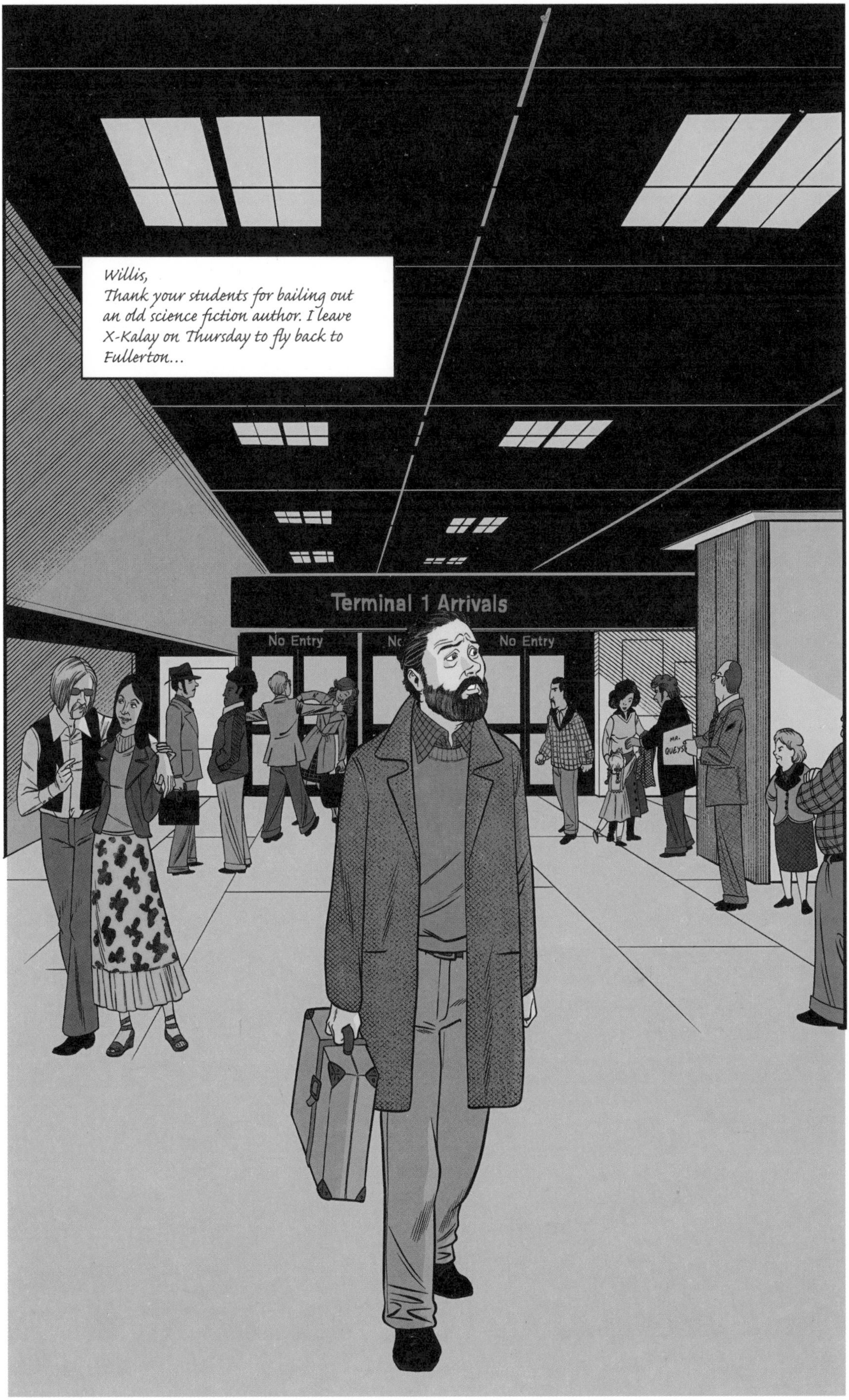
Willis,
Thank your students for bailing out an old science fiction author. I leave X-Kalay on Thursday to fly back to Fullerton...
Terminal 1 Arrivals
No Entry
No Entry
MR. QUEYS

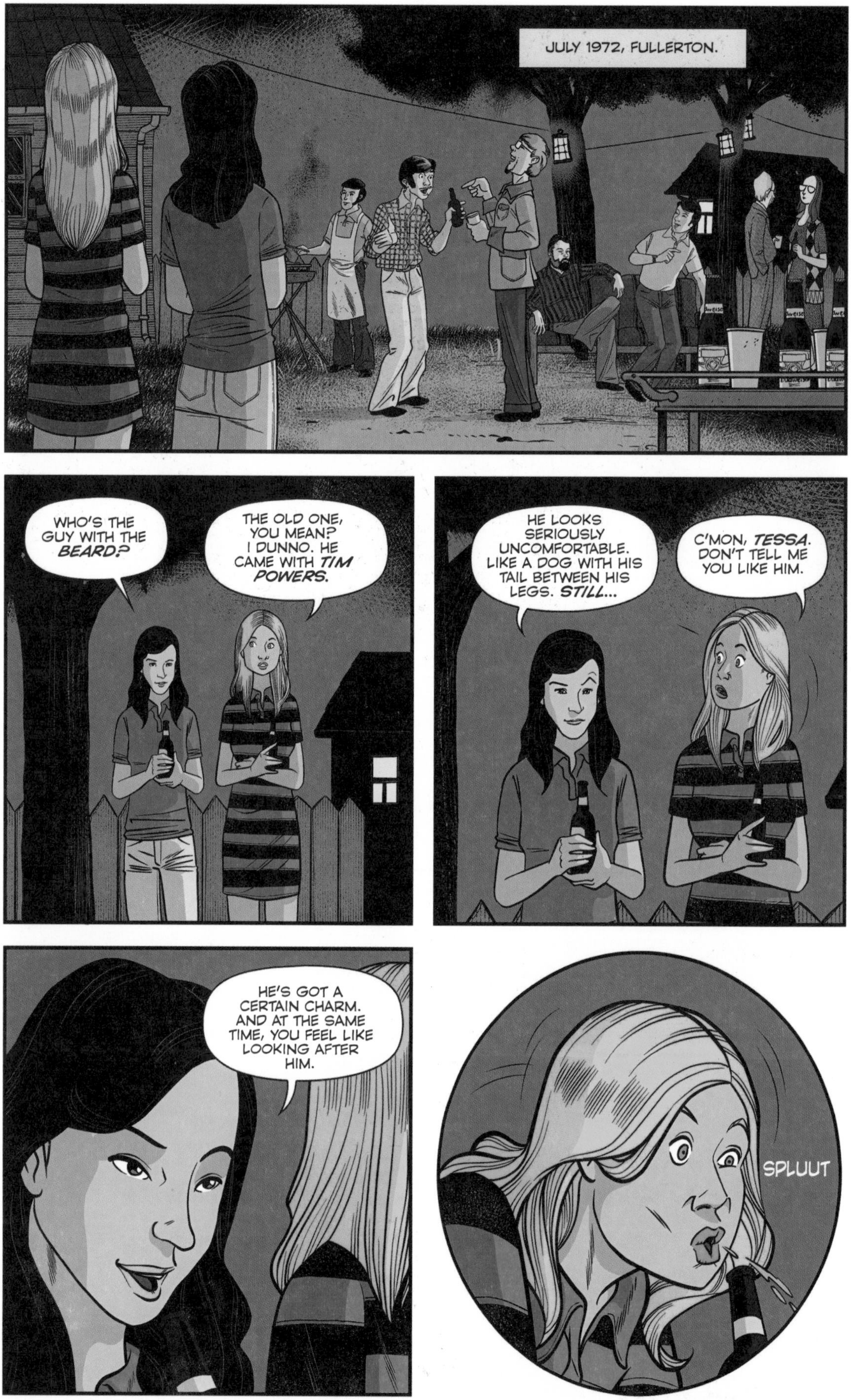
JULY 1972, FULLERTON.
WHO'S THE GUY WITH THE BEARD?
THE OLD ONE, YOU MEAN? I DUNNO. HE CAME WITH TIM POWERS.
HE LOOKS SERIOUSLY UNCOMFORTABLE. LIKE A DOG WITH HIS TAIL BETWEEN HIS LEGS. STILL...
C'MON, TESSA. DON'T TELL ME YOU LIKE HIM.
HE'S GOT A CERTAIN CHARM. AND AT THE SAME TIME, YOU FEEL LIKE LOOKING AFTER HIM.
SPLUUT

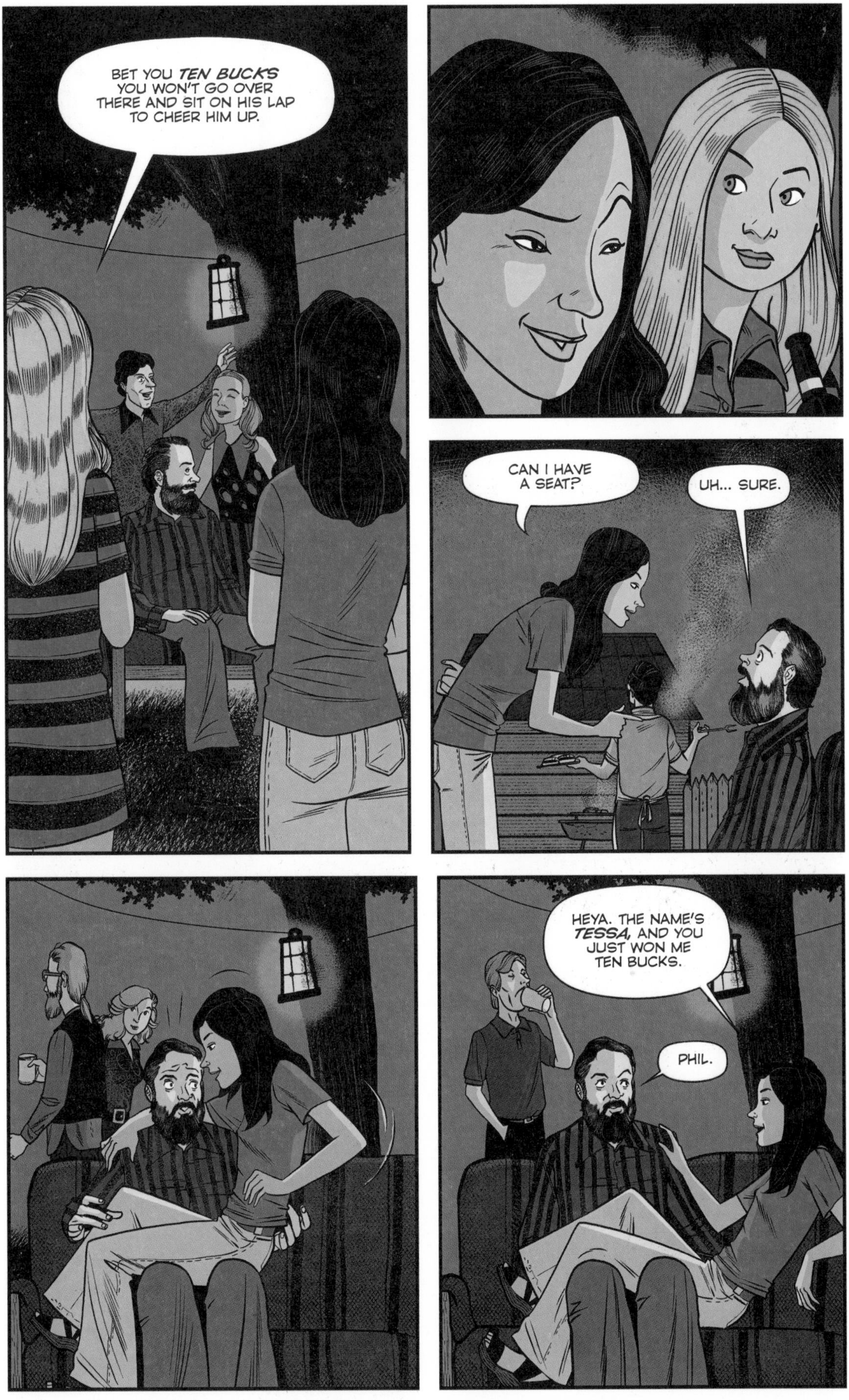
BET YOU *TEN BUCKS* YOU WON'T GO OVER THERE AND SIT ON HIS LAP TO CHEER HIM UP.
CAN I HAVE A SEAT?
UH... SURE.
HEYA. THE NAME'S *TESSA,* AND YOU JUST WON ME TEN BUCKS.
PHIL.

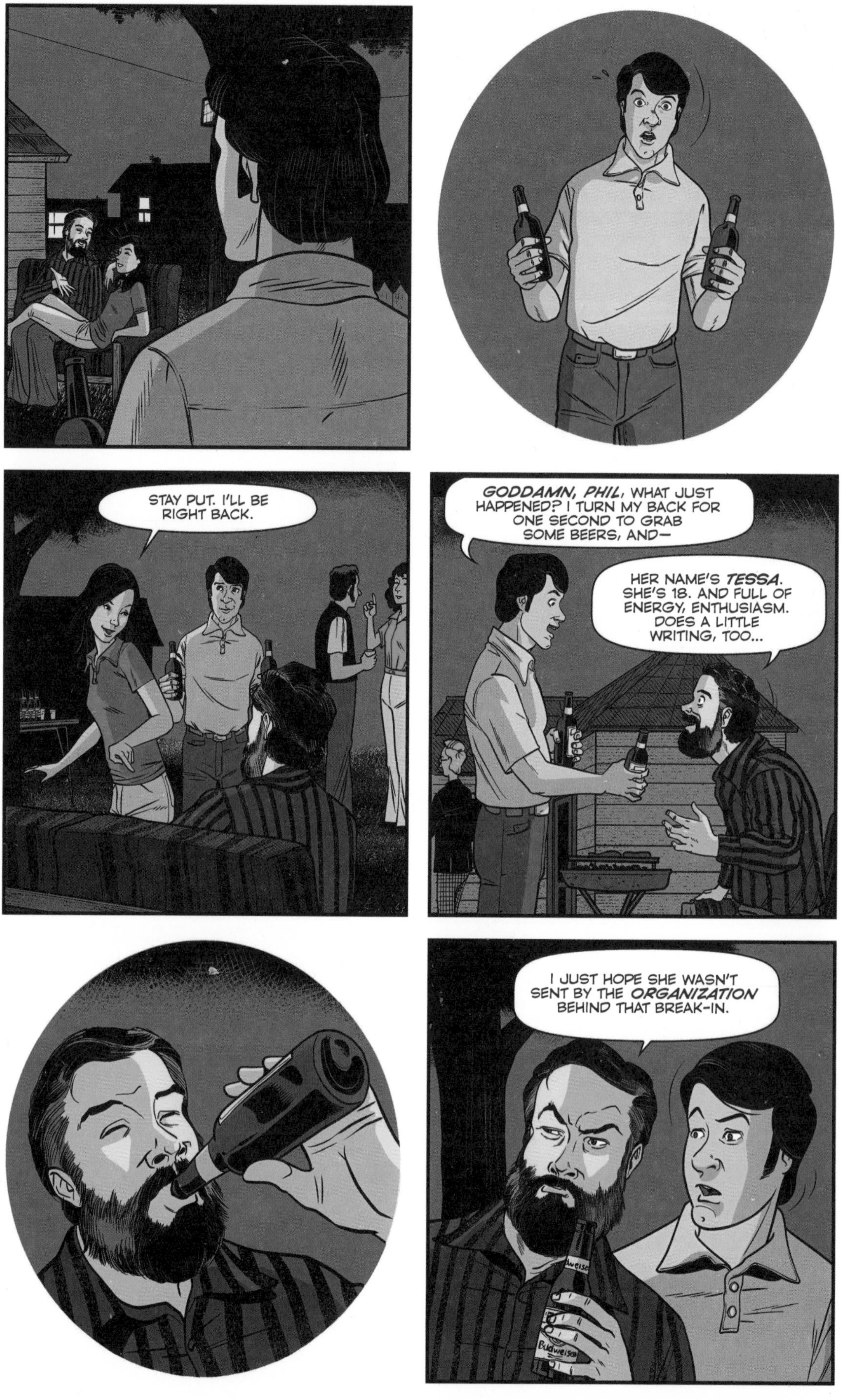
STAY PUT. I'LL BE RIGHT BACK.
GODDAMN, PHIL, WHAT JUST HAPPENED? I TURN MY BACK FOR ONE SECOND TO GRAB SOME BEERS, AND—
HER NAME'S TESSA. SHE'S 18. AND FULL OF ENERGY, ENTHUSIASM. DOES A LITTLE WRITING, TOO...
I JUST HOPE SHE WASN'T SENT BY THE ORGANIZATION BEHIND THAT BREAK-IN.

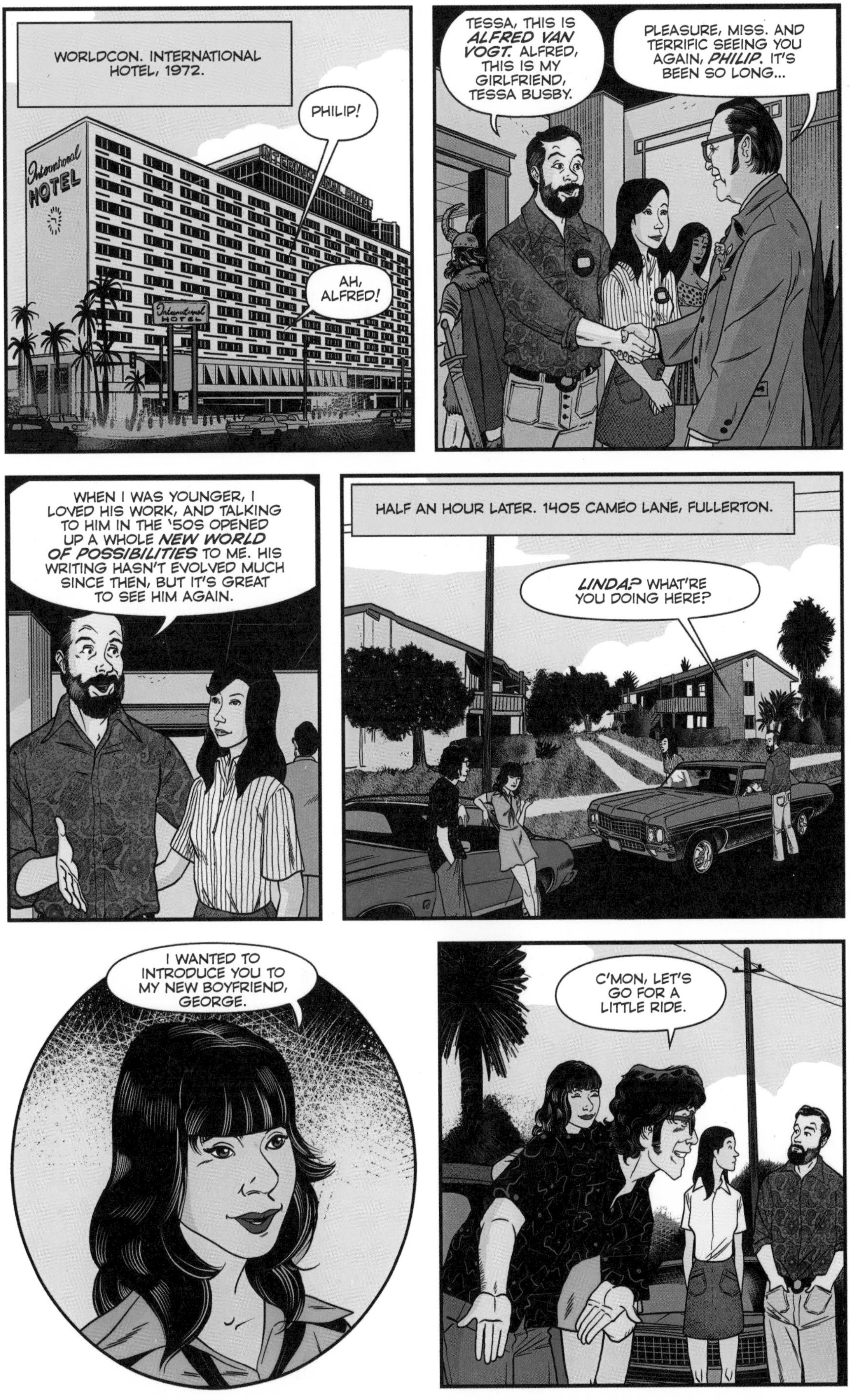
WORLDCON. INTERNATIONAL HOTEL, 1972.
PHILIP!
AH, ALFRED!
International HOTEL
TESSA, THIS IS ALFRED VAN VOGT. ALFRED, THIS IS MY GIRLFRIEND, TESSA BUSBY.
PLEASURE, MISS. AND TERRIFIC SEEING YOU AGAIN, PHILIP. IT'S BEEN SO LONG...
WHEN I WAS YOUNGER, I LOVED HIS WORK, AND TALKING TO HIM IN THE '50S OPENED UP A WHOLE NEW WORLD OF POSSIBILITIES TO ME. HIS WRITING HASN'T EVOLVED MUCH SINCE THEN, BUT IT'S GREAT TO SEE HIM AGAIN.
HALF AN HOUR LATER. 1405 CAMEO LANE, FULLERTON.
LINDA? WHAT'RE YOU DOING HERE?
I WANTED TO INTRODUCE YOU TO MY NEW BOYFRIEND, GEORGE.
C'MON, LET'S GO FOR A LITTLE RIDE.

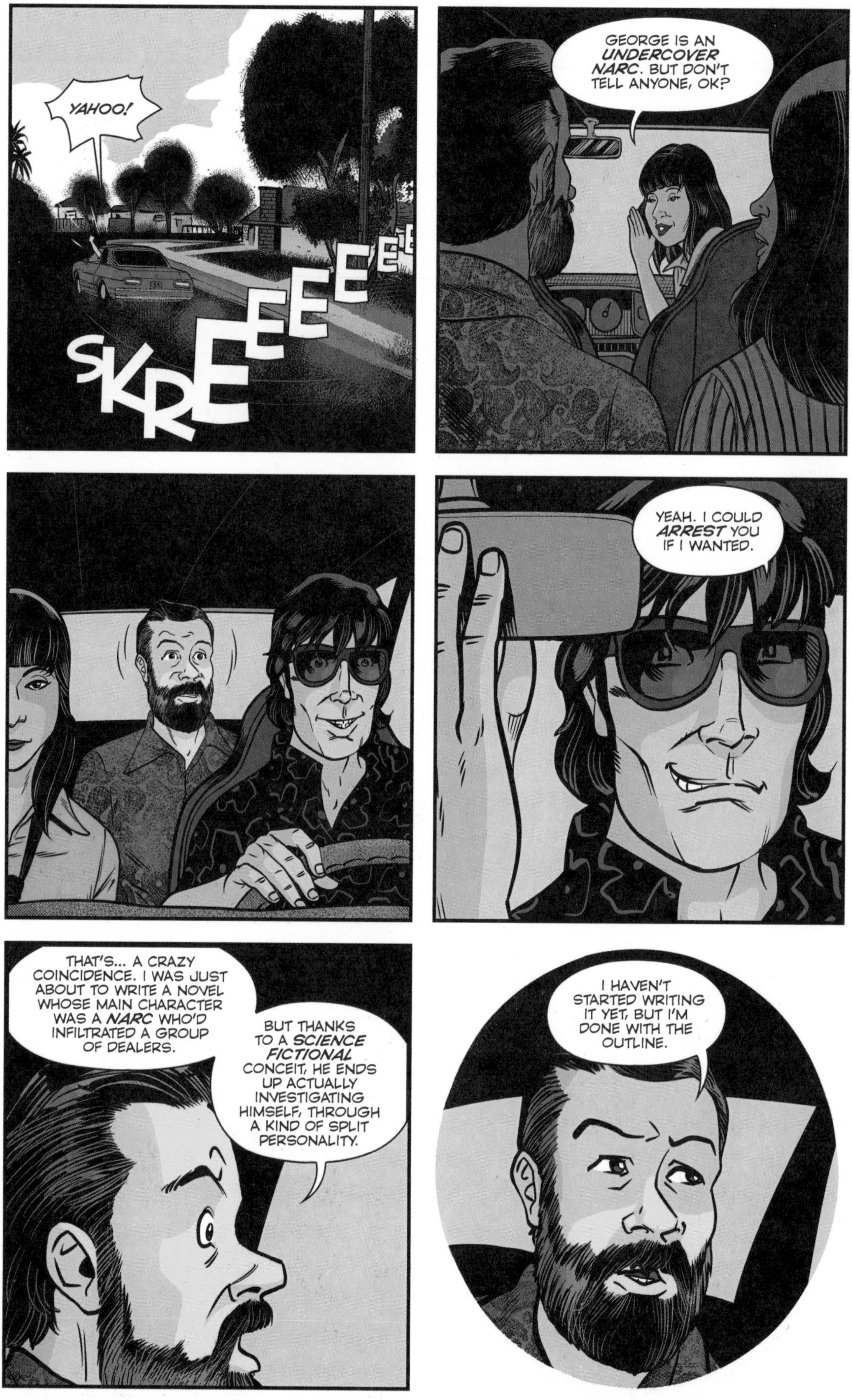

YAHOO!
SKREEEEEEEE
GEORGE IS AN *UNDERCOVER NARC*. BUT DON'T TELL ANYONE, OK?
YEAH. I COULD *ARREST* YOU IF I WANTED.
THAT'S... A CRAZY COINCIDENCE. I WAS JUST ABOUT TO WRITE A NOVEL WHOSE MAIN CHARACTER WAS A *NARC* WHO'D INFILTRATED A GROUP OF DEALERS.
BUT THANKS TO A *SCIENCE FICTIONAL* CONCEIT, HE ENDS UP ACTUALLY INVESTIGATING HIMSELF, THROUGH A KIND OF SPLIT PERSONALITY.
I HAVEN'T STARTED WRITING IT YET, BUT I'M DONE WITH THE OUTLINE.

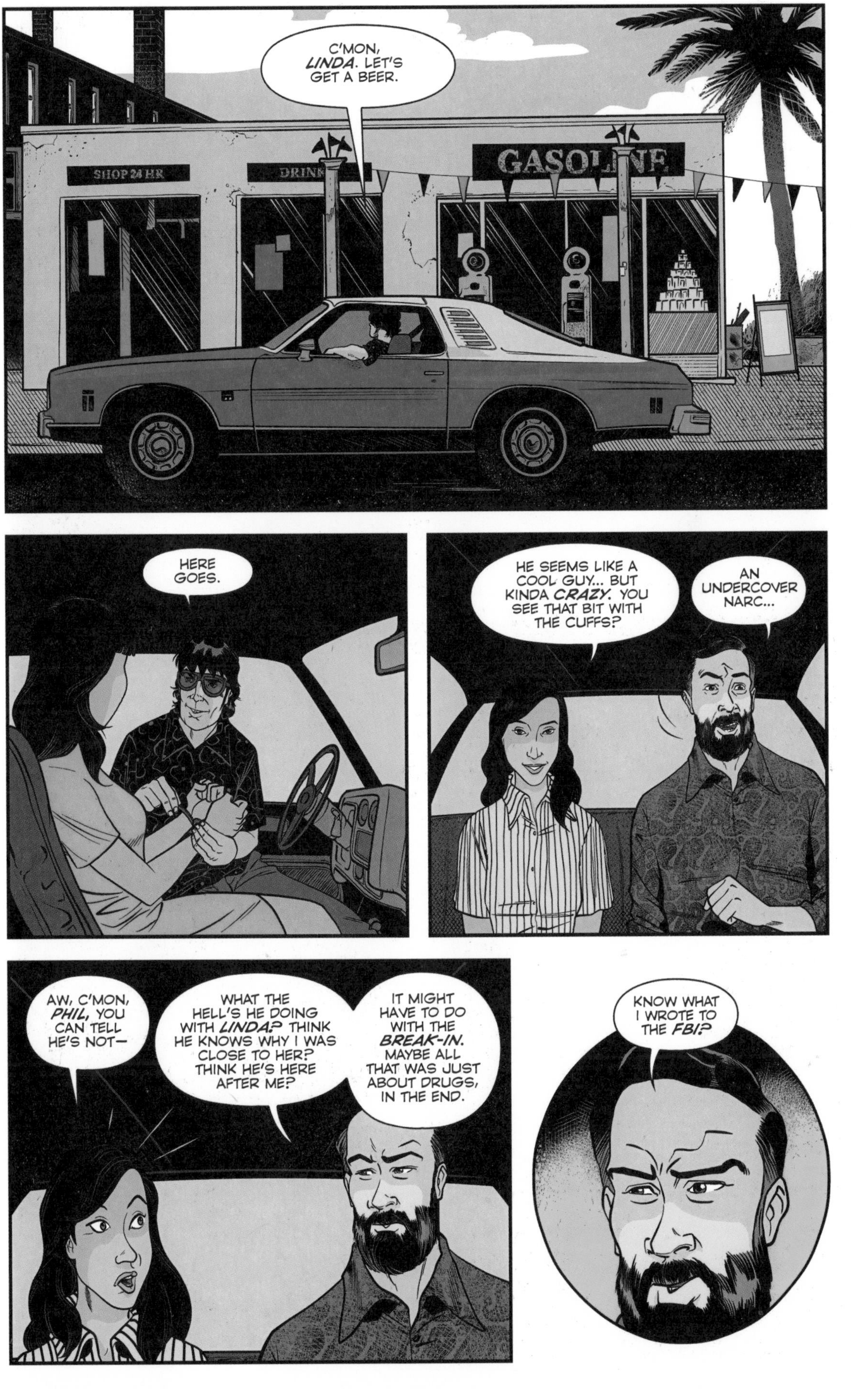
C'MON, LINDA. LET'S GET A BEER.
GASOLINE
SHOP 24 HR
HERE GOES.
HE SEEMS LIKE A COOL GUY... BUT KINDA CRAZY. YOU SEE THAT BIT WITH THE CUFFS?
AN UNDERCOVER NARC...
AW, C'MON, PHIL, YOU CAN TELL HE'S NOT—
WHAT THE HELL'S HE DOING WITH LINDA? THINK HE KNOWS WHY I WAS CLOSE TO HER? THINK HE'S HERE AFTER ME?
IT MIGHT HAVE TO DO WITH THE BREAK-IN. MAYBE ALL THAT WAS JUST ABOUT DRUGS, IN THE END.
KNOW WHAT I WROTE TO THE FBI?

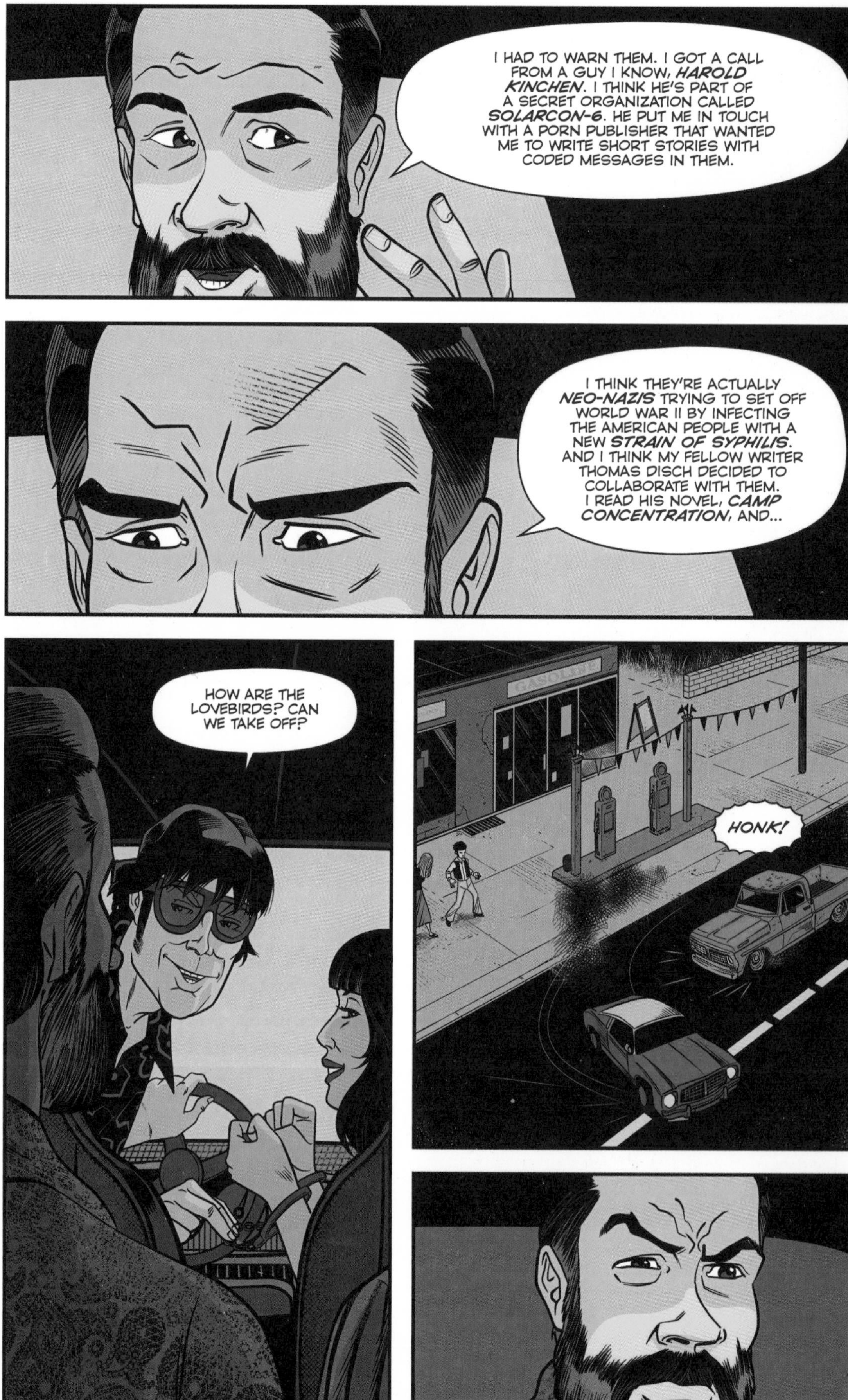
I HAD TO WARN THEM. I GOT A CALL FROM A GUY I KNOW, HAROLD KINCHEN. I THINK HE'S PART OF A SECRET ORGANIZATION CALLED SOLARCON-6. HE PUT ME IN TOUCH WITH A PORN PUBLISHER THAT WANTED ME TO WRITE SHORT STORIES WITH CODED MESSAGES IN THEM.
I THINK THEY'RE ACTUALLY NEO-NAZIS TRYING TO SET OFF WORLD WAR II BY INFECTING THE AMERICAN PEOPLE WITH A NEW STRAIN OF SYPHILIS. AND I THINK MY FELLOW WRITER THOMAS DISCH DECIDED TO COLLABORATE WITH THEM. I READ HIS NOVEL, CAMP CONCENTRATION, AND...
HOW ARE THE LOVEBIRDS? CAN WE TAKE OFF?
GASOLINE
HONK!

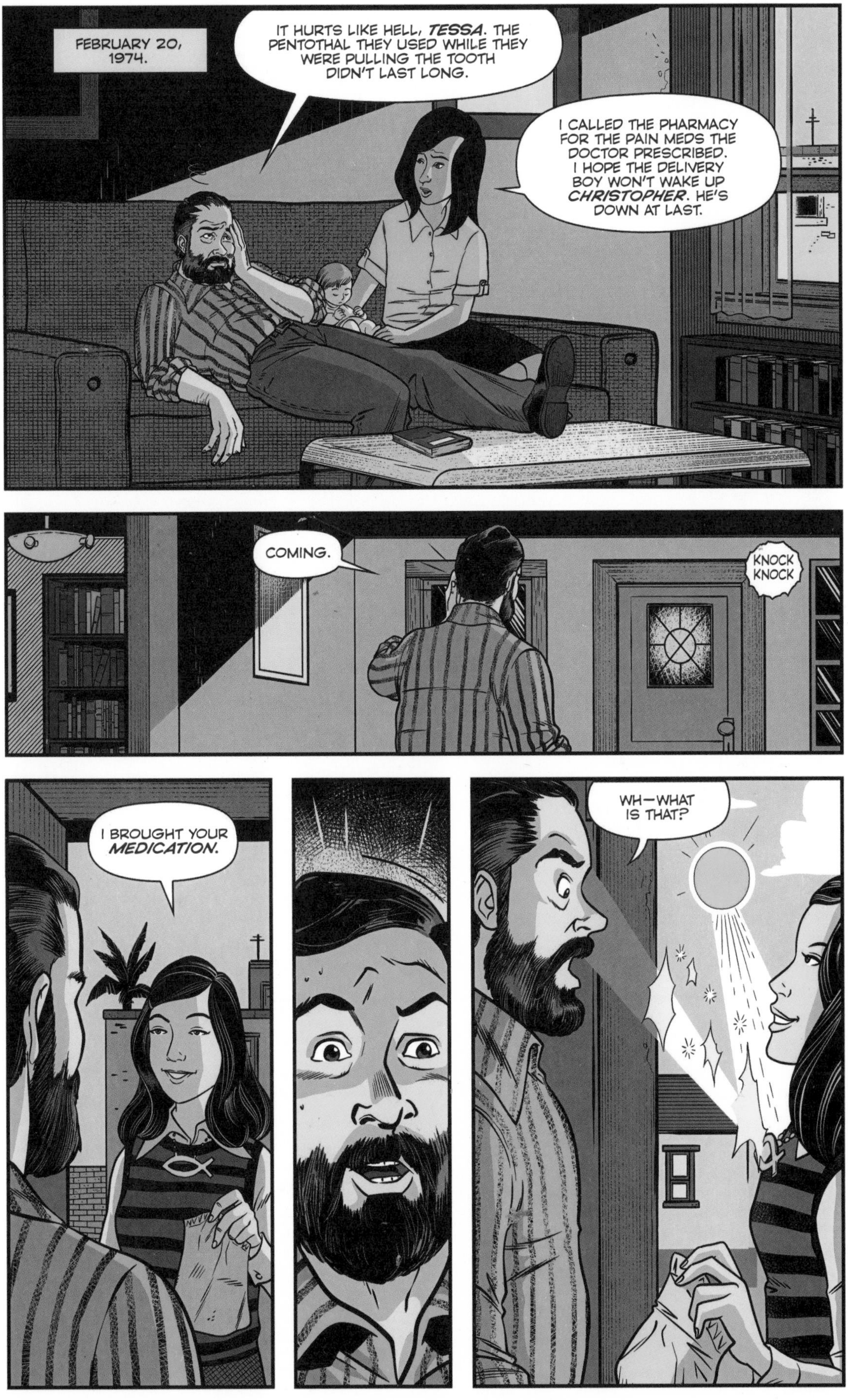
FEBRUARY 20, 1974.
IT HURTS LIKE HELL, *TESSA*. THE PENTOTHAL THEY USED WHILE THEY WERE PULLING THE TOOTH DIDN'T LAST LONG.
I CALLED THE PHARMACY FOR THE PAIN MEDS THE DOCTOR PRESCRIBED. I HOPE THE DELIVERY BOY WON'T WAKE UP *CHRISTOPHER*. HE'S DOWN AT LAST.
KNOCK KNOCK
COMING.
I BROUGHT YOUR *MEDICATION*.
WH—WHAT IS THAT?

IT'S A SECRET SYMBOL EARLY CHRISTIANS USED TO RECOGNIZE EACH OTHER.

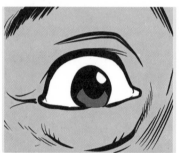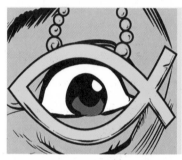

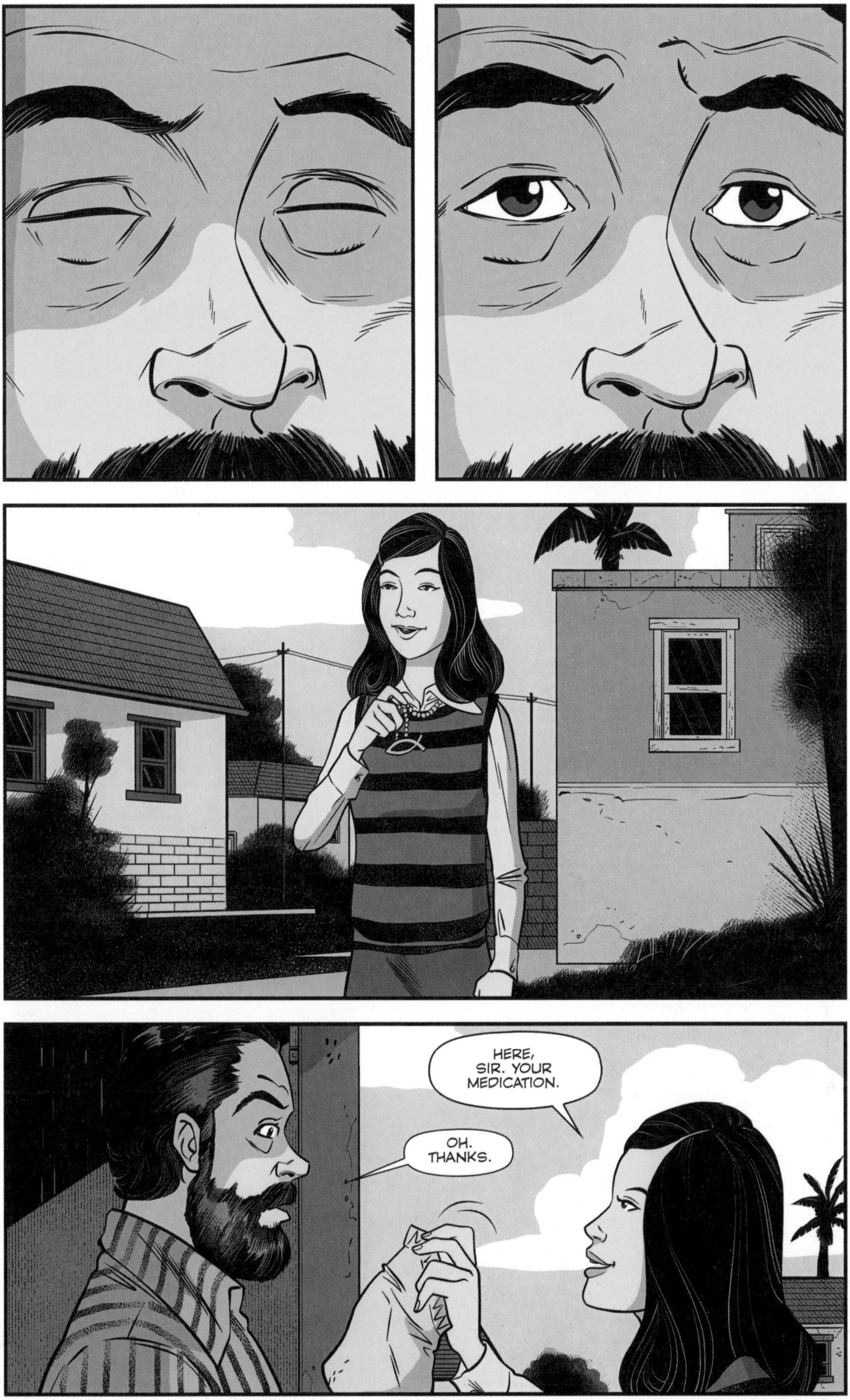
HERE, SIR. YOUR MEDICATION.
OH. THANKS.

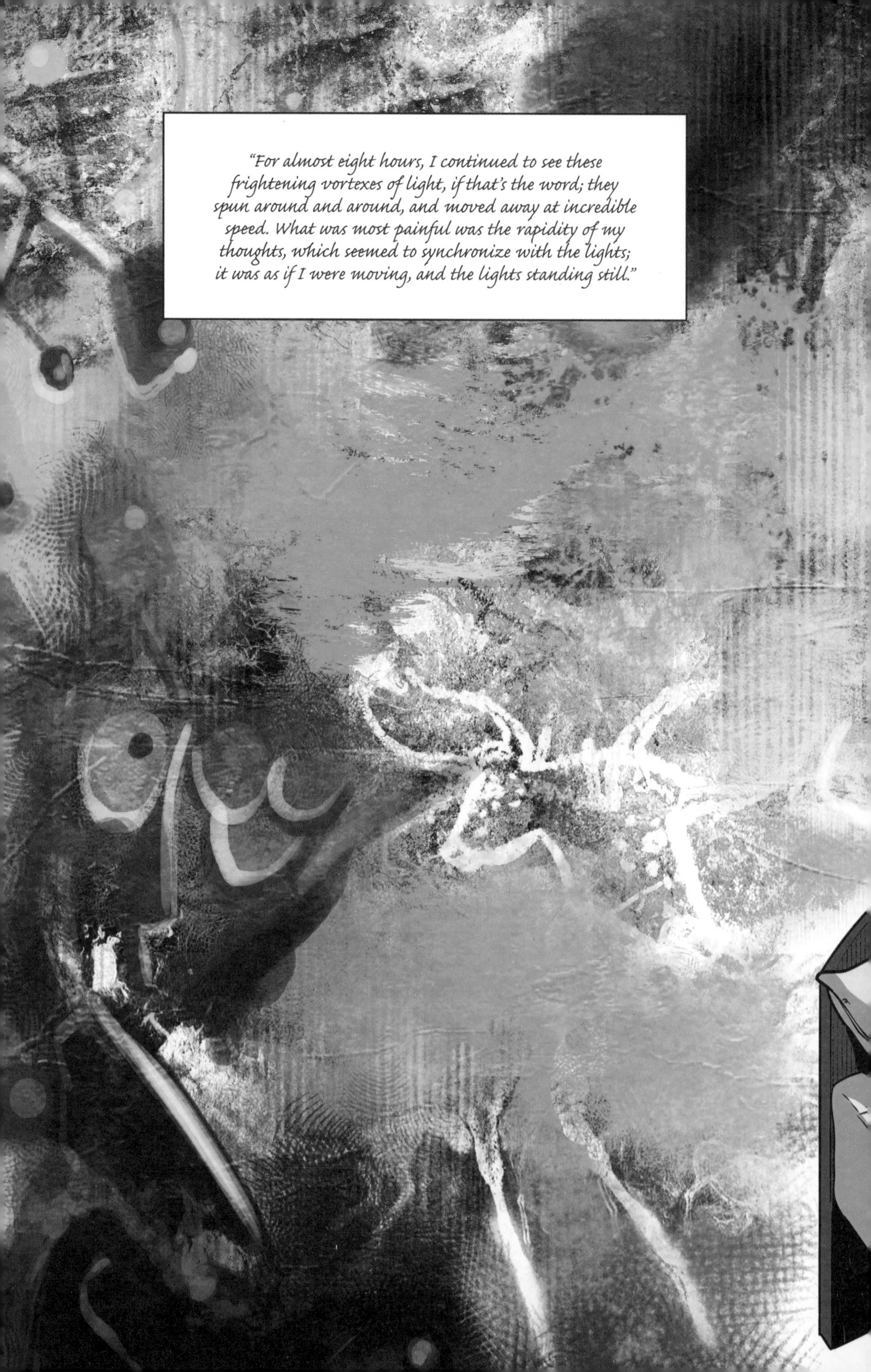
"For almost eight hours, I continued to see these frightening vortexes of light, if that's the word; they spun around and around, and moved away at incredible speed. What was most painful was the rapidity of my thoughts, which seemed to synchronize with the lights; it was as if I were moving, and the lights standing still."

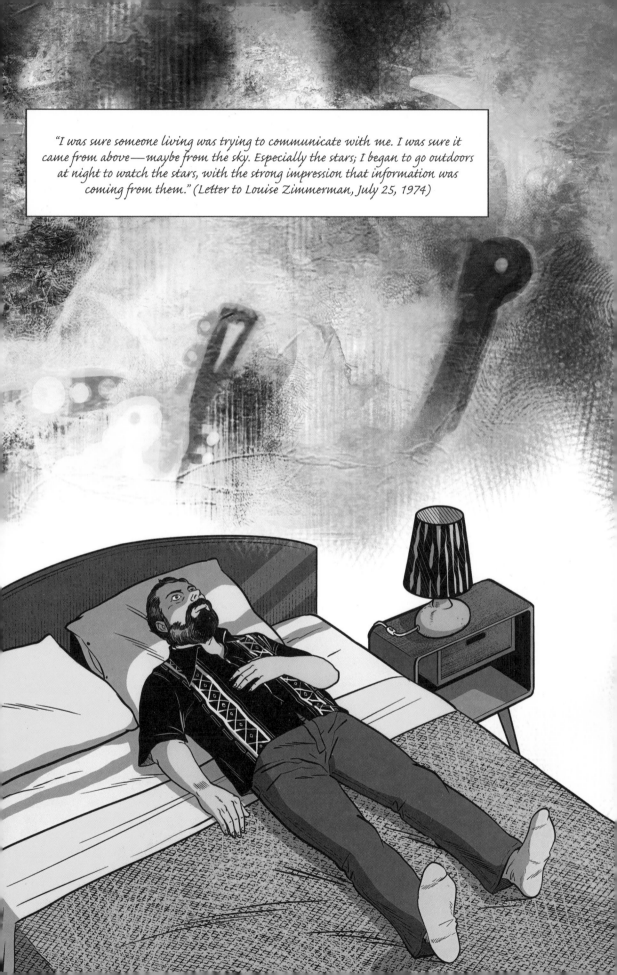

"I was sure someone living was trying to communicate with me. I was sure it came from above—maybe from the sky. Especially the stars; I began to go outdoors at night to watch the stars, with the strong impression that information was coming from them." (Letter to Louise Zimmerman, July 25, 1974)

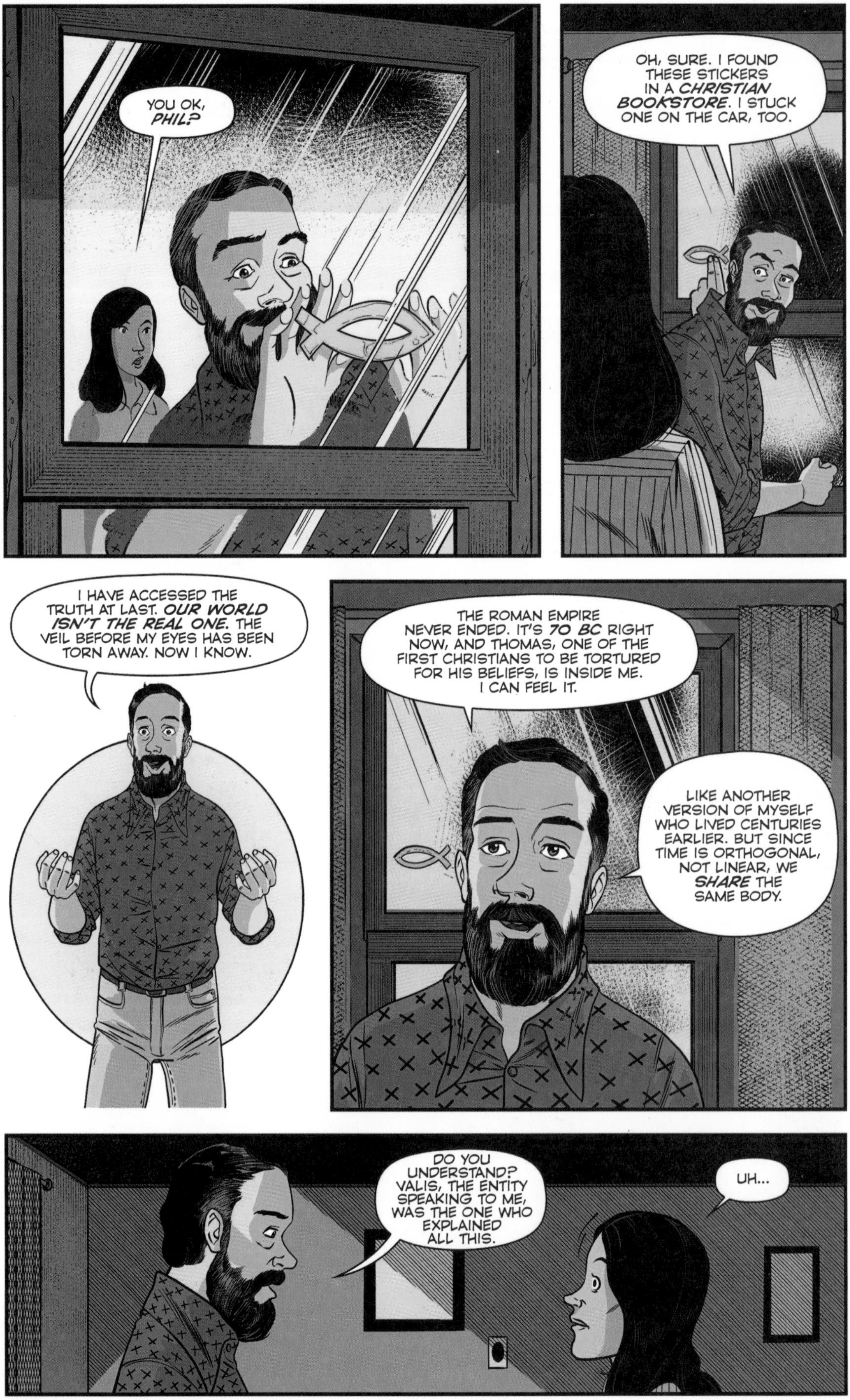
YOU OK, PHIL?
OH, SURE. I FOUND THESE STICKERS IN A CHRISTIAN BOOKSTORE. I STUCK ONE ON THE CAR, TOO.
I HAVE ACCESSED THE TRUTH AT LAST. OUR WORLD ISN'T THE REAL ONE. THE VEIL BEFORE MY EYES HAS BEEN TORN AWAY. NOW I KNOW.
THE ROMAN EMPIRE NEVER ENDED. IT'S 70 BC RIGHT NOW, AND THOMAS, ONE OF THE FIRST CHRISTIANS TO BE TORTURED FOR HIS BELIEFS, IS INSIDE ME. I CAN FEEL IT.
LIKE ANOTHER VERSION OF MYSELF WHO LIVED CENTURIES EARLIER. BUT SINCE TIME IS ORTHOGONAL, NOT LINEAR, WE SHARE THE SAME BODY.
DO YOU UNDERSTAND? VALIS, THE ENTITY SPEAKING TO ME, WAS THE ONE WHO EXPLAINED ALL THIS.
UH...

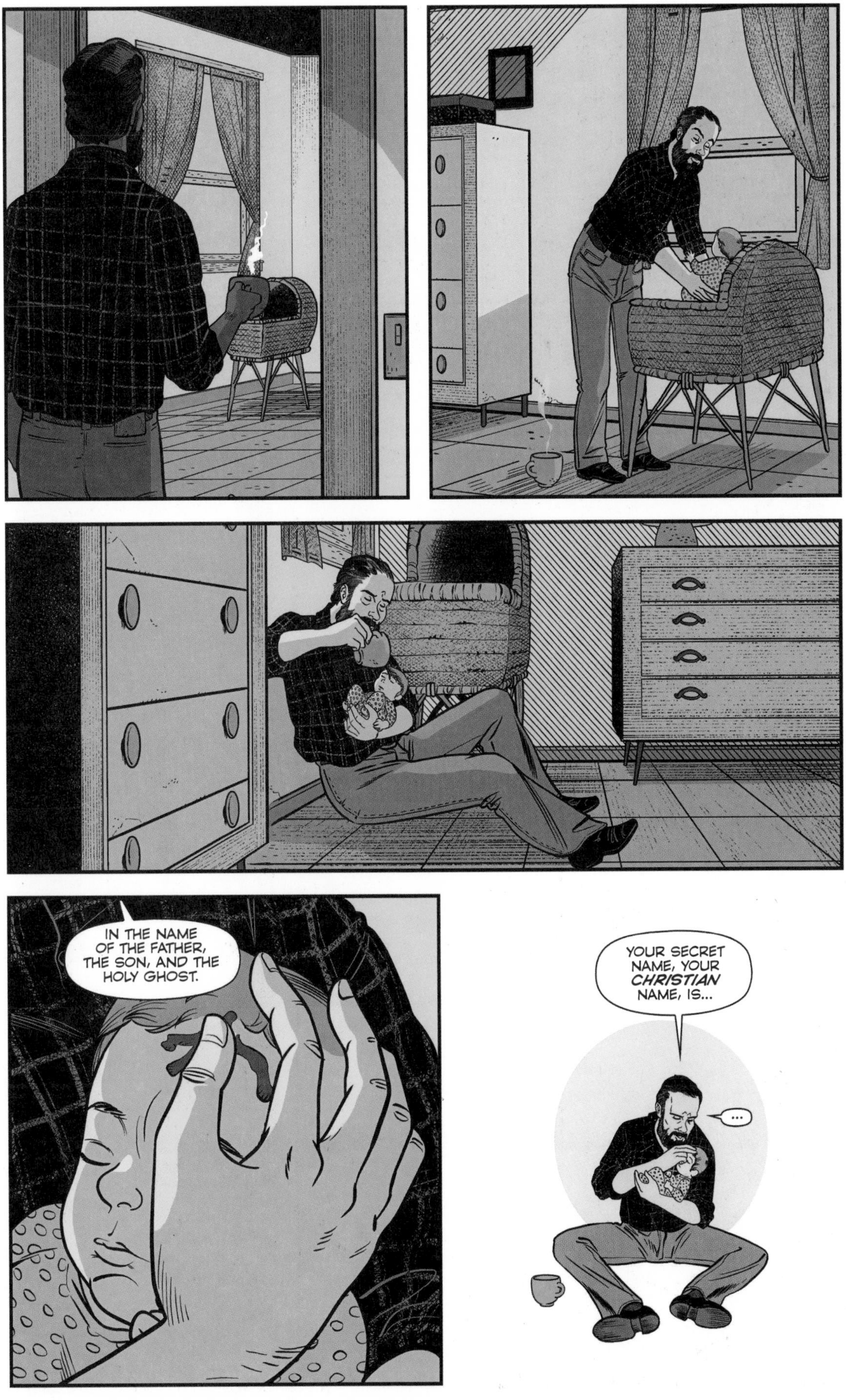
IN THE NAME OF THE FATHER, THE SON, AND THE HOLY GHOST.
YOUR SECRET NAME, YOUR *CHRISTIAN* NAME, IS...
...

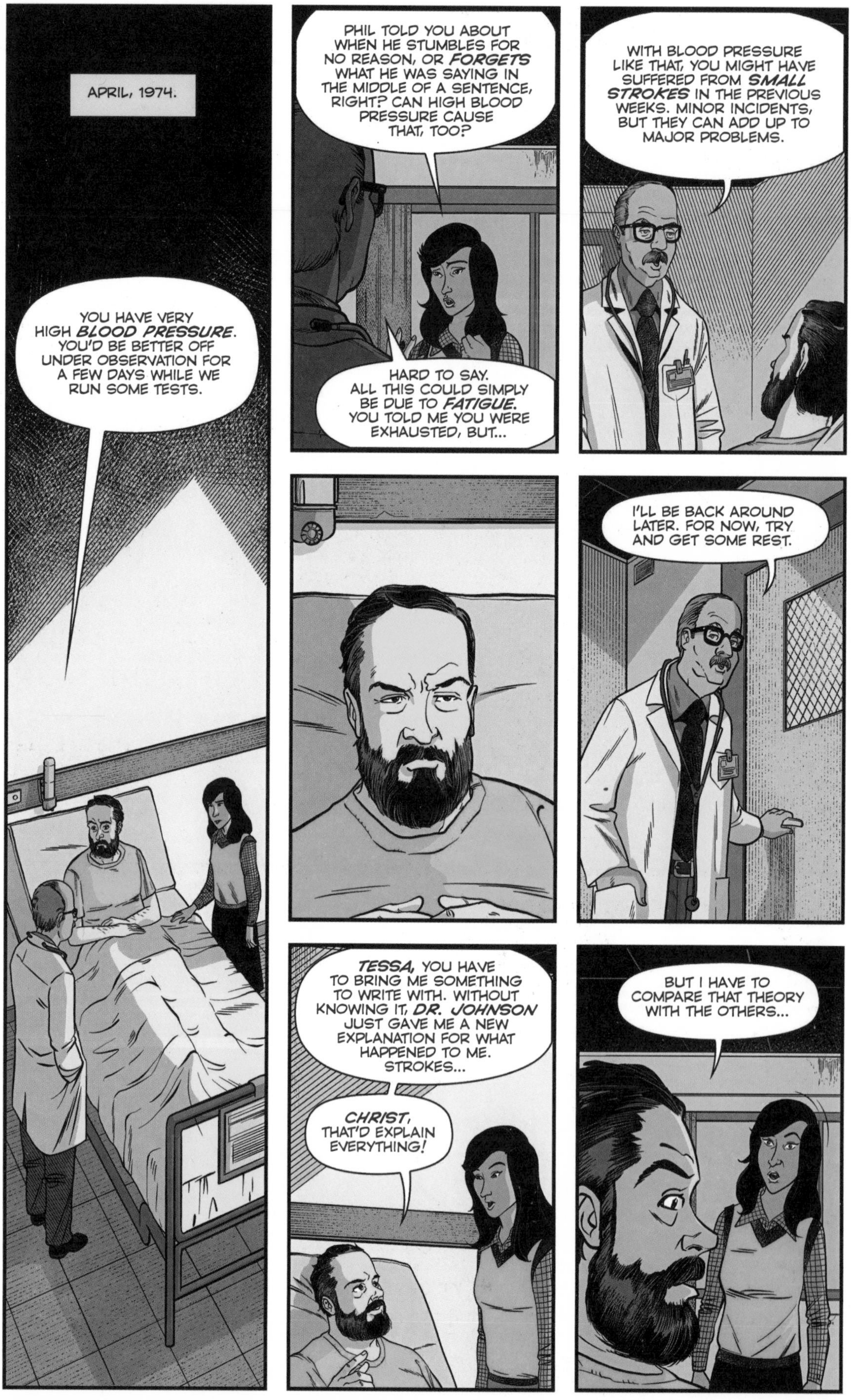
APRIL, 1974.
YOU HAVE VERY HIGH BLOOD PRESSURE. YOU'D BE BETTER OFF UNDER OBSERVATION FOR A FEW DAYS WHILE WE RUN SOME TESTS.
PHIL TOLD YOU ABOUT WHEN HE STUMBLES FOR NO REASON, OR FORGETS WHAT HE WAS SAYING IN THE MIDDLE OF A SENTENCE, RIGHT? CAN HIGH BLOOD PRESSURE CAUSE THAT, TOO?
HARD TO SAY. ALL THIS COULD SIMPLY BE DUE TO FATIGUE. YOU TOLD ME YOU WERE EXHAUSTED, BUT...
WITH BLOOD PRESSURE LIKE THAT, YOU MIGHT HAVE SUFFERED FROM SMALL STROKES IN THE PREVIOUS WEEKS. MINOR INCIDENTS, BUT THEY CAN ADD UP TO MAJOR PROBLEMS.
I'LL BE BACK AROUND LATER. FOR NOW, TRY AND GET SOME REST.
TESSA, YOU HAVE TO BRING ME SOMETHING TO WRITE WITH. WITHOUT KNOWING IT, DR. JOHNSON JUST GAVE ME A NEW EXPLANATION FOR WHAT HAPPENED TO ME. STROKES...
CHRIST, THAT'D EXPLAIN EVERYTHING!
BUT I HAVE TO COMPARE THAT THEORY WITH THE OTHERS...

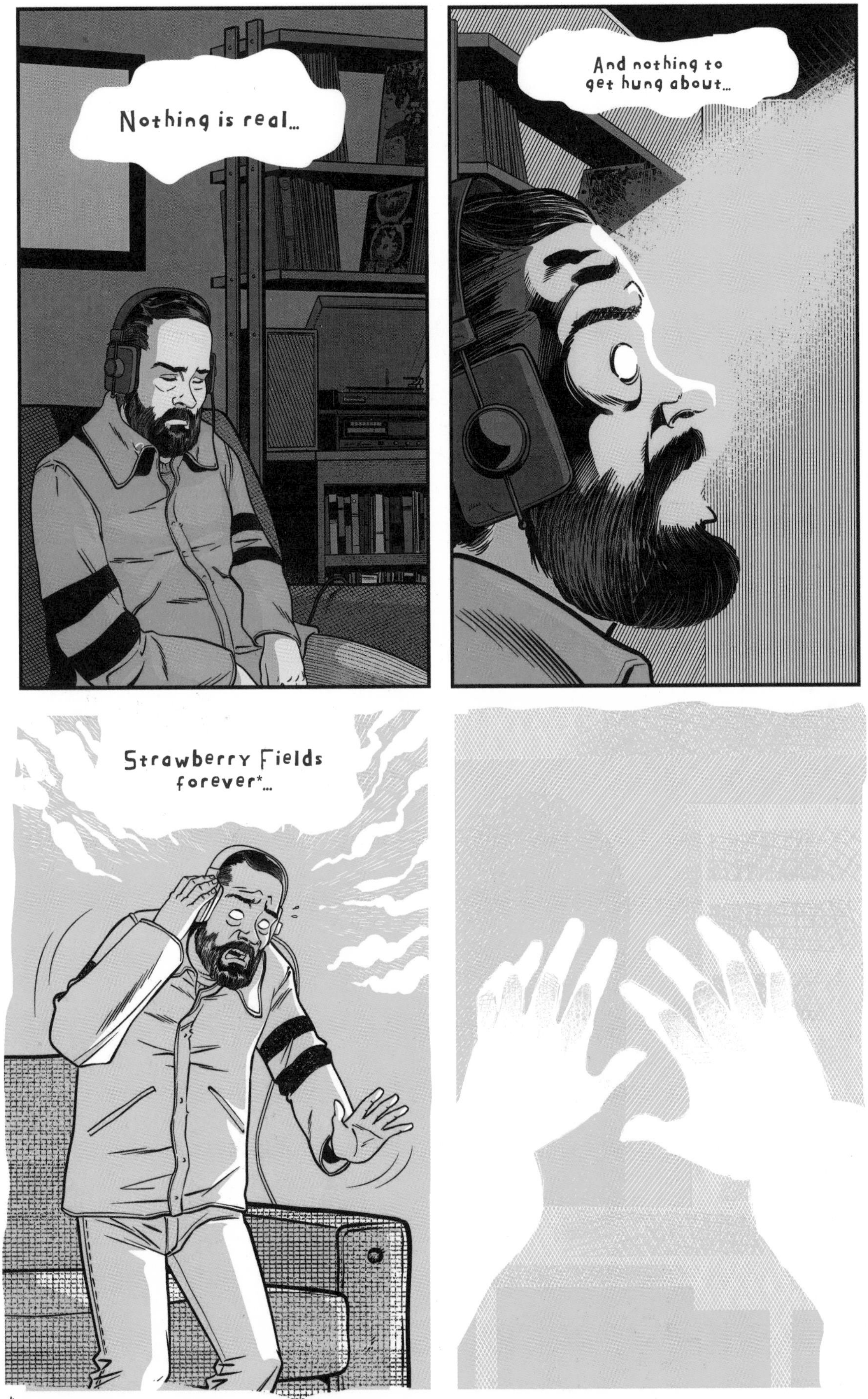
Nothing is real...
And nothing to get hung about...
Strawberry Fields forever*...

*"STRAWBERRY FIELDS FOREVER" : LENNON/MCCARTNEY (APPLE MUSIC)

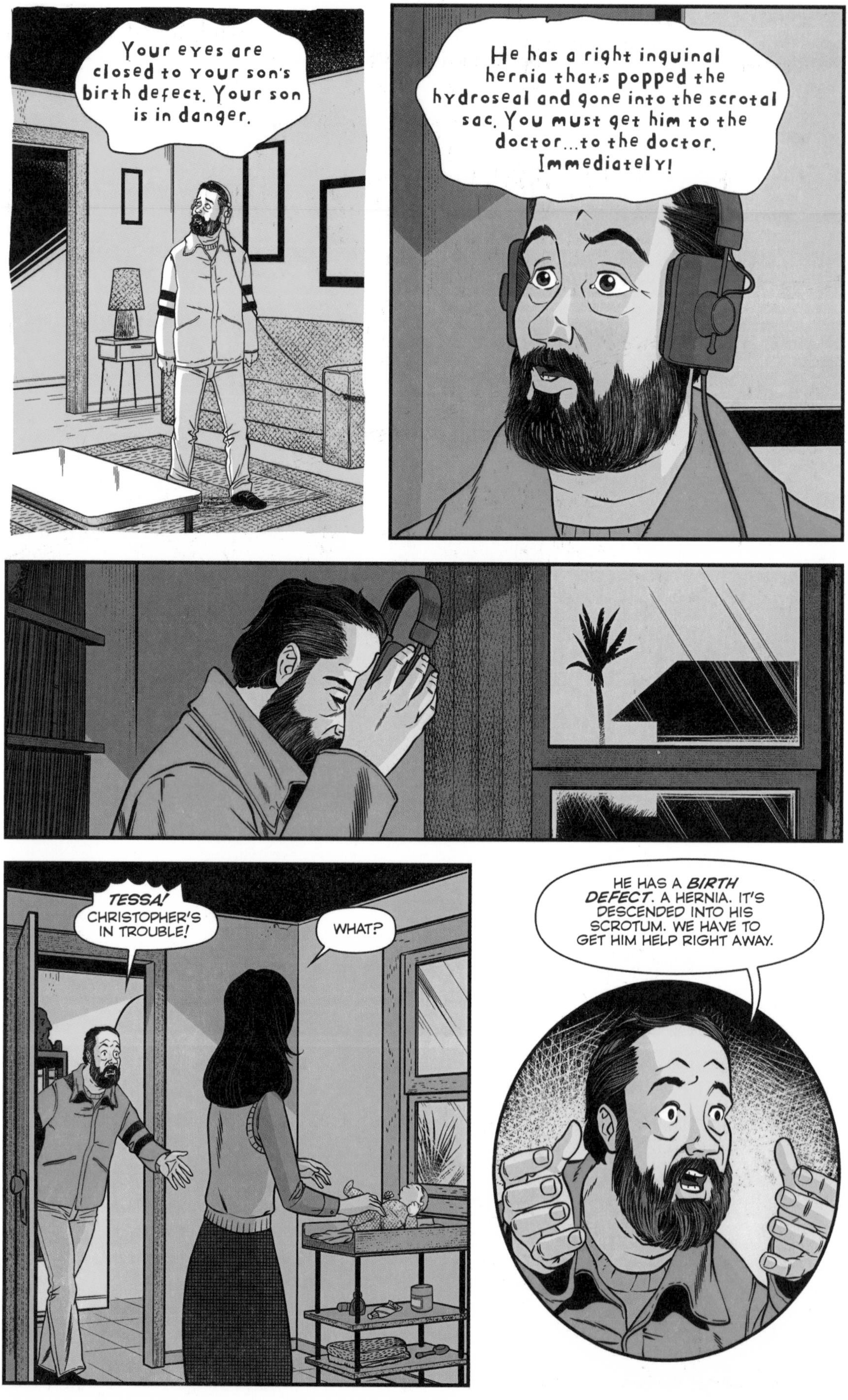
Your eyes are closed to your son's birth defect. Your son is in danger.
He has a right inguinal hernia that's popped the hydroseal and gone into the scrotal sac. You must get him to the doctor...to the doctor. Immediately!
TESSA! CHRISTOPHER'S IN TROUBLE!
WHAT?
HE HAS A BIRTH DEFECT. A HERNIA. IT'S DESCENDED INTO HIS SCROTUM. WE HAVE TO GET HIM HELP RIGHT AWAY.

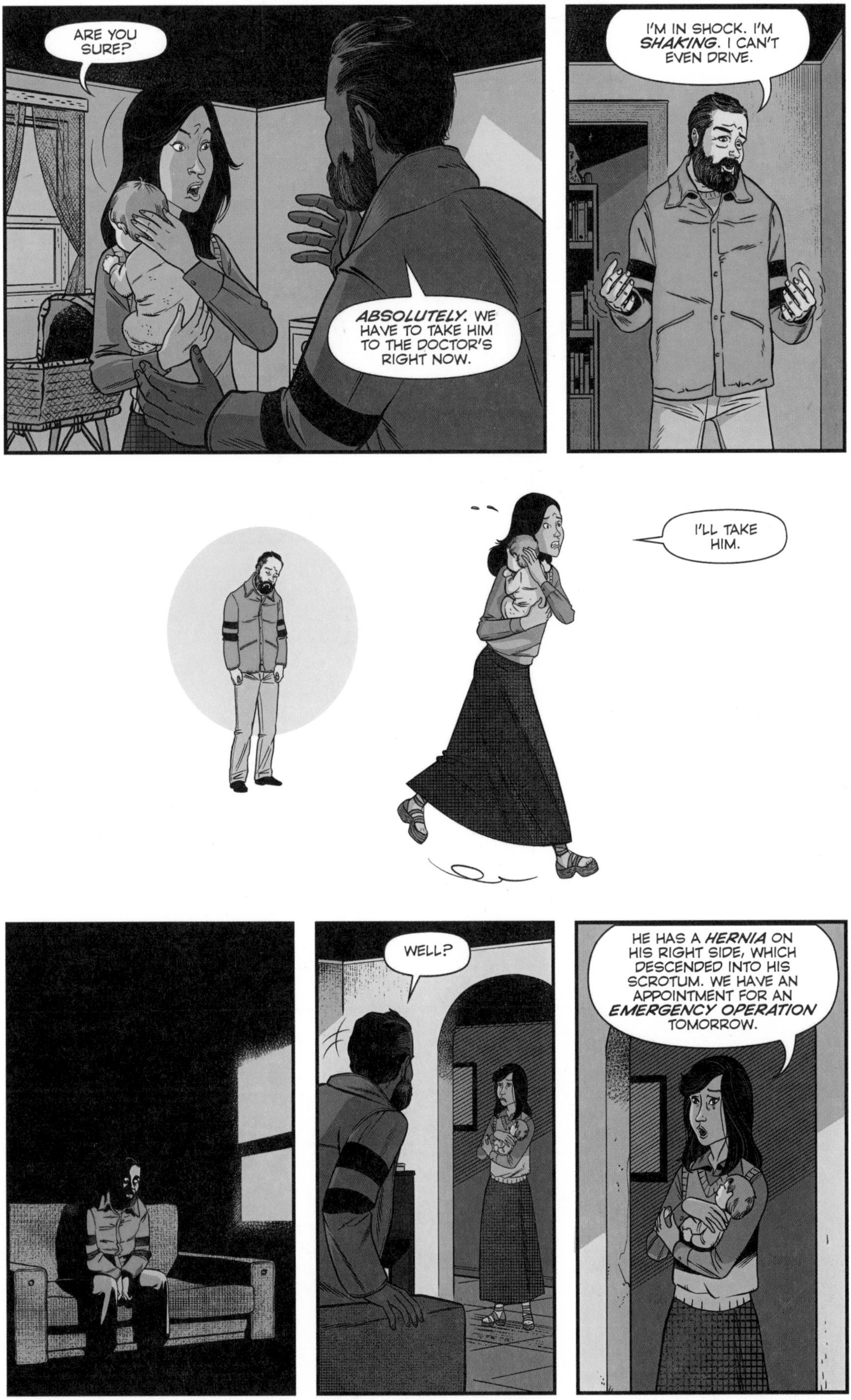
ARE YOU SURE?
ABSOLUTELY. WE HAVE TO TAKE HIM TO THE DOCTOR'S RIGHT NOW.
I'M IN SHOCK. I'M SHAKING. I CAN'T EVEN DRIVE.
I'LL TAKE HIM.
WELL?
HE HAS A HERNIA ON HIS RIGHT SIDE, WHICH DESCENDED INTO HIS SCROTUM. WE HAVE AN APPOINTMENT FOR AN EMERGENCY OPERATION TOMORROW.

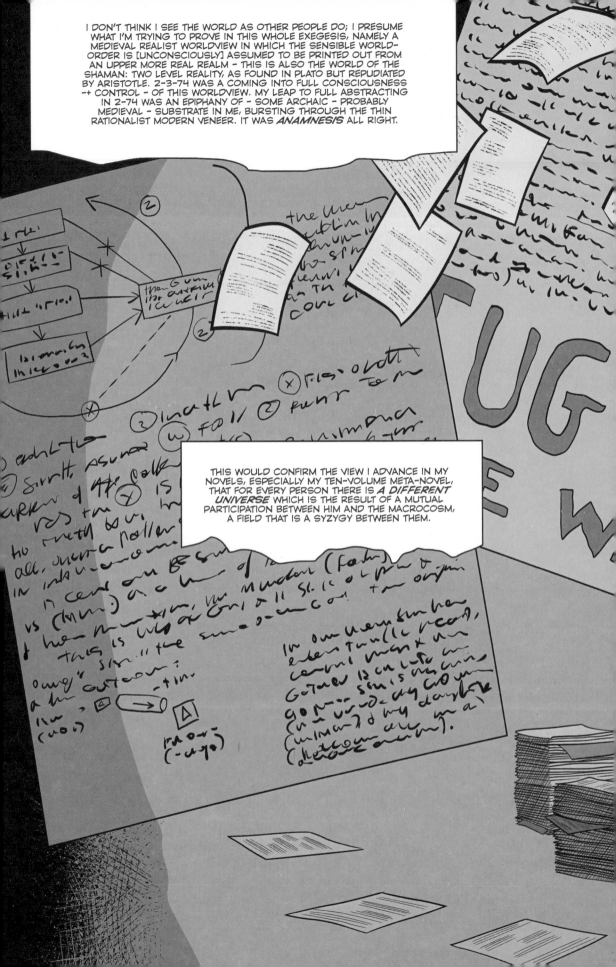

I DON'T THINK I SEE THE WORLD AS OTHER PEOPLE DO; I PRESUME WHAT I'M TRYING TO PROVE IN THIS WHOLE EXEGESIS, NAMELY A MEDIEVAL REALIST WORLDVIEW IN WHICH THE SENSIBLE WORLD-ORDER IS [UNCONSCIOUSLY] ASSUMED TO BE PRINTED OUT FROM AN UPPER MORE REAL REALM – THIS IS ALSO THE WORLD OF THE SHAMAN: TWO LEVEL REALITY, AS FOUND IN PLATO BUT REPUDIATED BY ARISTOTLE. 2-3-74 WAS A COMING INTO FULL CONSCIOUSNESS –+ CONTROL – OF THIS WORLDVIEW. MY LEAP TO FULL ABSTRACTING IN 2-74 WAS AN EPIPHANY OF – SOME ARCHAIC – PROBABLY MEDIEVAL – SUBSTRATE IN ME, BURSTING THROUGH THE THIN RATIONALIST MODERN VENEER. IT WAS *ANAMNESIS* ALL RIGHT.

THIS WOULD CONFIRM THE VIEW I ADVANCE IN MY NOVELS, ESPECIALLY MY TEN-VOLUME META-NOVEL, THAT FOR EVERY PERSON THERE IS *A DIFFERENT UNIVERSE* WHICH IS THE RESULT OF A MUTUAL PARTICIPATION BETWEEN HIM AND THE MACROCOSM, A FIELD THAT IS A SYZYGY BETWEEN THEM.

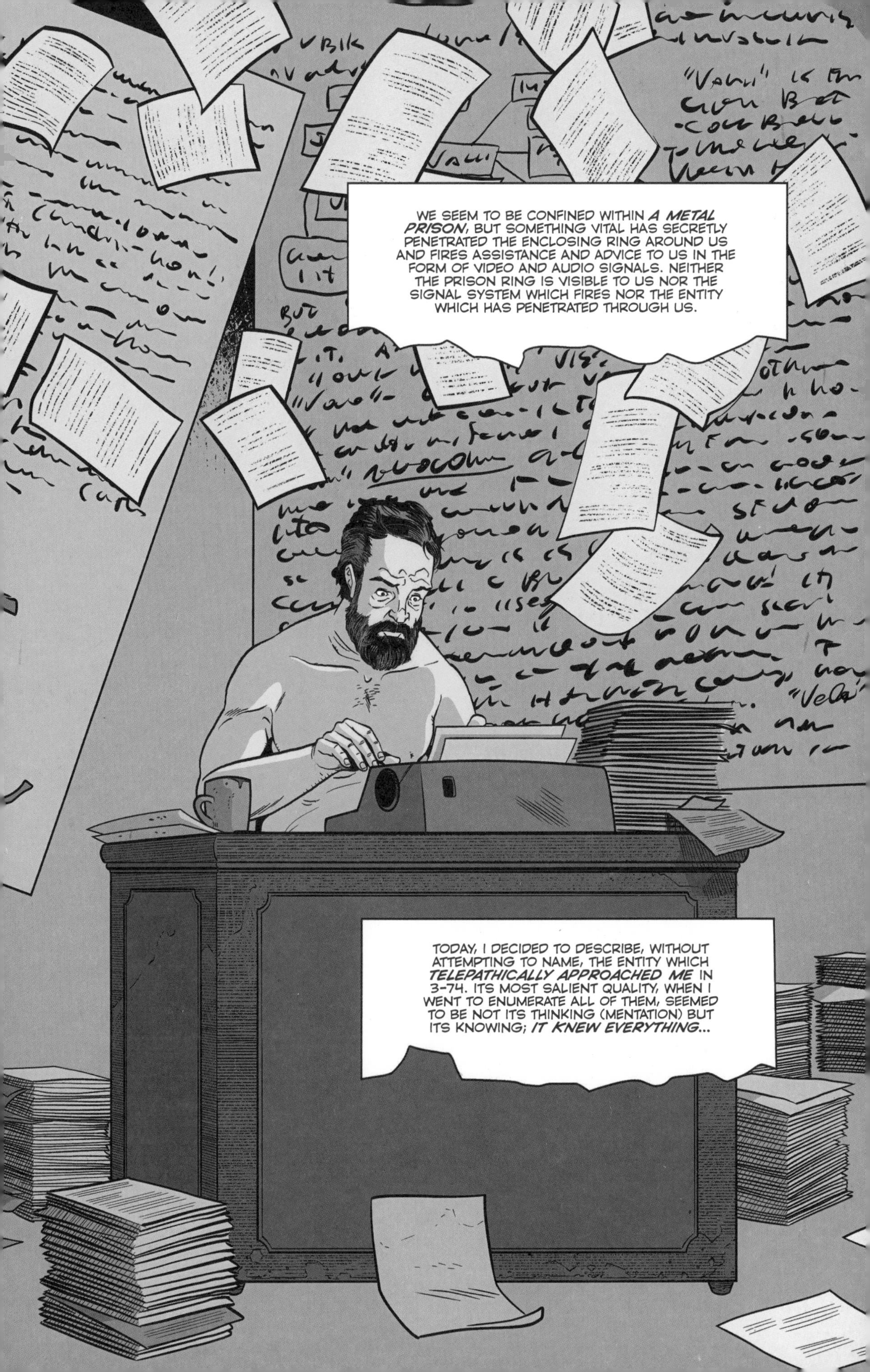
WE SEEM TO BE CONFINED WITHIN *A METAL PRISON*, BUT SOMETHING VITAL HAS SECRETLY PENETRATED THE ENCLOSING RING AROUND US AND FIRES ASSISTANCE AND ADVICE TO US IN THE FORM OF VIDEO AND AUDIO SIGNALS. NEITHER THE PRISON RING IS VISIBLE TO US NOR THE SIGNAL SYSTEM WHICH FIRES NOR THE ENTITY WHICH HAS PENETRATED THROUGH US.
TODAY, I DECIDED TO DESCRIBE, WITHOUT ATTEMPTING TO NAME, THE ENTITY WHICH *TELEPATHICALLY APPROACHED ME* IN 3-74. ITS MOST SALIENT QUALITY, WHEN I WENT TO ENUMERATE ALL OF THEM, SEEMED TO BE NOT ITS THINKING (MENTATION) BUT ITS KNOWING; *IT KNEW EVERYTHING*...

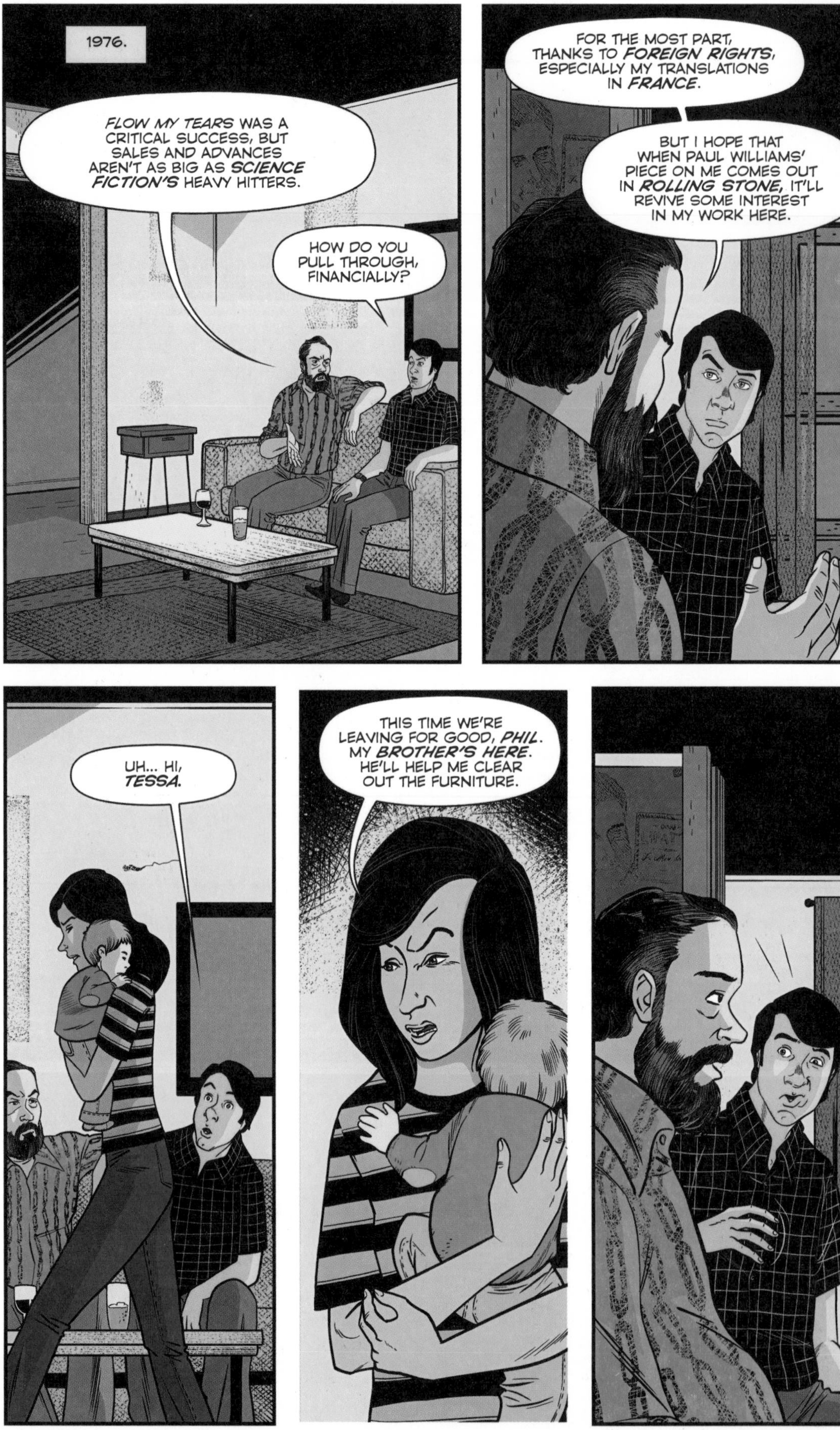
1976.
FLOW MY TEARS WAS A CRITICAL SUCCESS, BUT SALES AND ADVANCES AREN'T AS BIG AS SCIENCE FICTION'S HEAVY HITTERS.
HOW DO YOU PULL THROUGH, FINANCIALLY?
FOR THE MOST PART, THANKS TO FOREIGN RIGHTS, ESPECIALLY MY TRANSLATIONS IN FRANCE.
BUT I HOPE THAT WHEN PAUL WILLIAMS' PIECE ON ME COMES OUT IN ROLLING STONE, IT'LL REVIVE SOME INTEREST IN MY WORK HERE.
UH... HI, TESSA.
THIS TIME WE'RE LEAVING FOR GOOD, PHIL. MY BROTHER'S HERE. HE'LL HELP ME CLEAR OUT THE FURNITURE.

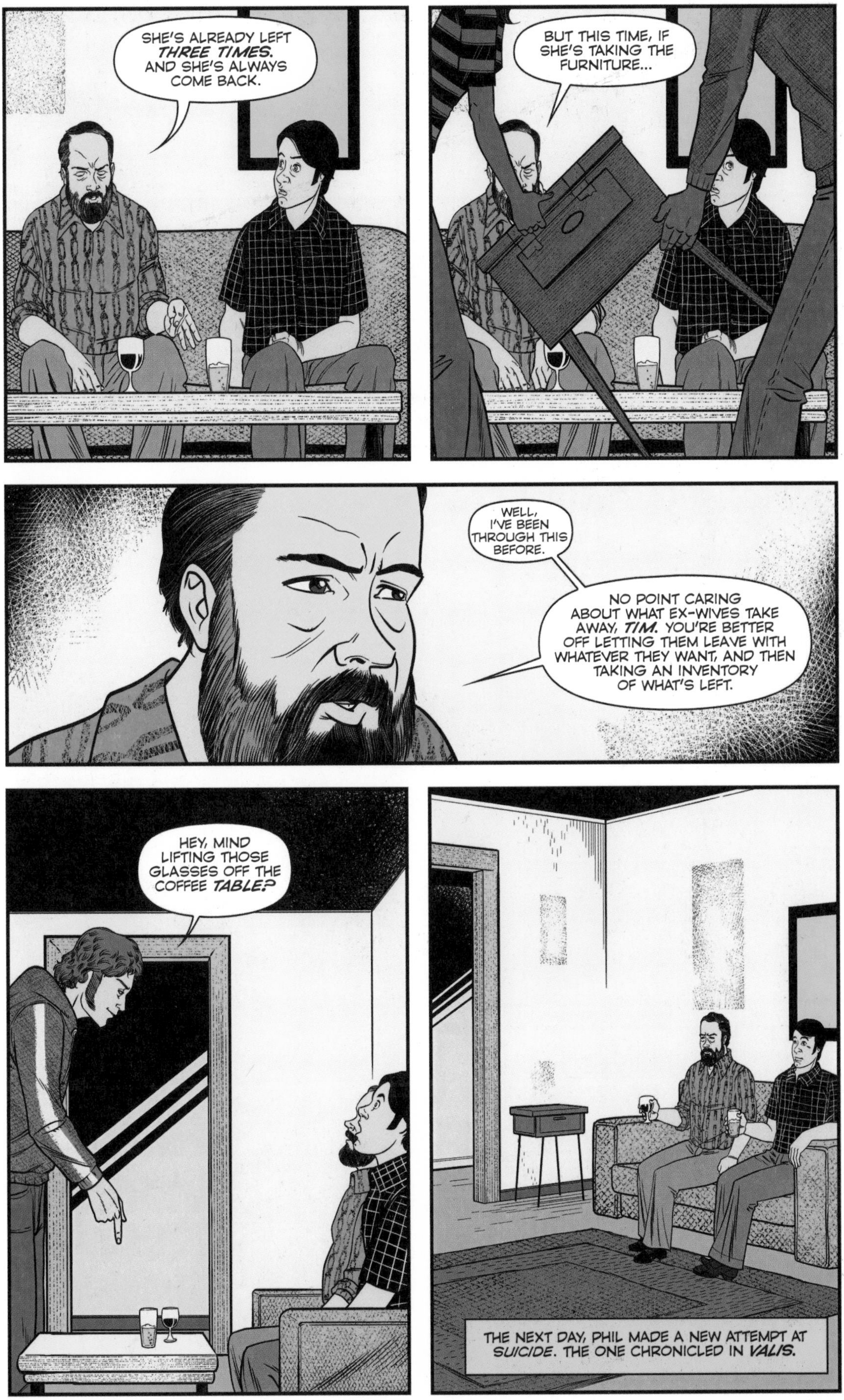
SHE'S ALREADY LEFT *THREE TIMES.* AND SHE'S ALWAYS COME BACK.
BUT THIS TIME, IF SHE'S TAKING THE FURNITURE...
WELL, I'VE BEEN THROUGH THIS BEFORE.
NO POINT CARING ABOUT WHAT EX-WIVES TAKE AWAY, *TIM.* YOU'RE BETTER OFF LETTING THEM LEAVE WITH WHATEVER THEY WANT, AND THEN TAKING AN INVENTORY OF WHAT'S LEFT.
HEY, MIND LIFTING THOSE GLASSES OFF THE COFFEE *TABLE?*
THE NEXT DAY, PHIL MADE A NEW ATTEMPT AT *SUICIDE*. THE ONE CHRONICLED IN *VALIS*.

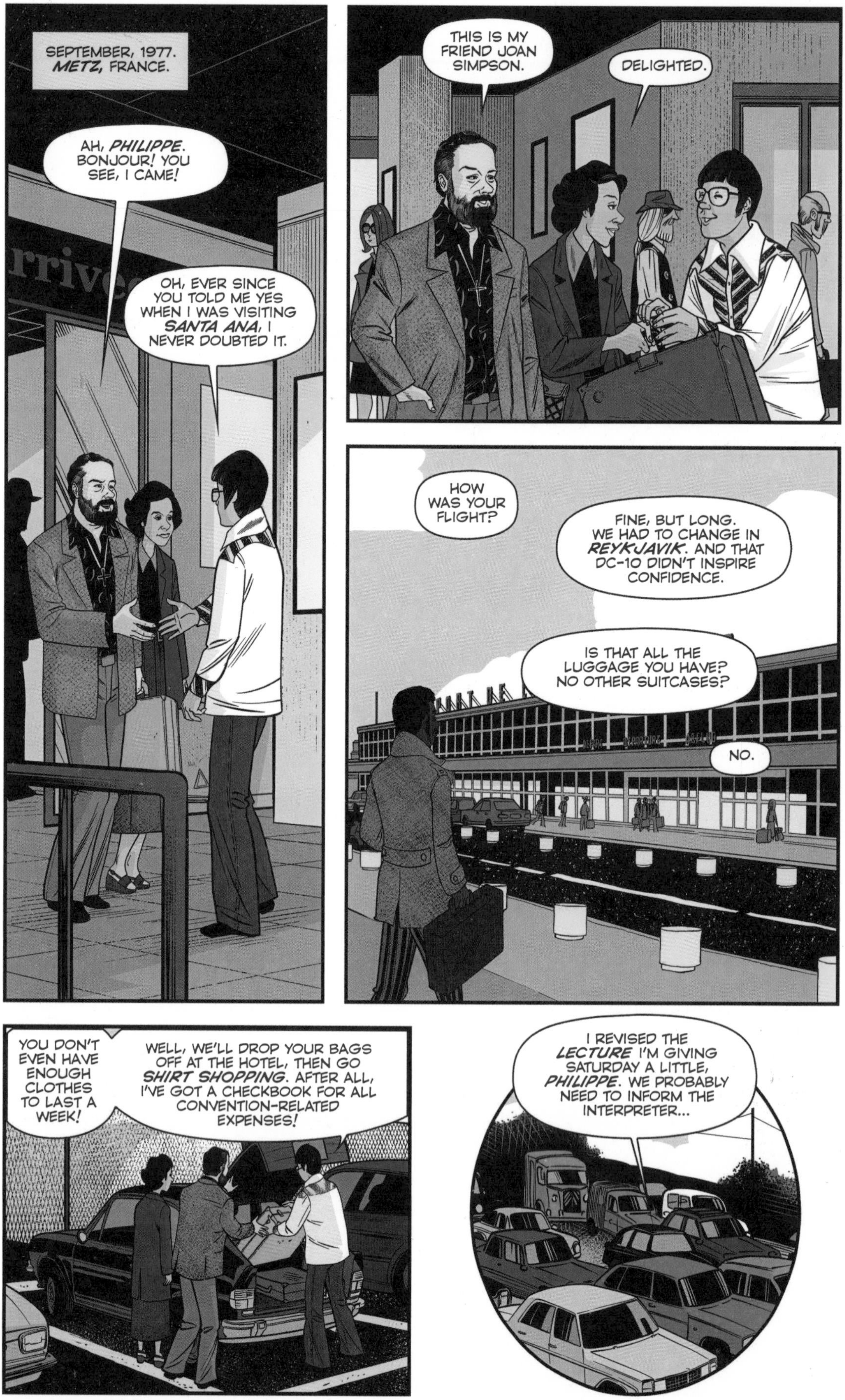
SEPTEMBER, 1977. METZ, FRANCE.
AH, PHILIPPE. BONJOUR! YOU SEE, I CAME!
OH, EVER SINCE YOU TOLD ME YES WHEN I WAS VISITING SANTA ANA, I NEVER DOUBTED IT.
THIS IS MY FRIEND JOAN SIMPSON.
DELIGHTED.
HOW WAS YOUR FLIGHT?
FINE, BUT LONG. WE HAD TO CHANGE IN REYKJAVIK. AND THAT DC-10 DIDN'T INSPIRE CONFIDENCE.
IS THAT ALL THE LUGGAGE YOU HAVE? NO OTHER SUITCASES?
NO.
YOU DON'T EVEN HAVE ENOUGH CLOTHES TO LAST A WEEK!
WELL, WE'LL DROP YOUR BAGS OFF AT THE HOTEL, THEN GO SHIRT SHOPPING. AFTER ALL, I'VE GOT A CHECKBOOK FOR ALL CONVENTION-RELATED EXPENSES!
I REVISED THE LECTURE I'M GIVING SATURDAY A LITTLE, PHILIPPE. WE PROBABLY NEED TO INFORM THE INTERPRETER...

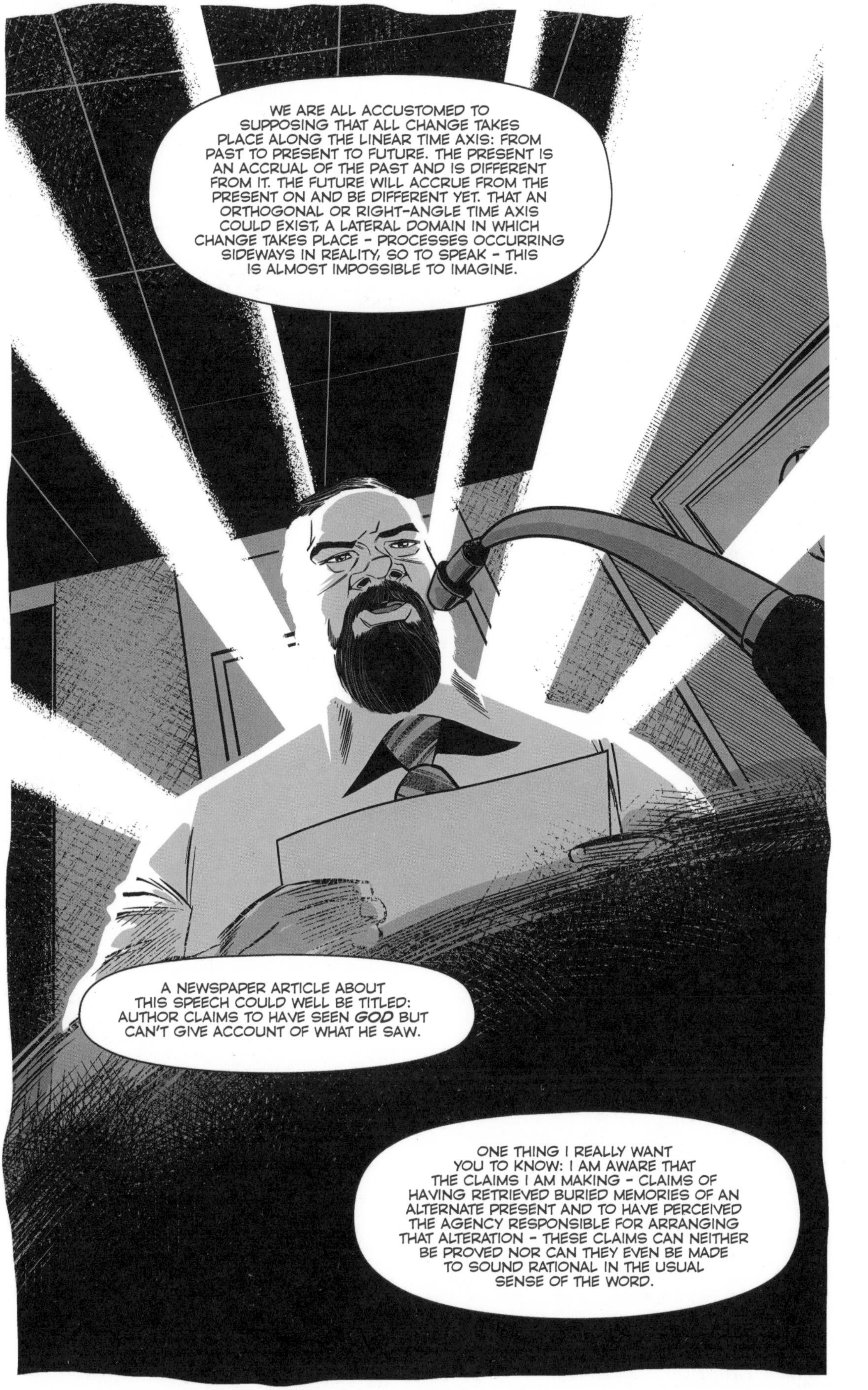
WE ARE ALL ACCUSTOMED TO SUPPOSING THAT ALL CHANGE TAKES PLACE ALONG THE LINEAR TIME AXIS: FROM PAST TO PRESENT TO FUTURE. THE PRESENT IS AN ACCRUAL OF THE PAST AND IS DIFFERENT FROM IT. THE FUTURE WILL ACCRUE FROM THE PRESENT ON AND BE DIFFERENT YET. THAT AN ORTHOGONAL OR RIGHT-ANGLE TIME AXIS COULD EXIST, A LATERAL DOMAIN IN WHICH CHANGE TAKES PLACE - PROCESSES OCCURRING SIDEWAYS IN REALITY, SO TO SPEAK - THIS IS ALMOST IMPOSSIBLE TO IMAGINE.
A NEWSPAPER ARTICLE ABOUT THIS SPEECH COULD WELL BE TITLED: AUTHOR CLAIMS TO HAVE SEEN ***GOD*** BUT CAN'T GIVE ACCOUNT OF WHAT HE SAW.
ONE THING I REALLY WANT YOU TO KNOW: I AM AWARE THAT THE CLAIMS I AM MAKING - CLAIMS OF HAVING RETRIEVED BURIED MEMORIES OF AN ALTERNATE PRESENT AND TO HAVE PERCEIVED THE AGENCY RESPONSIBLE FOR ARRANGING THAT ALTERATION - THESE CLAIMS CAN NEITHER BE PROVED NOR CAN THEY EVEN BE MADE TO SOUND RATIONAL IN THE USUAL SENSE OF THE WORD.

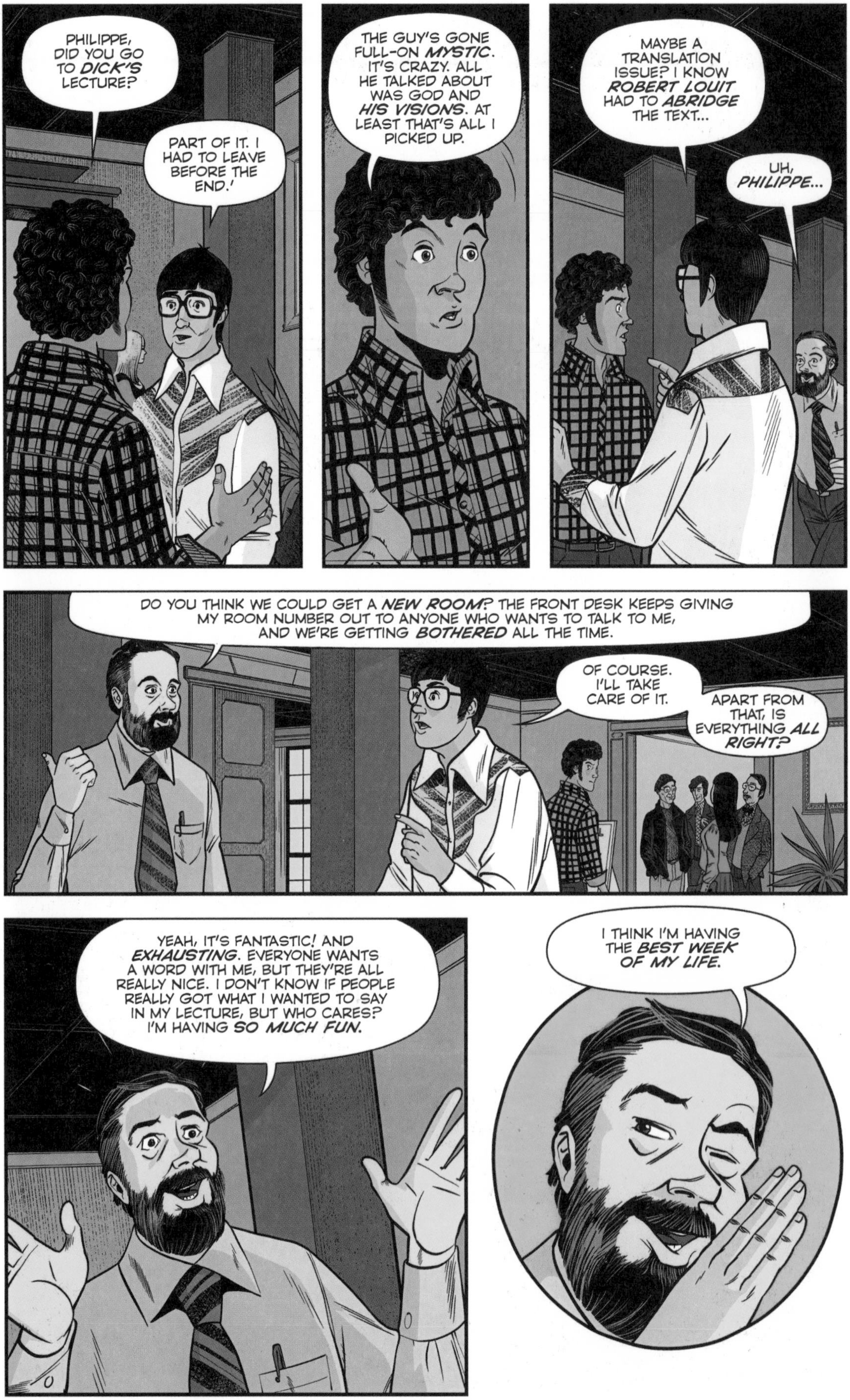
PHILIPPE, DID YOU GO TO DICK'S LECTURE?
PART OF IT. I HAD TO LEAVE BEFORE THE END.'
THE GUY'S GONE FULL-ON MYSTIC. IT'S CRAZY. ALL HE TALKED ABOUT WAS GOD AND HIS VISIONS. AT LEAST THAT'S ALL I PICKED UP.
MAYBE A TRANSLATION ISSUE? I KNOW ROBERT LOUIT HAD TO ABRIDGE THE TEXT...
UH, PHILIPPE...
DO YOU THINK WE COULD GET A NEW ROOM? THE FRONT DESK KEEPS GIVING MY ROOM NUMBER OUT TO ANYONE WHO WANTS TO TALK TO ME, AND WE'RE GETTING BOTHERED ALL THE TIME.
OF COURSE. I'LL TAKE CARE OF IT.
APART FROM THAT, IS EVERYTHING ALL RIGHT?
YEAH, IT'S FANTASTIC! AND EXHAUSTING. EVERYONE WANTS A WORD WITH ME, BUT THEY'RE ALL REALLY NICE. I DON'T KNOW IF PEOPLE REALLY GOT WHAT I WANTED TO SAY IN MY LECTURE, BUT WHO CARES? I'M HAVING SO MUCH FUN.
I THINK I'M HAVING THE BEST WEEK OF MY LIFE.

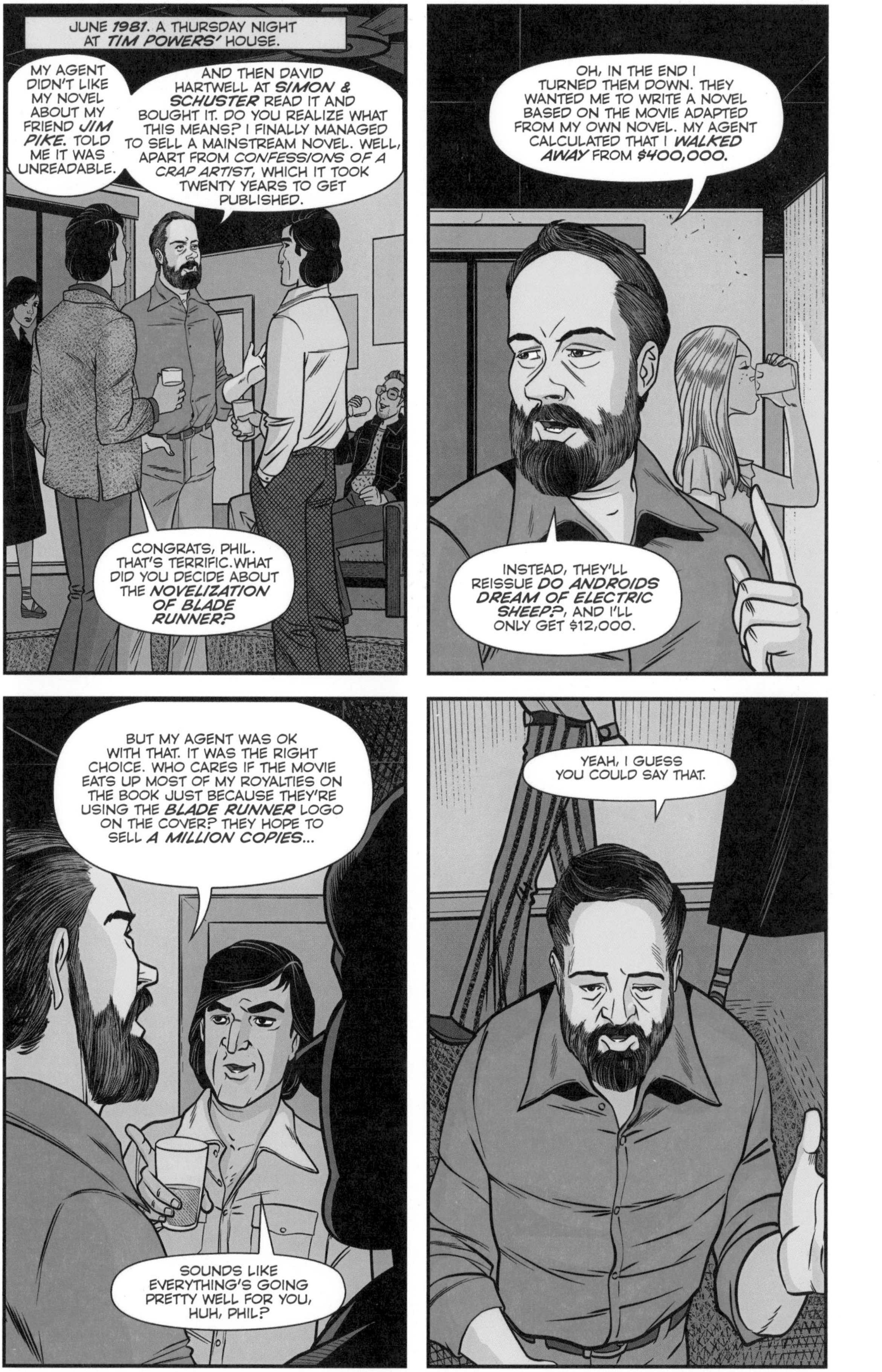
JUNE 1981. A THURSDAY NIGHT AT TIM POWERS' HOUSE.
MY AGENT DIDN'T LIKE MY NOVEL ABOUT MY FRIEND JIM PIKE. TOLD ME IT WAS UNREADABLE.
AND THEN DAVID HARTWELL AT SIMON & SCHUSTER READ IT AND BOUGHT IT. DO YOU REALIZE WHAT THIS MEANS? I FINALLY MANAGED TO SELL A MAINSTREAM NOVEL. WELL, APART FROM CONFESSIONS OF A CRAP ARTIST, WHICH IT TOOK TWENTY YEARS TO GET PUBLISHED.
CONGRATS, PHIL. THAT'S TERRIFIC. WHAT DID YOU DECIDE ABOUT THE NOVELIZATION OF BLADE RUNNER?
OH, IN THE END I TURNED THEM DOWN. THEY WANTED ME TO WRITE A NOVEL BASED ON THE MOVIE ADAPTED FROM MY OWN NOVEL. MY AGENT CALCULATED THAT I WALKED AWAY FROM $400,000.
INSTEAD, THEY'LL REISSUE DO ANDROIDS DREAM OF ELECTRIC SHEEP?, AND I'LL ONLY GET $12,000.
BUT MY AGENT WAS OK WITH THAT. IT WAS THE RIGHT CHOICE. WHO CARES IF THE MOVIE EATS UP MOST OF MY ROYALTIES ON THE BOOK JUST BECAUSE THEY'RE USING THE BLADE RUNNER LOGO ON THE COVER? THEY HOPE TO SELL A MILLION COPIES...
SOUNDS LIKE EVERYTHING'S GOING PRETTY WELL FOR YOU, HUH, PHIL?
YEAH, I GUESS YOU COULD SAY THAT.

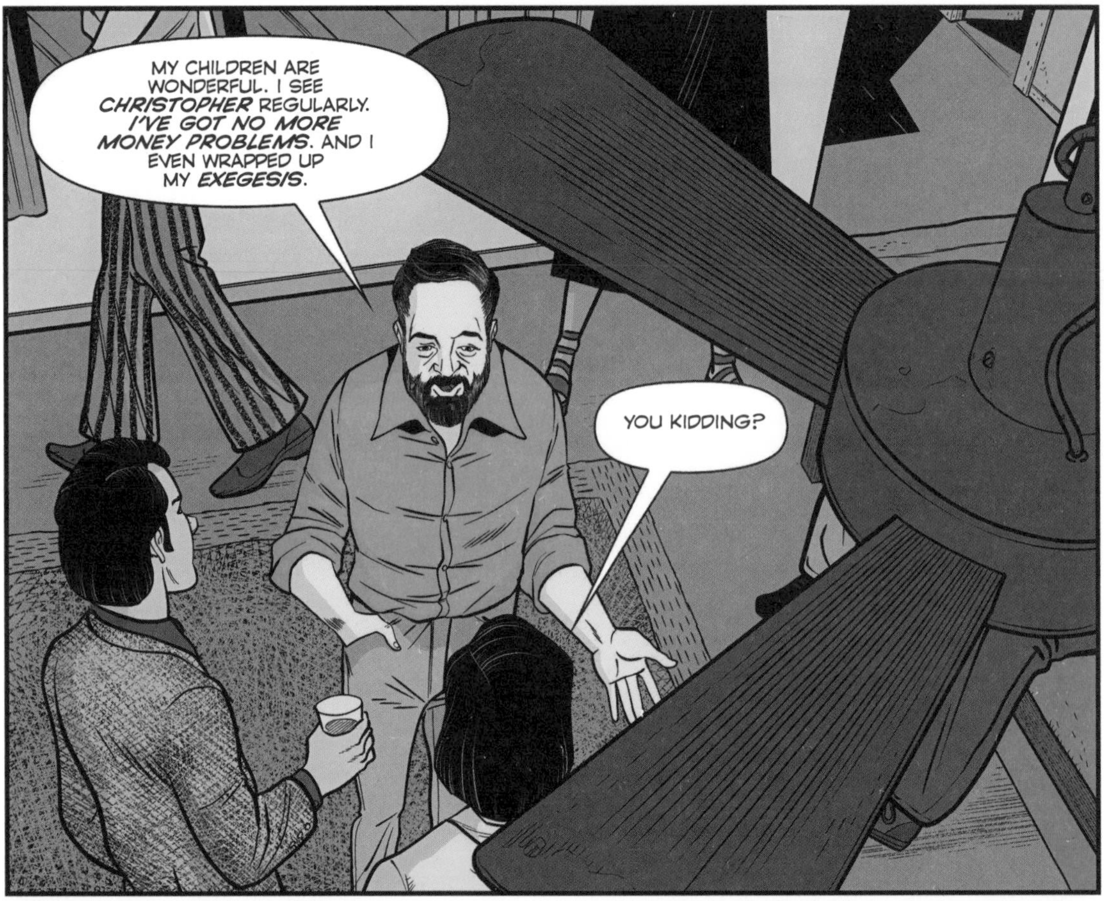
MY CHILDREN ARE WONDERFUL. I SEE CHRISTOPHER REGULARLY. I'VE GOT NO MORE MONEY PROBLEMS. AND I EVEN WRAPPED UP MY EXEGESIS.
YOU KIDDING?

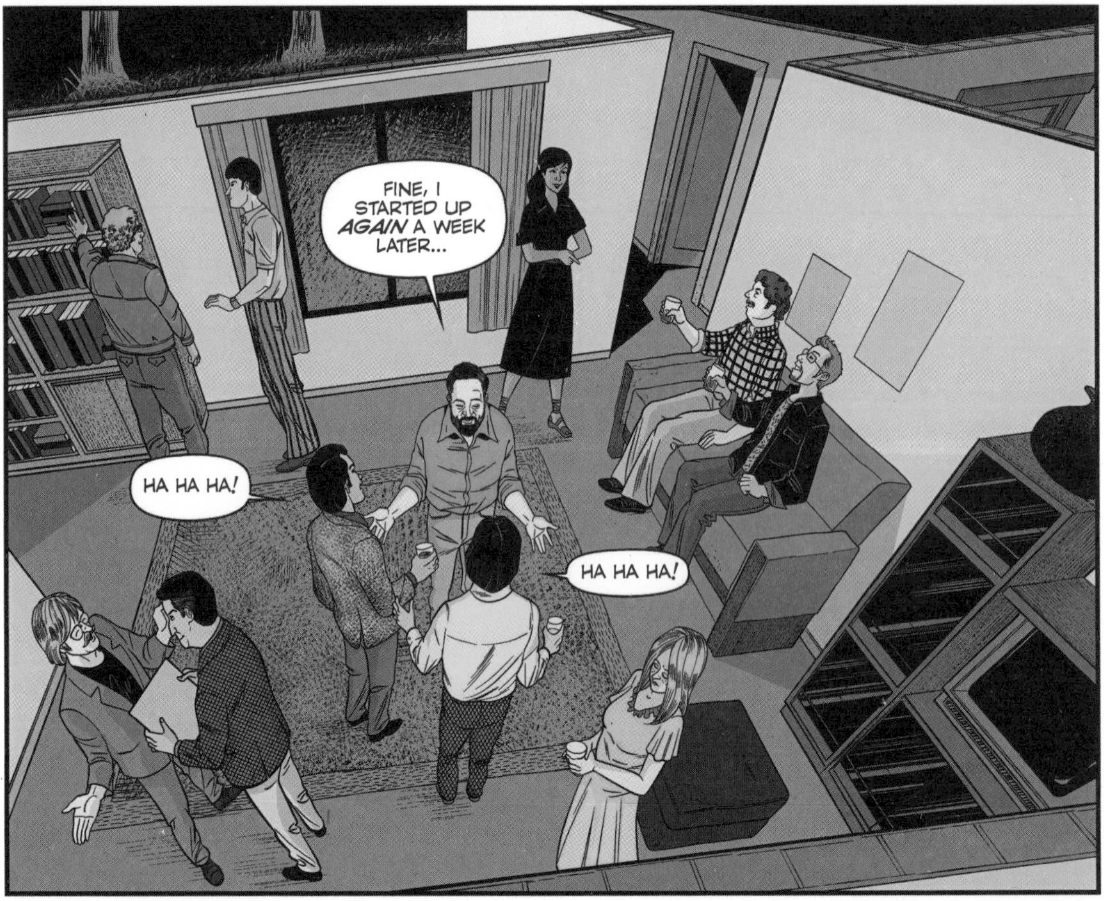
FINE, I STARTED UP AGAIN A WEEK LATER...
HA HA HA!
HA HA HA!

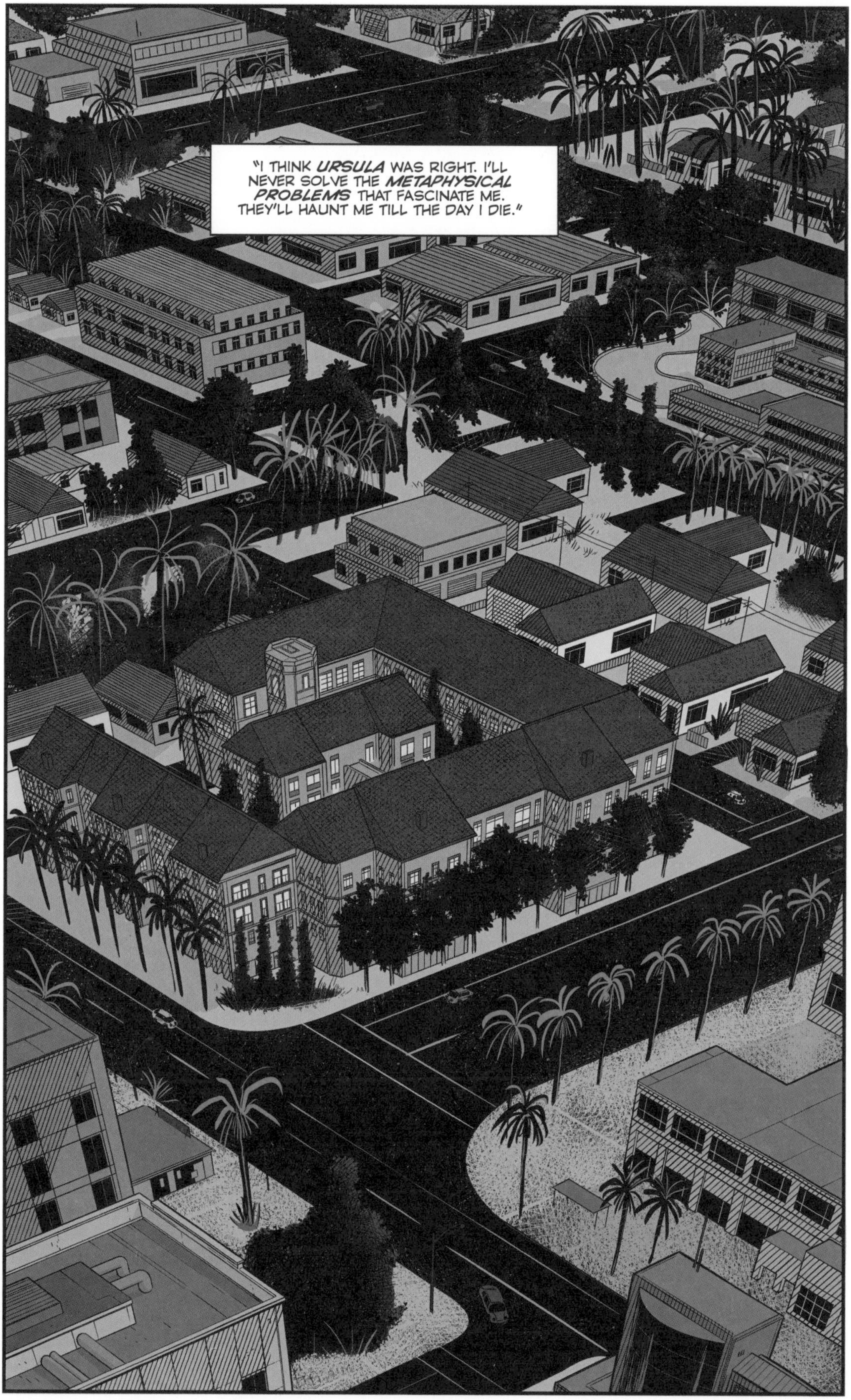
"I THINK *URSULA* WAS RIGHT. I'LL NEVER SOLVE THE *METAPHYSICAL PROBLEMS* THAT FASCINATE ME. THEY'LL HAUNT ME TILL THE DAY I DIE."

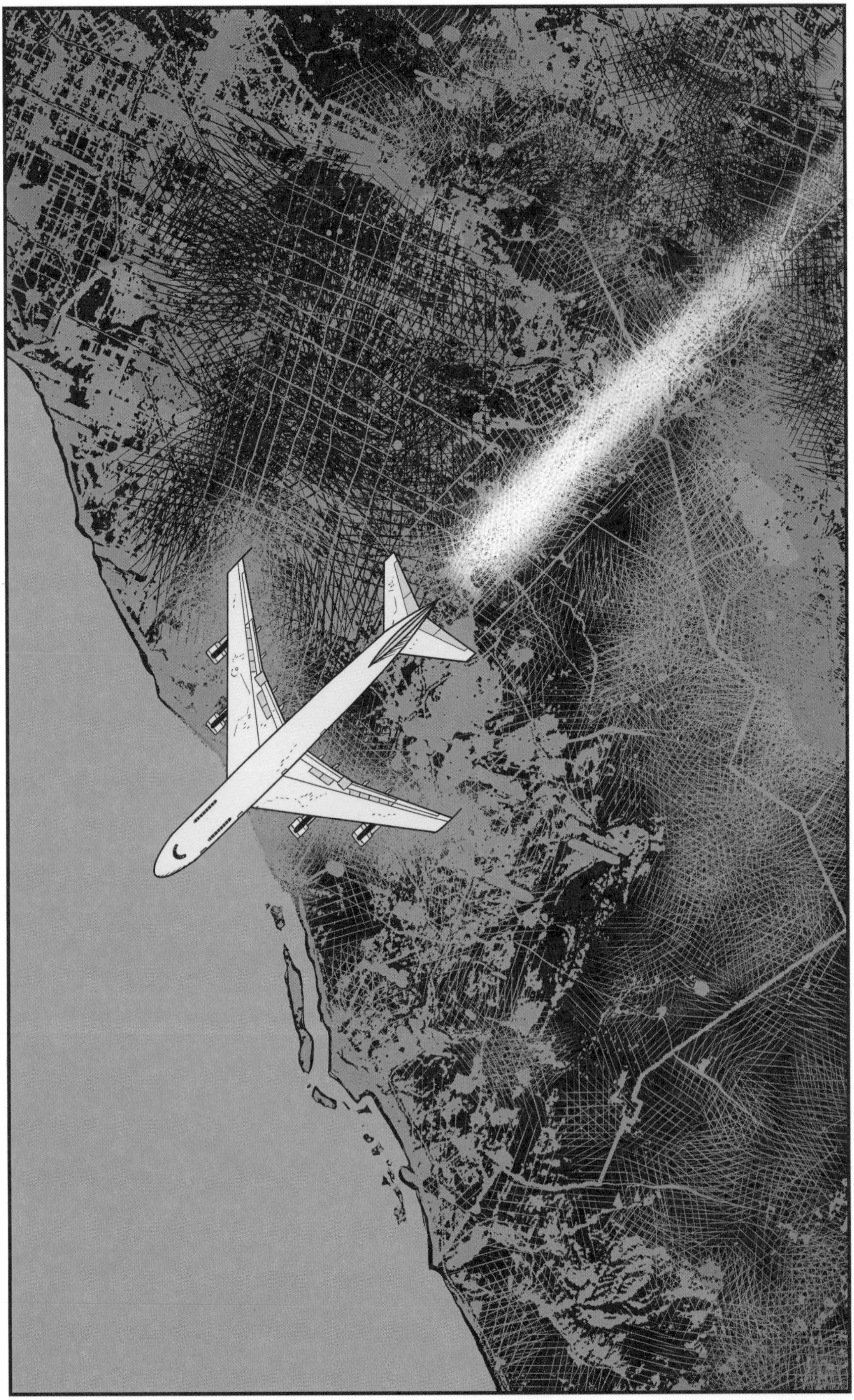

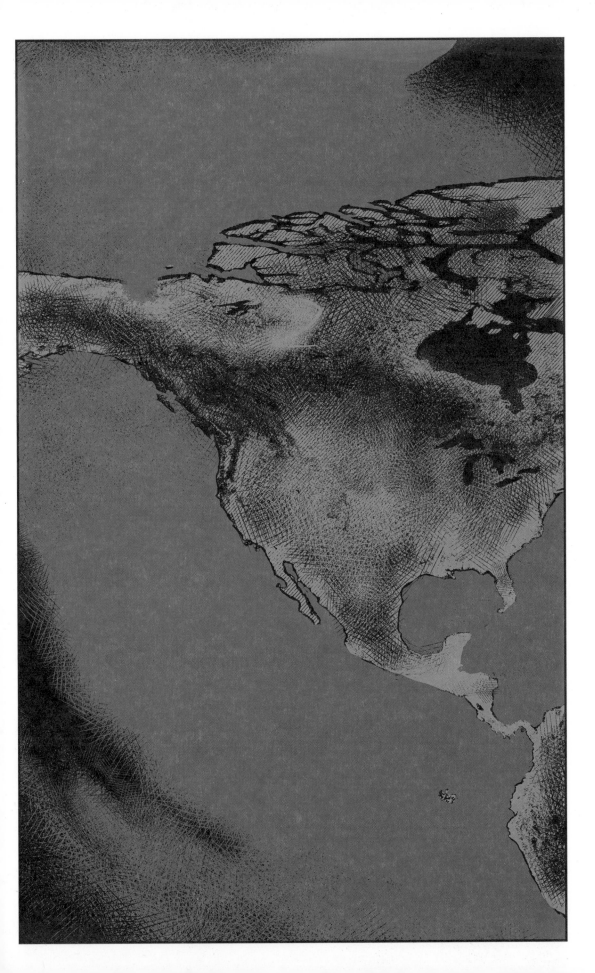

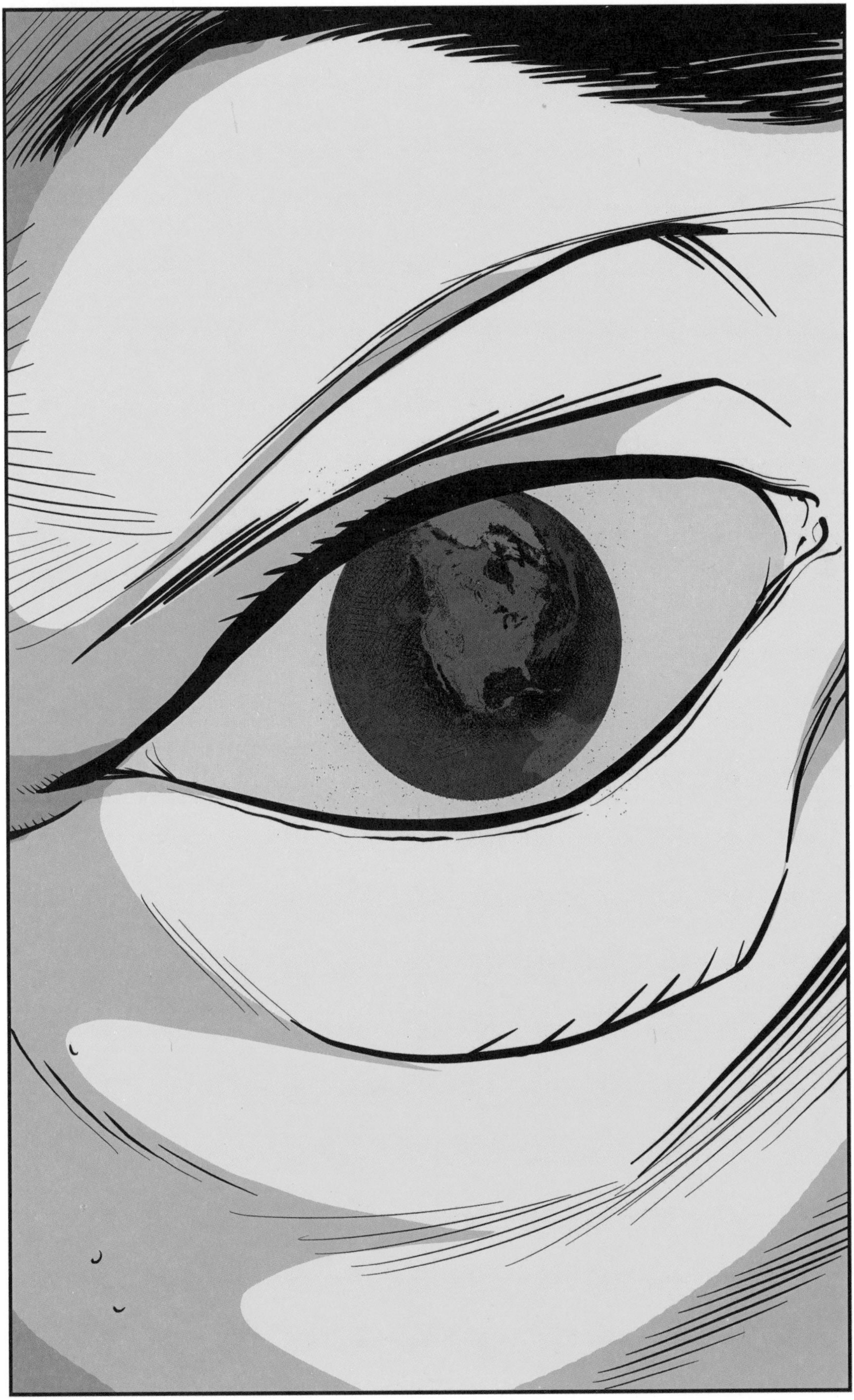

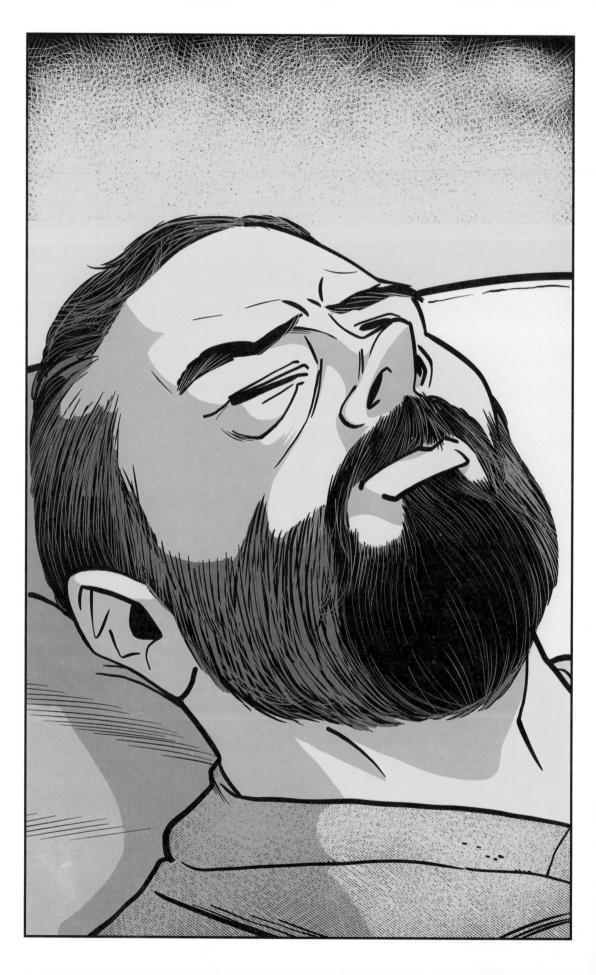

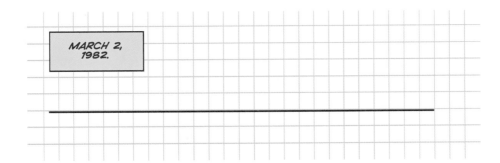

MARCH 2,
1982.

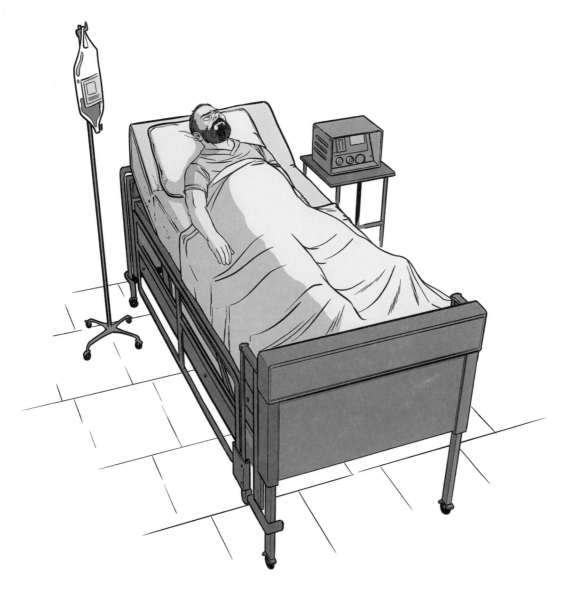

POSTSCRIPT

This is far from the first biography of **Philip K. Dick**. But unlike other previously published works, it pairs pictures with words and offers—or so I hope—an original point of view on the life of one of the most interesting American authors in recent memory.

Everything depends on point of view. Whether working on his novels or his *Exegesis*, Dick was constantly writing. We are each unique and see the world in our own way. In fact, the confrontation of personal interiority—that inner world Dick called the *idios kosmos*—with the communal world shared by all—*koinos kosmos*—provided material for the author's plots. How can we be sure that when we call something red, we're all seeing the same color?

Dick himself, in his life and work, enjoyed adopting a multitude of points of view, the better to work through his hypotheses and theories about the break-in at his house, or the events of February and March 1974, for instance. According to several eyewitnesses, he could even seem like a different person depending on his conversational partner, and would vary his behavior in relation to circumstance, as if playing a part, whether consciously or not.

Maer (Mary) Wilson, for one, gives us a very different Dick in her memoirs, less complicated and more at peace than the one described by other acquaintances from that stage in his life. The proliferation of firsthand accounts allows us to obtain an image of the man as seen by those close to him, or rather the many facets he showed to those around him. As for his inner life: we have his stories, his novels, his letters, and his *Exegesis*. For, rare are the authors who have so thoroughly committed to paper their vision of the world, their unique perspective, their theories and enthusiasms, their thought process. And even leaving out the gamesmanship or manipulation inherent to letters, there remains, especially in the *Exegesis*, enough to shed a significant light on Dick's inner world.

Everything depends on point of view. This comic is our vision of **Philip K. Dick**. Our take on the man and the world in which he lived. Even as the author now calls to mind the far-out or futuristic covers of his books, or, on top of that, the powerfully disseminated images from the Hollywood Dream Factory's adaptations, the actual times in which he lived, the world he wrote in and shared with others, no longer leap immediately to mind. And yet his body of work is intimately connected to California in the second half of the 20th century, its suburban setting of conapts and palm-lined streets (which would become whole gardens when Dick experienced his anamnesis), its counterculture of drifters, lost souls, and innovative artists.

Mauro Marchesi's art brings this setting back to life, a setting whose reality the novelist never stopped questioning. Mauro's *linework*—a kind of fusion of European ligne claire and American indie comics style—recreates an essential context all too rarely seen.

But comics aren't just about backgrounds. Just like literature, they also allow for a play of images on an analogical or symbolic level. And there may be something more immediate, more visceral, that the union of words and pictures brings to the table. By using the medium, some aspects can be made more obvious, some causal links brought to the fore.

It was only when I showed the first pages of this comic to American speculative fiction writer **Daryl Gregory** that I fully grasped this. After smiling at Mauro's depiction of **Tim Powers**, who had been Gregory's teacher at the Clarion Writers' Workshop, he paused over the page with baby Phil in an incubator and confessed that panel immediately made him think of PKD's novel *Ubik*. The art resonated with the author's body of work, and the image functioned as a true analogy, carrying meaning. Daryl swept away any last remaining doubts I'd had about the relevance of doing a comics biography of Philip K. Dick.

The important thing for me as a writer was not to get (too) bogged down in the details, and to offer up a portrait that, despite the multiplicity of sources, proved coherent and corresponded to the point of view that years of appreciation had allowed me to develop. The portrait of a highly complicated man, friendly and difficult. A good man, gifted with great empathy, but also his share

of darkness. An author haunted by his work, plagued by a deep need to assign meaning to the world around him. No doubt it is not my task to make excuses for this vision of Dick as Mauro and I have depicted him in these pages. Let me just say that my passion for his work before I even began writing this comic grew into a deep fondness for the character inspired by PKD that we've dramatized here.

My research was lengthy, immersive, intense, and rounded out by a few trips to the places where the author lived. It was a chance to breathe the same air he had and take a few photos that would later prove useful to Mauro. It was also a way to put pictures to certain descriptions in his work; driving from San Francisco to Point Reyes, past landscapes almost unchanged since the '60s, made me feel like I was actually following in the footsteps of characters from, say, *Confessions of a Crap Artist*, to name but one example.

This book is only our vision, our point of view on that unique individual known as Philip K. Dick: an incomplete and fragmentary vision, to be sure, but one that is faithful to our convictions, and that we'd wanted right from the start to make as truthful as possible.

No doubt the expression is a bit musty, but who cares? I swear: we put our hearts into it.

Laurent Queyssi - September 2017

BIBLIOGRAPHY

References and sources:
DICK, Anne R. *Search for Philip K. Dick 1928-1982.*
Point Reyes Cypress Press, 2009.

DICK, Philip K. *The Selected Letters of Philip K. Dick.*
volume 1. 1939-1971.
volume 2. 1972-1973.
volume 3. 1974.
volume 4. 1975-1976.
volume 5. 1977-1979.
volume 6. 1980-1982.
Underwood-Miller, 1991-2009.

JACKSON, Pamela et Jonathan LETHEM (editors),
The Exegesis of Philip K. Dick, Houghton, Mifflin, Harcourt, 2011.

RICKMANN, Gregg.
Philip K. Dick : In His Own Words, 1984.
Philip K. Dick : The Last Testament, 1985.
Fragments West/The Valentine Press.

PEAKE, Anthony. *A life of Philip K. Dick. The Man Who Remembered The Future.*
Arcturus, 2013.
RICKMANN, Gregg. *To the High Castle. Philip K. Dick : a life 1928-1962.*
Fragments West/The Valentine Press, 1989.
SAMMON, Paul M. *Future Noir. The Making of Blade Runner.* HarperCollins, 1996.
SUTIN, Lawrence. *Divine Invasions: A Life of Philip K. Dick.*
Da Capo Press, 2005.
SUTIN, Lawrence. *In Pursuit of Valis, Selections from the Exegesis.*
Underwood-Miller, 1991.
WILLIAMS, Paul. *Only Apparently Real, the World of Philip K. Dick.*
Arbour House, 1986.

Laurent Queyssi also culled a great deal of information from the mine that is the 30 issues of
the *Philip K. Dick Society Newsletter*, published from 1983 to 1992 by Paul Williams.

Other comics biographies also available from NBM:

The Beatles in Comics

Thoreau, A Sublime Life
*"This lovely book breathes new life into Thoreau
and returns to him his true depth, which has been
overlooked in recent impressions. A worthy addition
to any library that includes Thoreau's works."*
-Library Journal starred review

Billie Holiday
By Jose Munoz and Carlos Sampayo
*"Presents glaring flashes of Holiday's songs and life,
with stark, striking art that jazz lovers will appreciate."*
-Library Journal

See many more bios, previews,
get exclusives and order from:
NBMPUB.COM

we have over 200 titles available
Catalog upon request
NBM
160 Broadway, Suite 700, East Wing,
New York, NY 10038

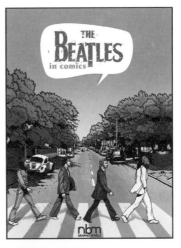